# *Verdi*

*Unlocking the Masters Series, No. 26*

Series Editor: Robert

# *Verdi*

## *The Operas and Choral Works*

Victor Lederer

af

AMADEUS
PRESS

An Imprint of Hal Leonard Corporation

Published in 2014 by Amadeus Press
An Imprint of Hal Leonard Corporation
7777 West Bluemound Road
Milwaukee, WI 53213

Trade Book Division Editorial Offices
33 Plymouth St., Montclair, NJ 07042


Printed in the United States of America


Book design by Snow Creative Services


Library of Congress Cataloging-in-Publication Data

Lederer, Victor.
   Verdi : the operas and choral works / Victor Lederer.
      pages cm. — (Unlocking the masters series ; no. 26)
   Includes bibliographical references.
   ISBN 978-1-57467-440-8
   1. Verdi, Giuseppe, 1813–1901. Operas. 2. Verdi, Giuseppe, 1813–1901. Vocal music.
3. Opera—19th century. 4. Choral music—19th century. I. Title.
   ML410.V4L36 2014
   782.1092—dc23
                                                                    2014027514

www.amadeuspress.com

# Contents

Acknowledgments vii

Chapter 1. Verdi and the Culmination of Italian Opera 1

Chapter 2. Verdi's Life and Character 13

Chapter 3. The Major Early Operas: *Nabucco, Ernani,* and *Macbeth* 23

Chapter 4. The "Galley" Operas 41

Chapter 5. The Transition to the Middle Period: *Luisa Miller* and *Stiffelio; Aroldo* 67

Chapter 6. The Big Three of the Middle Period: *Rigoletto, Il trovatore,* and *La traviata* 83

Chapter 7. Broadening the Scope: *I vespri siciliani* and *Un ballo in maschera* 111

Chapter 8. The Late Middle Period: *La forza del destino* and *Simon Boccanegra* 131

Chapter 9. Choral Works: The Manzoni Requiem and the *Quattro pezzi sacri* 155

Chapter 10. The Great Political Tragedy: *Don Carlo* 167

Chapter 11. A Farewell to Grand Opera: *Aida* 185

Chapter 12. Shakespearean Tragedy: *Otello* 199

Chapter 13. Shakespearean Comedy: *Falstaff* 217

Chapter 14. Listening to Verdi 235

Notes 239

Selected Bibliography 243

CD Track Listing 245

# Acknowledgments

Love of the composer's work goes back decades, at least to when Robert Berman advised me to "listen to much Verdi." Thanks go to my dear old pal Michael Davis, and to his late mother, Regina Resnik—Verdians of high pedigree—for guiding me through the early days of a lifelong obsession; and to Bernie Rose for an invaluable walk through the vocal score of *Otello*. Thanks also to copyeditor Iris Bass. Thanks, as always, to my children: Karen, Paul, and Kate. Thanks to my sister-in-law Marilyn Thypin; and thanks especially to my wife, Elaine, for her patience with this long, loud project. Finally, this book is dedicated to Bob Levine, who could—and perhaps should—have written it.

# Verdi and the Culmination of Italian Opera

Sooner or later we learn that in this world popularity and quality do not go hand in hand—far from it, in fact. But in the case of Verdi, they do. Giuseppe Verdi, probably the most popular operatic composer of all, brought Italian opera to its peak, single-handedly saving and reanimating this beloved musical genre for the better part of a century. Italian opera of the 1840s, when Verdi came on the scene, was a hodgepodge of formulas spun out by mostly forgotten composers who were at the mercy of fickle audiences, self-promoting singers, and impresarios whose chief personal quality was greed. A few fine composers—Rossini, Bellini, and Donizetti—had by their individuality and hard work carved out niches for themselves, achieving popularity that spread beyond Italy, over Europe, and across the Atlantic. But with the arrival of ambitious new ideas about musical drama, chiefly those of Wagner, German opera had become the avant-garde, what the cool kids, even in Italy, wanted to see. While even the finest works by Italians still sounded beautiful, they were rarely daring. With his musical and dramatic genius and force of character, Verdi gave Italian opera's tired conventions new life, while continually raising its standards, ultimately adding sixteen indestructible operas (of the twenty-eight he composed) to the repertory.

Verdi's music combines lyricism with power, helping it reach its vast and well-deserved popularity. His operas grab you by the throat, demanding your attention and making submission to their beauty and force your only course. They're not always subtle, but that's not generally a quality associated with Italian opera. Verdi refined his style continually, though, and his final opera, *Falstaff*, is nothing if not subtle. Opera, the Italian variety in particular, may be unsubtle, but it is the best musical form for the direct expression of emotions, at which it is unsurpassed. By any analysis, it's one of the most important limbs of the Western musical tree; you can perhaps think of it as standing opposite to German-Austrian instrumental music, which runs to the abstract and intellectual. German opera, the fruit of the romantic era, is moody, grandiose, often mystical. But the goals of Italian opera are the expression of emotions, often in showy ways, and sheer entertainment.

To say that opera in Italy fills a much wider position in the national culture than it does in the United States seems a truism; it's also safe to say that nothing in American culture, where the boundaries between "high" and "low" are written in stone, is analogous to opera in Italy, where it's accepted by millions as an essential element of their upbringing and national heritage. While Americans and others seem irritated or amused up to a point, or bored by opera; others feel intimidated, and many seem to be put off by its artificiality. But of course, placed in the proper light, any art—and any sport—can appear unnatural. There's more than a bit of blood sport in being an opera fan in Italy, where fine performances are cheered, and bad ones booed enthusiastically; and where the ability of tenors and sopranos to execute fast passagework and hit high notes with ease and power—or their failure to do so—are applauded or condemned vigorously during performances. Verdi's popularity in Italy arises, as we'll see, not only from his role as perhaps Italy's greatest composer, but also as a symbol of the national spirit during the unification struggles of the mid-nineteenth century.

Opera's noble purpose is to say in music what everyone feels—no more, no less. The big solo numbers, or arias, typically express an emotion that the character is experiencing. In a duet, each character's emotion should be clarified and heightened by the music. Termed *affects*, these are the feelings we've all known from early in our own lives: happiness, grief, anger, fear, and all the others. (It seems curious that opera should not gain a wider response in an age and a society in which open emotional expression is accorded high value.) By Verdi's time, emphasis had begun to shift toward the expression of more complex psychological and dramatic truth, an art Verdi excelled at and brought to transcendent levels of mimesis.

The voice dominates Italian opera, and it is the dominant element of Verdi's style. His works are written for singers, who at best inhabit their roles and hope to become known as great Lady Macbeths, Rigolettos, or

Aidas. Verdi's mastery of the orchestra was immense, as well, and three of the operatic overtures (*Luisa Miller, I vespri siciliani,* and *La forza del destino*) are played in the concert hall. With the exception of a few piano fantasies on Verdian themes by Franz Liszt, there are no suites of material lifted from the operas and played by the orchestra without a singer: the idea itself is preposterous. The opposite holds true for Verdi's contemporary and fellow operatic titan Richard Wagner, whose music has always been excerpted and transcribed for orchestra without voice, and Wagner's music generally stands up well to the treatment. Verdi came to maturity in an era in which the bel canto style dominated; the phrase means "beautiful singing," and it's characterized by elaborate and difficult vocal parts, with lots of high notes for the high voices and decoration of all vocal parts. The voice is what's on display in bel canto operas, and much of what singers are asked to do requires not only vocal power, but also agility and subtlety. The popularity of singers in Italy, entirely comparable to that of professional athletes, typically rewards those who have mastered this difficult style of singing. As we'll see, some of Verdi's operas display bel canto characteristics, though he came into his prime as the style was losing its hold on the public. But even if he had been born a few years earlier, his development as a composer of musical drama would have strained the inherent limitations of the style.

The musical drama known as opera developed in the courts of Italy in the late sixteenth century as an attempt to re-create music that was thought to have accompanied classical Greek dramas. The Italian word *opera* translates plainly as the noun "work." The madrigal composers Jacopo Peri and Giulio Caccini kicked things off in Florence. The first great operatic composer was Claudio Monteverdi, whose three surviving operas (*L'Orfeo, Il ritorno d'Ulisse in patria,* and *L'incoronazione di Poppea*), like most of his music, mock their age, leaping across the centuries with their beauty, force, and fierce immediacy of expression. Another very great composer, Monteverdi forms a fitting ancestor to Verdi, these two giants marking the beginning and end of Italian opera's golden age. (Readers not yet acquainted with Monteverdi need to remedy that quickly.) The Italian operatic banner was carried in the seventeenth century by Francesco Cavalli and Pietro Antonio Cesti. At the royal court of France a grand, highly ornamented vocal and instrumental style, with plenty of dancing, different from the more straightforward Italian melodic model, developed under Jean-Baptiste Lully, born Giovanni Battista Lulli in Florence. Like the Italian, the elegant French operatic manner would live on into the early twentieth century. In the early and mid-nineteenth century, the Paris Opéra (with Milan's La Scala) was one of the two most important opera houses in the world. It was the goal of every important opera composer, including Verdi and Wagner, to write for the Paris Opéra, and the French style of the day influenced Verdi. In the high baroque period, the German-born George Frideric Handel built his career writing Italian operas in London, most of which have come happily back into the repertory; except for the big choruses, his well-loved oratorios are operatic treatments of Biblical stories. Handel's forms and melodically direct treatment of the affects also hold up well for modern listeners, though, as with other high baroque operas, there's little stage action. Italian style dominated the melodic thinking of Wolfgang Amadeus Mozart, whose graceful melodies for instrumental works are usually based on Italianate ideas. Three of Mozart's greatest operas (*Le nozze di Figaro*, *Don Giovanni*, and *Così fan tutte*) have Italian librettos, as do the fine but more old-fashioned *Idomeneo* and *La clemenza di Tito*, and contain much Italianate melody, but this master's style is so complex and idiosyncratic that it stands apart from the mainstream of the Italian (or any) operatic style. For all its grandeur, Beethoven's only opera, *Fidelio*, is also unidiomatic. With the folk tale–based *Der Freischütz* of Carl Maria von Weber (1821), we see the path of German opera diverging definitively from Italian or French models.

As mentioned earlier, three distinguished composers, all masters of bel canto, preceded Verdi in the mainstream Italian style of the first half of the nineteenth century. Gioachino Rossini is best known for his comedies, including *Il barbiere di Siviglia* and *La Cenerentola*, the latter based on the Cinderella tale. Known as *opera buffa*—comic opera—these are sublime in their way, with Rossini's depth of musical characterization sometimes rivaling Mozart's. But performances of Rossini's *opere serie*—serious works—over the past few decades have shown a composer of greater range. Like most opera composers of the day, this skilled, fast producer wound up in Paris, writing for the theaters there. His last opera, *Guillaume Tell*, has long been appreciated, at least in parts. Rich, famous, and exhausted, Rossini retired at age thirty-seven. He remained in Paris, composing occasionally, producing over the rest of his long life at least two masterworks, the Stabat Mater and a wonderful *Petite messe solennelle*. Rossini's style is lyrical but elegant, fluent yet a bit nervous, making great demands on singers' speed and stamina.

Vincenzo Bellini's short life and relatively low productivity belie his enormous influence on just about every composer of his time, and on many who followed. The Sicilian-born Bellini's skill was at writing breathtakingly long, expressive, and beautiful melodies, inside which the hearer seems to float, time suspended. The most famous is probably "Casta diva" from *Norma*, but all his works are packed with them. Verdi himself wrote admiringly of Bellini's "*lunghe, lunghe, lunghe*"—long—melodies, emulating them openly; even Wagner praised Bellini and conducted his *Norma*. Newbies may find Bellini's style hard to appreciate at first—again, you have to remember that it's about the voice, first and foremost. Once you do, though, you're hooked. Bellini's unsophisticated musical technique somehow works as part of his charm. More than a few listeners have come to know Verdi by working backward, starting with the late masterworks. The same approach might work for Bellini, whose last opera (*I Puritani*, soon after the Parisian premiere of which the composer died at age thirty-three) reflects a broadening of the young master's skills as an orchestrator and harmonist, with no abatement of his prodigious lyric gift.

Finally, Gaetano Donizetti, composer of more than sixty operas, was the predecessor Verdi modeled himself most closely on, especially early in his career. Donizetti was another master of bel canto, but as that style began to wane in popularity during his brief but furiously busy career, he shifted to a faster paced, more dramatic operatic manner that Verdi would conquer, while displaying a structural tightness and rhythmic drive that he admired and learned from. Donizetti's most famous operas are the bel canto tragedy *Lucia di Lammermoor*, best known for its mad scene for the heroine; *La favorite*; and the excellent comedies *La fille du régiment*, *L'elisir d'amore*, and *Don Pasquale*. The two operas with French titles (*La favorite* and *La fille du régiment*) were written when the composer was in Paris in 1840. As with Rossini, performers and audiences have found that there's more to Donizetti than the handful of operas that were popular for a century, finding much to admire in *Anna Bolena*, *Roberto Devereux*, *Caterina Cornaro*, and *Lucrezia Borgia*, among the fifty-odd others.

A number of Rossini's brilliant opera overtures have found a life of their own in the concert hall; Figaro's aria "Largo al factotum" from *Barbiere* is also well known; Bellini and Donizetti belong exclusively to consumers of opera. But Verdi appeals to a far broader base in ways that reach past the formal structures in which his predecessors worked, speaking directly and intensely to anyone who loves or even just responds to music and permits him- or herself to feel. Verdi's music has an emotional catch that's too strong to be denied. And, though he began his career working with the structures of scene and aria cherished by Italian audiences, his successes at home and abroad allowed him to loosen these forms as the plot and musical development of each story demanded. Although not thought of as a revolutionary composer, Verdi revolutionized Italian opera by pushing himself, his singers, librettists, opera directors, and finally audiences to accepting greater musical and dramatic truth with each successive work. Verdi's tireless push for truth in musical drama is one of his greatest legacies and most endearing qualities as an artist.

Perhaps Rossini's music, polished and entertaining, exerts the strongest pull of the three bel canto masters. But none of the three has anything close to the red-blooded Verdi's ability to grab us by the throat. This directness comes from his lyricism and his power, underpinned by his ferocious rhythmic drive. The lyricism is heard in is his extraordinary melodies, from such catchy tunes as "La donna è mobile" from *Rigoletto* to the blazing melodic arches that animate the other middle and late operas. There's no question that Verdi knew how to write and deploy melodies that go straight through us. Then, his deployment of rhythm displays fierce energy, balancing the melodies and animating the dramas. As we look at the operas individually, you'll see just how crucial rhythm is to Verdi's success.

The conventions of Italian opera called for frequent dramatic reversals to let composers portray contrasting emotions. As a result, plots can be preposterous, even in Verdi's case as late as *Forza* and *Simon Boccanegra*. The point is not to pick them apart for absurdities, but to view them as settings for the expression by the voice of primal emotions. Also, you'll find that as Verdi's music gets stronger, the plots seem less silly.

Words take longer to deliver when sung than spoken. Operatic time is therefore an expanded version of "real" time, onto which the glory of music is placed. This fact Verdi accepted, but he worried about it, knowing how easy it is for an audience to become bored. As a result, he pressed his music dramas ahead with an urgency all his own. Time and again, his correspondence with his librettists shows his dread of dullness. As a result, his works, even the long ones, such as *Don Carlo*, move along swiftly, build climactically, then get on to the next scene. This is a major quality in a dramatic artist, and a gift to operatic beginners.

Another strength of Verdi's is his mastery at depicting psychological conflict. A da capo aria by Handel, Jean-Philippe Rameau, or Alessandro Scarlatti will express one emotion, one affect in its outer sections; the middle part will contrast slightly with it in mood and musical texture. But the emotions expressed in both parts will be plain, pure, and nameable. With Mozart, all that changed. Reflecting that people often say one thing—what they think they're supposed to say—but feel something entirely different, Mozart's characters sing with pinpoint psychological accuracy. Verdi was equally adept at the depiction in music of a split psyche. This skill will be shown repeatedly in our looks at the individual operas, but to give one extraordinary example, throughout *Otello*, Iago and Otello must constantly feign emotions. Iago is good—too good—at it; Otello himself utterly incapable of containing his feelings, as Verdi shows, through music of devastating insight and power.

The split within all of us between responsibility and our private desires is one of opera's major themes, typically as background or setup for a tragic love story. You'll find it at work in any opera with royalty or political leaders as characters, which includes many in the repertory. (Sometimes, as in *Otello* and *Falstaff*, the protagonist-hero stands in as the royal figure.) Verdi exploited this dichotomy with ever-greater force and profundity from the beginning to the end of his long career, with *Don Carlo* as perhaps its consummate expression. Verdi was fiercely anticlerical, a posture that spilled over into his work. We'll hear heroes and heroines in *Il trovatore*, *Don Carlo*, and *Aida* locked in futile struggles with oppressive and reactionary priesthoods that crush their lives and loves. And, finally, parents and—or more accurately versus—children, with particularly poignant relationships between fathers and daughters, is another theme Verdi took up regularly and vividly.

The darkness that shadows Verdi's work from beginning to (nearly) the end speaks clearly to something inside us. We respond to the composer's pessimism, in the expression of which none of his Italian predecessors come close. More than mere entertainment, his operas address terrible truths about human existence. Yet there's more to Verdi than fatalism:

his characters, like Shakespeare's, Monteverdi's, Mozart's, or Wagner's, seem to live and breathe, and the composer's love for them in their rages, passions, and follies remains clear. Verdi may be dark, but he's always humane. Among the dark emotions, his expressions of anger stand alongside those of Beethoven and Wagner as some of the most convincing in music. For Verdi's Italian predecessors, anger is an affect to be picked up, then dropped as the libretto proceeds. When Verdi's characters express anger, the emotion's expression is of another order, of frightening force and accuracy of depiction.

Richard Wagner, Verdi's exact contemporary (born on May 22, 1813, less than five months before Verdi) makes up the other half of one of the remarkable sets of twin masters in Western music. Wagner's reforms of the arts of music and musical drama were enormous. It was Wagner who, with *Lohengrin* (1850) first dispensed with individual numbering of scenes, arias, and choruses from his operas. Most significantly, though, Wagner kicked apart the framework of the old-fashioned harmonic structure. If you look in a textbook study of musical history, you'll learn that the German is, from a purely developmental standpoint, the more significant composer. "The discrepancy between intrinsic worth and historical significance is perhaps greater with Verdi than with any important composer except J. S. Bach,"[1] the author of one overview in which Wagner gets ten pages acknowledges in his five-paragraph summary of Verdi. Wagner's higher historical profile has more to do with his mold-breaking approach to harmony than to his changes in operatic structure, which Verdi pretty much paralleled. Wagner's achievement was to make dissonance—the sound of tones that clash—a standard element of harmonic vocabulary. To hear how Wagner changed music's course, you need to listen to *Tristan und Isolde*. In this extraordinary music drama—a seminal work in Western music and culture—you'll hear dissonance deployed in a way that was new, with passages in dissonant harmony far longer than any composer had ever asked an audience to tolerate. *Tristan* turned dissonance into a new type of consonance. No composer who is not a great harmonic practitioner can belong to the top rank, and by any measure, Verdi is a magnificent harmonist. His harmonic backdrops are richly expressive, and he moved between keys with great freedom and dramatic effect; as he got older, his boldness at moving from key to key grew quite remarkable. But he did not alter the harmonic underpinning of Western music, as Wagner did.

Wagner and Verdi may be the two greatest masters of the high romantic era, and certainly Verdi's romantic-era chops can be heard in the sweep and richness of the Requiem or the love duets from *Ballo* and *Otello*. But to the end of his career, Verdi also displayed a strong classical bent, sounding at times like the keen student of Haydn, Mozart, and Beethoven he was.

Wagner may win the prize for harmonic daring, but you'll surely find yourself persuaded, as you endure the twelve-minute monologue of King Marke that brings act 2 of *Tristan*, an opera that has little in the way of conventional action, to a dead halt, that Verdi had the better feel for what works onstage. Verdi kept things moving even when faced with trite or awkward junctures of plot. Wagner didn't know when to quit, flogging us with concepts or having characters recap the plot; the librettos to his operas, which he wrote, range from profound (as in act 3 of *Tristan*) to laughable. The straightforward librettos to *Rigoletto* and *Traviata*, written by Francesco Maria Piave under Verdi's close supervision, get the job done with never a lapse into dullness. This is not to posit a matchup between these two giants, merely to point out that Wagner's theorizing and tendency to run on overcame his dramatic judgment at times; as you'll see, there are lumpy moments in Verdi, too. Surely the proper approach for the music lover is to revere both masters and appreciate the coincidence of these titanic imaginations' working in the same arena at the same time.

Wagner's influence on Verdi seems minimal; Verdi never really sounds anything like Wagner. As noted, the German may have run a bit ahead in breaking the bonds of the scene, but Verdi, stuck early in his career with the rigid structures of Italian operas, worked from the start to loosen them and to allow his music dramas to move with the urgency he imagined for them. Verdi was able to set all the creative conditions for his final operas, *Otello* and *Falstaff*, and both fly along faster than anything by Wagner. Perhaps more influential on Verdi was the Paris Opéra, which he knew well and composed several works for. Unlike Italians, French audiences appreciated novelty, and Verdi spent much time in Paris, hearing operas by his French contemporaries. And apparently the important opera orchestras of Paris played better than did those in Italy. So, Verdi was able to write more demandingly for them, and to demand better of Italian orchestras when he returned to compose for Italian theaters.

Verdi composed twenty-eight operas between *Oberto, Conte di San Bonifacio*, in 1839, and *Falstaff*, in 1893. Two of the twenty-eight are substantial revisions, with new titles, of existing operas. Of the twenty-eight, sixteen are the most significant, and, with the exception of the underrated *Stiffelio*, it is with these that this book—an overview, after all—will deal. It's unfortunate to have to make such distinctions, but the twelve lesser works are rarely performed; there are recordings and DVDs for readers who feel they must see and hear them. The breaking of Verdi's works into two tiers is not my whim; it has long and generally been recognized as accurately applying to the operas' relative merits. I will describe the twelve lesser works in chapter 4, focusing on their high points, of which there are many. But the sixteen big operas are so vast and rich that as you'll see there's plenty in them to hear and think about. Verdi completed a Requiem in 1874 that stands among his finest and most beloved works; it's operatic in idiom though not in form. His final compositions, the *Quattro sacri pezzi*—Four Sacred Pieces, composed between 1888 and 1897, are Verdi's sublime final works. We'll look at these and the Requiem in chapter 9.

Any discussion of Verdi and his works needs beautifully sung examples. For that, the compact disc at the back of the book offers examples by some of the great Verdi singers of the last century. We'll take a brief look at Verdi singers and their styles and make a few more recommendations for further listening and viewing in chapter 14.

A list of Verdi's operas follows. I also give the dates of their first performances, translations of the titles where they seem useful, and whether they are considered important or lesser works.

- *Oberto, Conte di San Bonifacio* (1839); lesser
- *Un giorno di regno* (King for a Day; 1840); lesser
- *Nabucco* (1842); important
- *I Lombardi alla prima crociata* (The Lombards on the First Crusade; 1843); lesser
- *Ernani* (1844); important
- *I due Foscari* (The Two Foscari; 1844); lesser
- *Giovanna d'Arco* (Joan of Arc; 1845); lesser
- *Alzira* (1845); lesser
- *Attila* (1846); lesser
- *Macbeth* (1847; revised in 1865); important
- *I masnadieri* (The Robbers; 1847); lesser

- *Jérusalem* (1847; a revision in French of *I Lombardi*); lesser
- *Il corsaro* (The Corsair; 1848); lesser
- *La battaglia di Legnano* (The Battle of Legnano; 1849); lesser
- *Luisa Miller* (1849); important
- *Stiffelio* (1850); classed among the lesser works, but we'll look at it among the important ones
- *Rigoletto* (1851); important
- *Il trovatore* (The Troubadour; 1853); important
- *La traviata* (The Lost One; 1853); important
- *Les vêpres siciliennes/I vespri siciliani* (The Sicilian Vespers; 1855); written for the Paris Opéra and translated into Italian the following year; important
- *Simon Boccanegra* (1857); revised extensively in 1881; important
- *Aroldo* (1857); a thorough revision of *Stiffelio* and the last of the lesser works
- *Un ballo in maschera* (A Masked Ball; 1859); important
- *La forza del destino* (The Force of Destiny; 1862); important
- *Don Carlos*, also titled *Don Carlo* (1867 to 1887); important. As with *I vespri siciliani*, the original opera was written in French, then translated into Italian and revised over two decades.
- *Aida* (1871); important
- *Otello* (1887); important
- *Falstaff* (1893); important

We'll look at Verdi's productivity in chapter 2, which discusses his life, as well as at other points in the book; but you can see as you look over the list that he worked at a furious pace in the first half of his career, then less regularly on new operas after 1850, though he often revised older ones. A glance at the table of contents will show you how the book is organized, but before the four late masterpieces (*Don Carlo* through *Falstaff*), each of which get its own chapter, it makes sense to group the works in pairs and threes. The three important early operas work well as one chapter; *Rigoletto*, *Trovatore*, and *Traviata*, big and familiar, are probably too much for a single chapter. But they form so clear a turning point to Verdi's mature style that it's useful to consider them together.

# Verdi's Life and Character

High ambition, hard work, and genius provided the elements for Verdi's rise. But the tragic deaths of his first wife and their two children that struck in his early maturity marked him indelibly with sorrow and shaped his dark vision as a musical dramatist. Little is known of Verdi's temperament before these personal tragedies occurred in 1838 through 1840. But the stern face of later portraits, whether painted, drawn, or photographed, seem to reflect a personality consistent with their outward appearance.

Verdi was cautious and even shy in his dealings with the world, avoiding journalists and well-wishers. He was close to his inner circle, yet behaved tyrannically at home with his second wife, Giuseppina, and their servants.[1] He feuded bitterly with people, including his parents, in his hometown of Busseto, yet planted himself and Giuseppina there, when he could have lived anywhere. The paradoxes go on; and although Verdi didn't advertise it, he was, quite exceptionally for a nineteenth-century Italian, an atheist.[2] Although Verdi's career describes a pretty direct upward course in his popular success, artistic recognition, and wealth, his personal life was troubled. Much of his difficulties in the world seem to have stemmed from his willfulness: like everyone, he wanted things his way. As a respected artist, he was generally able to get what he wanted. But outside the world of the theater, he seems rarely to have considered the reaction an unpopular personal decision might provoke.

Verdi was born on October 9 or 10, 1813, in Le Roncole, a hamlet near the town of Busseto in the province of Parma in north-central Italy. His parents, Carlo and Luigia, owned an inn and grocery; so while far from rich, they were not poor, either. Verdi's musical gifts showed early, and by age nine he played the organ in the village church. Sent to Busseto for school, he there attracted the attention of Antonio Barezzi, a wealthy merchant. Barezzi would become Verdi's patron, father-in-law, and ultimately almost a second father. Barezzi first advanced Verdi's cause as a musician, trying to secure for him a place and scholarship at the Milan Conservatory. Verdi's application was rejected, however, and he began to study privately with Vincenzo Lavigna, a teacher in Milan. Milan's opera houses provided Verdi with the opportunity to attend operas daily, marking him decisively with the understanding that the audience must never be allowed to tire of the music or stage action.

Verdi had also made contact with Bartolomeo Merelli, director of the La Scala opera house in Milan, expressing to Merelli his desire to compose an opera. It was some time during this period that Merelli put into Verdi's hands the libretto to *Oberto, Conte di San Bonifacio*. Verdi worked on it in Busseto and Milan in 1838 and 1839, and his first opera was produced at La Scala on November 17, 1839. *Oberto* was well reviewed, and apparently more than a moderate success at the box office, and Merelli contracted with the rookie composer for three more operas. Verdi plunged into the second, *Un giorno di regno*, in early 1840.

In 1836, Verdi had married his patron Barezzi's daughter, Margherita. Margherita gave birth to a daughter, Virginia, in March 1837, and a son, Icilio, in July 1838. But Virginia died that August. Icilio died in October 1839, marking the second of the three crushing tragedies that deprived the composer of his first family. In June 1840, Margherita died as well. A shattered Verdi asked to be released from his operatic contract but Merelli persuaded him to go back to work, however, even though Verdi's grief worked against his writing a comedy. *Un giorno di regno* is a reasonably well-made if not masterful opera buffa—comic opera—that flopped at its premiere, partly due to weak casting. Yet Verdi's outlook would remain dark, as would his music, for the rest of his life: "But after all, in life isn't everything death? What else exists?"[3] he wrote to a friend, discussing the gloomy plot of *Il trovatore*. In early 1841 Merelli offered Verdi the libretto of *Nabucco*, which would be his first big hit. While composing the work, Verdi met Giuseppina Strepponi, a brilliant soprano notorious for her personal behavior, who would become his friend, then his mistress, and eventually his wife. Although her voice was in decline by the time they met, Strepponi sang the demanding role of Abigaille in the premiere of

*Nabucco* at La Scala on March 9, 1842, the event that established Verdi's reputation.

As the man of the hour, Verdi pushed himself to compose again and again, at least one opera a year, sometimes two and even three, over the next ten years. First was *I Lombardi alla prima crociata*, for La Scala. *Ernani*, for the Venetian theater La Fenice, was another big hit; as we'll see, it's a fiery work that holds up beautifully. *Ernani* is also the first opera he collaborated on with Francesco Maria Piave, the adapter and wordsmith whom Verdi prodded and bullied into producing ten texts that range in quality from mediocre to, in the case of *Rigoletto*, well above average. Next composed were *I due Foscari* for the Teatro Argentina in Rome, followed by *Giovanna d'Arco*. *Alzira*, for the Teatro San Carlo in Naples, is considered Verdi's worst; the composer himself thought so.[4]

Once an operatic subject was agreed on, Verdi would discuss the overall plan for the opera with his librettist. His letters show Verdi giving minute instructions to the collaborator, down to (in fact, particularly to) the syllable. Often Verdi had set the musical idea for Piave to backfill with text, Italian being more forgiving than English to such treatment. Piave was also one of the wary composer's few close friends, knowing him from early on, unawed by the man but genuinely happy for his success. The letters between the two reveal a playfulness that's rare in Verdi's correspondence.[5]

*Attila*, which premiered in May 1846 at La Fenice, falls among the master's minor works, but in a duet between the titular Hun and a Roman general Ezio, the latter sings, "You may take the universe, but leave Italy to me." The line struck a chord among patriots who hoped to see the Italian-speaking provinces united into a single nation, a movement known as the *Risorgimento*—Resurgence. Italy was a group of medium to small principalities under various rulers. Verdi was himself a firm supporter of the movement, though he kept clear of the battlefronts.

With *Macbeth*, composed for a Florentine opera house, Verdi reaches for and often, though not consistently, grasps sublimity. *Macbeth* is the first of his three operas based on works by Shakespeare; Verdi also had Salvatore Cammarano prepare (in 1850) a libretto for an operatic *King Lear*, which the composer toyed with over the years but never completed. That the master's fame was now international is shown by the next two operas, *I masnadieri* and *Jérusalem*, written for Her Majesty's Theatre in

London and the Paris Opéra, respectively. The latter in particular demonstrates Verdi's rise to prominence among Italian opera composers, as Paris was probably the most esteemed house in Europe. *Jérusalem* itself is a revision in French of *I Lombardi*. Verdi wrote *Il corsaro* for the Trieste opera house; the work premiered in October 1848.

*Corsaro* was followed in 1849 by the frankly patriotic *La battaglia di Legnano*. The composer's name was used as a coded acronym for Vittorio Emanuele, Re d'Italia, ruler of Savoy and Sardinia, under whom Italy would finally unify in 1861. The Italian movement began to boil along with much of the rest of Europe, in 1848. *La battaglia di Legnano*, with a libretto by Salvatore Cammarano, premiered in Rome in 1849, and was conceived unambiguously to work Italians into a patriotic fervor.

*Luisa Miller*, of 1849, to a libretto by Cammarano and based on an intimate drama by Schiller, marks an important advance in Verdi's style. The composer portrayed his mostly humble characters with new musical and dramatic warmth, with the relationship between Luisa and her father standing as one of the most touching father-daughter portrayals in Verdi's canon. The work was a success at its premiere in Naples, in December 1849. The next opera, *Stiffelio*, was and remains an unusual work. The subject, a Protestant minister who must forgive his wife for her infidelity, is a complex theme, more dramatic than tragic. *Stiffelio* premiered in November 1850 in Trieste. Neither subject nor treatment discouraged the initial audience, which received the work warmly. It did, however, displease the censors in other Italian cities, some of whom demanded the resetting of a scene in a church, not to mention a scene of confession. These headaches anticipated more that Verdi would endure in the creation of his next three operas.

With those operas—*Rigoletto*, *Il trovatore*, and *La traviata*—Verdi's genius reaches full bloom. These astonishing works, along with *Aida*, remain his most popular, and among the most popular of all operas. They also show the composer's gifts at their most wide-ranging: with *Rigoletto*, which first played in March 1851 at Venice's La Fenice, telling with force and economy of a hunchbacked court jester and daughter destroyed by a cynical ruler and his court. Verdi's treatment of the title character remains one of the most remarkable in opera. *Il trovatore* (Rome, January 1853) transfigures an old-fashioned libretto and stock characters with music of white heat. *La traviata*, which premiered in March 1853 at La Fenice, tells an intimate, contemporary story of a woman used and then thrown away by society.

Verdi complained in a letter to a friend that he had spent the years since the composition of *Nabucco* without "an hour's peace . . . in the galleys."[6] Indeed, a look at the list of operas in the previous chapter shows intense work from the start of his career through 1853, with one work following the next in close succession. But of course Verdi was enslaved by his own ambition. After *Traviata*, however, rich and established as the unchallenged master of Italian opera, Verdi began to look more selectively at his projects, and to take time off between.

In 1855, Verdi received a commission from the Paris Opéra for *Les vêpres siciliennes*. Following the French format, this is an expansive, five-act opera with a ballet. Few regard *Vêpres* (now usually heard in its Italian version, *I vespri siciliani*) as one of Verdi's most attractive works. But its spaciousness, with no loss of the composer's typical furious manner, does represent an expansion of his style, looking ahead to such big, scenic operas as *La forza del destino*, *Don Carlo*, and *Aida*. Composed to a libretto by Eugène Scribe, *Vêpres* premiered in Paris in June 1855.

Verdi's next opera, *Simon Boccanegra*, is based, like *Vespri*, on a historical theme from the Middle Ages, this time to a Piave libretto. Verdi struggled with this work, which, with a ridiculously complex plot and shortage of female roles, was poorly received at its opening in Venice in March 1857. Verdi reworked it in 1880 and 1881 with Arrigo Boito, who would later collaborate with him on *Otello* and *Falstaff*. That same year, Verdi revised *Stiffelio* into *Aroldo* for the Teatro Nuovo at Rimini.

Worried over the trouble he foresaw with censors, Verdi approached his next project, *Un ballo in maschera*, warily. The subject, the assassination of the King Gustavus III of Sweden in 1792, had been used dramatically before; but Verdi was correct to be cautious. He fought suggestions by his librettist, Antonio Somma, to set the ball in pre-Christian Scotland or Pomerania on the Baltic Sea, both of which sound ludicrous once one knows this elegant score. Ultimately, Verdi reset it in colonial Boston, with the governor rather than a king as the protagonist. Yet this brilliant opera stands as a landmark in Verdi's output, showing none of the difficulties that attended its creation. *Ballo*, which premiered in Rome in February 1859, has been appreciated since as one of the composer's greatest and most consistent works—with many recent productions set at the Swedish court, as originally intended.

Verdi began to say around this time that he was exhausted and ready to retire.[7] Although, of course, this was not the case, proposals for new works had to be raised discreetly. On August 29, 1859, Verdi secretly married Giuseppina, with a priest officiating, in a village on the border between Piemonte and Switzerland. There's no indication of why the wedding took place, Verdi's unconventional views on marriage and priests not having changed. He was then part of a committee that called on King Vittorio Emanuele of Savoy, requesting that his home state of Parma be attached to the new Italian nation. He also served in Italy's Chamber of Deputies, attending dutifully though rarely speaking, and retiring from politics in 1865.

In 1860 Verdi began to scout for a new project. The Imperial Theater in St. Petersburg offered a project with wide creative latitude; the fee was irresistibly high, and travel expenses to Russia were paid. This was the start of *La forza del destino*, the sprawling slice of life set in eighteenth-century Spain, in which the characters are pawns of a coincidence-loving fate. *Forza* received its premiere in St. Petersburg in November 1862. There's an amusing photograph of a stone-faced Verdi in St. Petersburg, dressed in a fur hat and a floor-length fur-collared coat.

Verdi's next operatic project was a revision of *Macbeth* for one of the Parisian theaters. The result is a slightly awkward but still impressive mixture of his early and middle styles, with ballets for witches thrown in, dance elements still in demand by Parisian audiences. It's the version performed today. Verdi retained a deep affection for this work, which was reborn in Paris in April 1865.

His next operatic project would result in one of his greatest operas, *Don Carlo*, as well as marking the start of his flexible, rich, and complex late style. Based (like *Luisa Miller* and *I masnadieri*) on a play by Schiller, this extraordinary work probes its six important characters with a new depth of insight and all the old passion. Originally conceived as *Don Carlos* for the Paris Opéra to a libretto in French by Camille du Locle, this masterpiece would be reworked several times over the next two decades, Verdi changing the music of the ending, putting it into Italian, and reducing its scale from the vast five-act French version to four acts. *Don Carlo* is appreciated and revered as one of Verdi's most characteristic masterworks, as well as his most spacious. It had its premiere in Paris in March 1867.

That year and the next were unhappy personally to Verdi: both his own father, Carlo, and Antonio Barezzi, his father-in-law and patron, died in 1867. In 1868, he was introduced to one of his literary idols, the novelist Alessandro Manzoni, author of *The Betrothed*. Verdi revered Manzoni, whose death in 1873 provided a new dedicatee for a Requiem he'd originally planned to honor Rossini. The composer made revisions to *La forza del destino*, which was introduced to Italy in February 1869.

*Aida* was commissioned to celebrate the opening of the Cairo Opera House.[8] This tragic love story combines intimacy with the sweep of the triumphal scene, while showing the composer's new mastery of the orchestra as well as a piquant harmonic coloring that accorded well with European ideas about how "exotic" music should sound, though Verdi's sophistication keeps the score in beautiful balance. His regular collaborator Piave had suffered a stroke in 1869, and so the composer turned to Antonio Ghislanzoni for this libretto. Verdi was not present for the world premiere in Cairo in December 1871, but supervised the Italian premiere at La Scala in 1872.

Around this time Teresa Stolz, a Czech soprano, enters the narrative. Stolz sang Aida in the Italian premiere, and many times afterward; she and Verdi worked together professionally on many occasions in the years that followed. And Stolz may have been his mistress. Such, at any rate, was the speculation in the Italian press, which in 1875 surmised a rendezvous in Florence between Verdi and Stolz. Letters show that his wife, Peppina's jealousy was indeed roused, though she and Stolz eventually became friends. Stolz and Verdi remained close companions after Peppina's death in 1897. Verdi's single, excellent string quartet comes from this period. Written when the composer "had nothing to do,"[9] this fine chamber work is well worth hearing.

The Requiem idea from five years before had percolated in his imagination, because when Manzoni died in 1873, Verdi began work on the great Mass for the dead that remains one of his most beloved works. The paradox of this atheist and anticlerical genius composing in a religious form is wonderful;[10] but the composer stuck to his dramatic manner, which has been called many times, with heavy irony, his "greatest opera." As you'll hear, Verdi makes a terrified humanity the protagonist of the existential drama.

The Requiem had its premiere in Milan on May 22, 1874, the anniversary of Manzoni's death, deepening respect for the composer across Europe.

Verdi had worked with the writer and composer Arrigo Boito in 1862, when Boito provided the composer with a text for Verdi's single occasional piece, the *Inno delle nazioni*—the Hymn of the Nations. Verdi paid Boito, thanked him politely for his work, and the matter seemed closed. In 1863 Boito wrote a satirical poem deploring the state of Italian music; as its leading figure by a wide margin, Verdi assumed the poem was about him. There were no relations to speak of between the two in any case, but after this it seemed unlikely that they might collaborate on Verdi's last two operas. Verdi's publisher Giulio Ricordi saw in Boito a potential collaborator and writer of sufficient talent and musical knowledge to assist the still vigorous Verdi. Ricordi had Boito write an outline for *Otello*, then used Verdi's dissatisfaction with *Simon Boccanegra* to nominate Boito to fix the libretto. Verdi revised *Simon Boccanegra* into the version that premiered at La Scala in March 1881, and is always the one performed today. Although the plot is still too complicated, the world gained a fierce and powerful work in Verdi's late style. And now the master had a librettist whose gifts matched his own.

Even so, Verdi had to be coaxed into and through the *Otello* project. Although eager to return to Shakespeare, the composer complained that he was too old to start on a task so large. Again, the publisher Ricordi and Boito had to suggest gently that the composer, clearly at the height of his powers, was up to the job. In 1884, after several years of discussion and hesitation, Verdi began work on the opera, acting surprised when he was productive. Verdi finished *Otello* late in 1886, and it had its premiere at La Scala on February 5, 1887. If there was a dramatic subject suited to Verdi's gifts, it's the high passion and poetry of *Othello*; the grandeur of *Otello*, the pinnacle of Italian lyric drama, was obvious from that first night.

Boito's contribution to the success of *Otello* was of a different order than that of any of Verdi's previous librettists, and the composer knew it, bringing the writer onstage to share the cheering at the premiere. With Boito, no mere wordsmith, on board, it was only a matter of time before the two collaborators were discussing the possibility of one more work, a comedy based on Sir John Falstaff, the sublime Shakespearean character from *The Merry Wives of Windsor* and the two *Henry IV* history plays. As was his way, Verdi voiced doubts, but, knowing that he had the rare chance to round out his creative life in a most beautiful fashion, he was itching to get at it. Boito's libretto for *Otello* is a masterpiece of compression, concision, and dramatic momentum, but his for *Falstaff* is even more astonishing. The plot follows that of *The Merry Wives of Windsor*, into which Boito inserts bits from the histories that deepen the characters' motivation. The text is full of verbal explosions, which Verdi takes full advantage of in the score. It's hard to think of anything by any composer that moves faster, and *Falstaff*, perhaps more than any major opera, repays regular hearings and long acquaintance. The other side of that coin is that it's impossible to grasp its countless subtleties on first hearing. So, while initial audiences listened respectfully, *Falstaff* wasn't universally adored at its premiere at La Scala on February 9, 1893, or in the decade or so that followed. With the advent of recordings, its greatness became obvious.

Verdi spent the rest of his life working on the four settings of Catholic texts he had begun in 1889, the *Quattro pezzi sacri*; revising his works for new productions; and supervising a production here and there. Peppina died on November 14, 1897, at Sant'Agata. Verdi watched over the construction of the Rest Home for Musicians in Milan, which he built and endowed, and where he and Peppina are buried. He died in Milan, on January 27, 1901, a week after suffering a stroke. A crowd estimated at 200,000 accompanied the coffin to the municipal cemetery where he was initially buried, and a larger one a month later, when Verdi and Peppina were reinterred in the Musicians' Rest Home.

# The Major Early Operas
## Nabucco, Ernani, and Macbeth

E
ach of the three most significant operas of Verdi's early period has a character quite different from the other two. *Nabucco* and *Ernani* both, however, feature plots loaded with disguises, mistaken and hidden identities, recognitions, and reversals that strike modern listeners as ridiculous. These were standard devices for operas of the 1840s and the preceding decades, narrative contortions allowing composers to portray as many emotional affects as possible in an evening's entertainment, and, more important at the time, letting singers show off their voice and skills at vocal display. Absurd yet predictable, these stories are not terribly different from those of TV sitcoms or police dramas, where you know who'll be zany or when in the course of the hour the real killer will be exposed. The young Verdi accepted these conventions, while altering them, mostly by tightening here and there. Admired from the start for his melodic fertility and skill at evoking moods, he was in no position to turn the Italian operatic world upside down—he probably didn't even think in those terms. But, driven by an overriding fear of boring his audience, Verdi accelerated the pace of these creaky tales, not including *Macbeth*, of course. And his fierce rhythmic drive already sets these works apart stylistically.

## Nabucco

Two ironies are attached to story of the opera that made Verdi famous. The first is that the work's real title is *Nabucodonosor*—an Italianization of the name of the Babylonian king Nebuchadnezzar. The shortened name was bestowed in 1844 by a theater in Corfu,[1] and has stuck. Also, the nostalgic chorus "Va, pensiero"—Fly, thought—was not initially the favorite. It seems that a bigger impression was made by the thunderous "Immenso Jehova," the opera's penultimate number.[2] The nationalistic flavor of "Va, pensiero," implicitly comparing enslaved Hebrews with Italians under foreign domination, stoked the aspirations of the unification movement in the years that followed, raising the chorus to anthemlike status.

The chorus plays an important role in *Nabucco*, frequently onstage, expressing the Israelites' hopes and fears; these spoke with additional meaning to Italian audiences of 1842 and the following years, as the unification movement gained momentum. No single character in the opera dominates the work to the same extent as does the chorus, not even Nabucco himself, alarming though Verdi's musical portrayal of him is at times. Among the solo parts, that of Abigaille is exceedingly difficult; Verdi's conceptions of her and Nabucco prepared the composer for Macbeth and his wife five years later.[3] Alternately furious and pitiful for Nabucco, and furious and tender for Abigaille, they're also the only vividly drawn characters in the opera. Abigaille is a late example of an angry opera seria female lead, like Cherubini's Medea or Elettra in Mozart's *Idomeneo*. Although operatic treatments of Biblical subjects, such as *Nabucco*, were unusual in Italian opera houses of the era, they were not unheard of, with Rossini's *Mosè in Egitto*—Moses in Egypt—of 1818 its best-known antecedent.

*Nabucco* holds together better than much of other early Verdi does, although it's uneven as well. It opens with a long, loose overture of the potpourri type, meaning it takes themes from the opera, putting them in a free-flowing montage to set a mood of seriousness well suited to the music drama, though the racing take on the chorus that ends the first act sounds like a cancan. What we think of as acts are called "parts" in the libretto and score, and the librettist Temistocle Solera gave a title to each. Right at the start of the first "part," titled "Jerusalem," the chorus assumes its primacy with a long passage where it expresses fear about Nabucco and his army, Verdi putting the harp to good use in the accompaniment. The high priest Zaccaria's aria that follows ("D'Egitto là sui lidi"—*There on the shores of Egypt*) is grand and dignified in its patient flow. The gurgling bassoon solo that accompanies the middle part of the aria may detract a bit from its intended solemnity, but Verdi already writes for the bass voice with distinction. Zaccaria's cabaletta (at this time in the composer's career, a slow aria is almost always followed by a quick-tempo, rhythmically incisive cabaletta), "Come notte a sol fulgente"—*As night before the bright sun*—in which the chorus participates, has a fierce energy.

With Abigaille's furious declaimed taunt of Ismaele and Fenena ("Prode guerrier!"—*Brave warrior!*), Verdi characterizes her volatility, pride, and rage in an elaborate vocal line of unequalled virtuosity. Abigaille's role—impressive when well sung, which isn't often—is so showy and difficult that it can distract from the drama. The trio for Fenena, Ismaele, and Abigaille that follows ("Io t'amava"—*I loved you*) is beautiful, too, though except for Abigaille, it lacks the differentiation of character Verdi would later achieve in such ensembles. A march of nervous energy tells of Nabucco's approach; his monologue, mocking the Israelites' god when he enters the temple ("O vinti, il capo a terra"—*O vanquished, bow down*) expresses his arrogance. The bitter debate between Zaccaria and Nabucco, here backed by the full ensemble, looks ahead to other great duels between low voices, in *Macbeth, Rigoletto, Simon Boccanegra,* and *Don Carlo.* And the energy of the rhythm in the fast part of the ensemble shows the composer's drive at its purest.

A snarling recitative for Abigaille opens the second act, or part, titled "The Unbeliever," on a strong note. This murderous passage ("Ben io t'invenni"—*Lucky I found you*) contains a huge, two-octave drop from high C to middle C, very unusual for Verdi, and the kind of difficulty this practical composer for the stage generally spared his singers. Although elaborately decorated, the soothing stepwise motion of her aria "Anch'io dischiuso un giorno"—*I, too, once opened my heart to joy*—is more typical of Verdi's style. The sweetly chattering woodwinds that accompany her anticipate a more famous aria of another daughter in love, the "Caro nome" of Gilda in *Rigoletto.* And the entire scene, in which Abigaille recalls her love for Ismaele, makes her sympathetic. The next, where she dispatches realpolitik with the High Priest of Baal and chorus, again with the vocal line greatly challenging, is fiery and fine. The second scene, with its prayer "Vieni, o Levita!"—*Come, Levites!*—for Zaccaria, in a free vocal line, accompanied by six cellos, marks another bold step in orchestral mastery for the young Verdi. His likely inspiration here is a famous passage in Rossini's *Guillaume Tell,* but the effect is completely different. The curse of Ismaele for contravening Zaccaria by the Levites is another passage of stunning rhythmic drive. And the ensemble that concludes the act, "Chi mi toglie il regio scettro?"—*Who has taken my royal scepter?*—in which Nabucco's crown is swept off his head, with the orchestra imitating the mysterious wind, displays real power. The freedom with which Verdi treats the mad Nabucco's vocal line is comparable to Abigaille's, without being as extreme. This ensemble is a good, early example of Verdi's tendency to compress and accelerate the musical pace at climactic moments, building excitement rather than defusing it with repetition or pompous expansions.

The third act ("The Prophecy") contains the chorus that's the opera's most famous moment, but there's much more to it. The duet between the mad and now pitiful Nabucco and the imperious Abigaille ("Uscite, o fidi miei"—*Leave us, my loyal subjects*) is tense and brilliantly characterized, though the tune to which her rejoicing is set is trivial. The king's line mixes pathos with recollections of his former commanding nature, while her vocal part leaps furiously, and is decorated with wild coloratura, another example of what makes this role so intimidating. The second scene opens with the haunting chorus that made Verdi famous: "Va, pensiero, sull'ali dorate"—*Fly, thought, on golden wings*. After a solemn orchestral introduction, its sinuous melody is stated quietly over a rocking accompaniment; the second verse, reminiscent of an Italian lullaby, is a bit louder and in full harmony. But the low volume is riveting, and far more affecting than a thunderous statement might be, and the contrast offered by the middle passage is not so strong as to break the reflective mood. Even young, Verdi's instinct for drama is notable, as he grabs his audience's attention by understating this crucial moment. The act ends with an impressive prophecy of doom for Babylon ("Del futuro nel buio discerno"—*I can see into the gloom of the future*) rendered in somber tones by Zaccaria. Verdi's orchestral accompaniment, though not particularly original, is a fine example of orchestral tone painting, a careful rendering of the divine wind that will destroy Babylon.

The final act ("The Shattered Idol") begins with a short but telling introduction in which the orchestra broods on themes heard before as the curtain rises on Nabucco, dozing uneasily. His monologue "Son pur queste mie membra"—*Yes, these are my limbs*—entails many changes of mood and expression as he recalls his anger at the Hebrews, then finds himself locked in his chamber, sees Fenena being brought to execution out of his window, then prays to the god of the Hebrews, is rescued by his guards, and resolves to save Fenena, all of which Verdi tracks minutely. Although the scene works pretty well dramatically, it's not the strongest musically. Nabucco's cabaletta "O prodi miei"—*My brave men*—is coarse but irresistibly exciting, thanks to its rhythmic drive. You'll hear a brass band in the mix, playing a somber march offstage. The *banda*, as it's called in Italian, is a small group of brass players used for coloristic effects. It's a convention of Italian stage works that Verdi made much use of, as late as *Aida*. He deploys the *banda* with ever more discretion—and to better effect—as his style developed, but here it sounds clumsy and old-fashioned.

The final scene of *Nabucco* opens with the sound of the *banda* playing the same funeral march for Fenena's impending execution. Her little prayer is sad, a bit corny, but brief, and delicately scored for pizzicato strings and woodwinds. Nabucco's pronouncement after the collapse of the statue of Baal ("Ah, torna Israello"—*Return, Israel*) is effectively set, as is the big prayer, "Immenso Jehova," for unaccompanied chorus. This, as noted, is where many nineteenth-century performances ended, the taste of the age considering it more uplifting than Abigaille's death scene. But that superb number ("Su me ... morente ... esanime ..."—*To me ... weak ... dying ...*) in which a chamberlike orchestra accompanies the singer, whose part, harmonized strikingly by the English horn, struggles before soaring high, is well worth hearing, so modern performances include it. Bucking operatic custom, Verdi does not provide Abigaille with a virtuosic cabaletta. This makes dramatic sense—she's dying, after all—but many sopranos of the era insisted on show-offy death scenes, and audiences liked them, too. Instead, Zaccaria and the chorus end the opera with another thunderous prediction of Babylon's fall.

## Ernani

The gravity of *Nabucco*'s biblical subject imposes some restraints on Verdi's naturally fiery style, but *Ernani* gives it free rein. A semimythical Spain—savage, exotic, backward—had long been a favorite operatic setting, including some of the best known and loved. The "Figaro" plays by Pierre-Augustin Caron de Beaumarchais, set in Seville, are the sources for Mozart's *Le nozze di Figaro* and Rossini's *Il barbiere di Siviglia*. Mozart's

*Don Giovanni* takes place in Seville, too. The Spanish setting, flavor, and fatalism are essential to the effect of Bizet's *Carmen*, also set in and around Seville. Wagner's *Parsifal* happens to be placed in the Spanish Pyrenees, but there's nothing remotely Spanish in the music of Wagner's solemn mystery play. Ravel's *L'heure espagnole*, an exquisite one-act comedy (the title of which loosely translates as "Spanish Time") is saturated in Iberian musical idioms. In Verdi's oeuvre, a number of important works, of which *Ernani* is the first, are set in Spain. The rages and improbable situations of *Il trovatore* echo those of *Ernani*, polished with nine years of experience. Later works are *Forza* and finally, *Don Carlo*, in which responsibilities weigh down royal passions.

*Ernani*, based on an 1830 play by Victor Hugo, is laden with twists of plot that don't even form the most ridiculous aspect of the story. That distinction belongs to the obsession with honor displayed by the title character and his nemesis, Silva, culminating in Ernani's keeping an oath to kill himself on Silva's demand. Nor is the alliance the two make midway through to kill their mutual enemy, Don Carlo, king of Spain, terribly credible. In fact, this tale contains enough inconsistencies and excesses from which one could make a long, long list. But the point is not to laugh at *Ernani*'s quaint dramatic conceits but to admire the fidelity, fire, and seriousness with which Verdi treats the story, bringing pasteboard characters to red-blooded life, making their absurd situations moving with his passionate score. *Nabucco* is an important milestone in Verdi's development that contains some great moments. Despite some rough edges, *Ernani* is a great opera.

Brief but dense, the prelude opens with the music of the fatal oath Ernani swears to Silva, stated menacingly by the brass. This is an early example of Verdi's finding the thread that pulls the drama together and treating it as a unifying element. What follows is a long, ripe melody, characterizing the love between Ernani and Elvira that reappears only once, in act 4. The oath motto returns to end the prelude ominously. Thus, Verdi compresses the most crucial elements of the story into three minutes of music that sets a tone of high expectation. Subtitled "The Bandit," the first act opens with a curtain-raising chorus ("Evviva, beviam"—*Hurrah, let's drink*) for Ernani's bandit crew. It's anything but subtle, but then it's not meant to be; it's there to grab your attention and crank up your pulse a few notches. Above all, it displays the composer's rhythmic drive in all its elemental force. Ernani then sings an aria apostrophizing his love for Elvira. In an opera brimming with great tunes, this one, "Come rugiada al cespite"—*Like dew on a cluster of faded flowers*—holds its own, making its point with the pleasing rise and fall of its melody and delicately scored orchestral accompaniment that Ernani loves her and hopes to snatch her from "old Silva." In the manly, energetic manner of the opening, the chorus tells him to buck up. But the cabaletta for Ernani that follows, "O tu che l'alma adora"—*You whom my spirit adores*—sounds cheap and coarse. Here we can see why Verdi tired of the cabaletta as the inevitable ending to every aria and scene, and why he created forms that spring from the dramatic situation, rather than imposing the same type of music on every event.

The second scene, set in the castle of Don Ruy Gomez de Silva, opens with Elvira musing sadly over her impending marriage to Silva, who loves her, but whom she decidedly does not love in return. Her aria "Ernani, Ernani, involami"—*Ernani, Ernani, carry me away from his loathsome embrace)*—(Track 1 on the compact disc at the back of the book) is surely the most famous in the opera. The sculpted melody moves first in a serpentine shape before arching up, then down. There's little urgency and no desperation in this dignified and memorable tune because Verdi ignores the sentiment expressed by Elvira in its spiky opening line, focusing instead on her dreams life of with Ernani, whom she swears to follow "through caves and moors." Beautiful, and deeply satisfying when well sung, "Ernani, Ernani, involami" is probably Verdi's earliest aria that displays complete vocal mastery. Be aware as you listen to the many high notes, and the coloratura runs that decorate the melodic line. All are difficult, particularly considering that this is Elvira's first appearance onstage. Even warmed up, the finest soprano can be nervous, as some tense live performances of the aria show. Thus, while Verdi rarely asks singers to perform crazy feats, his music even in this early work requires high skill and artistry. A chorus of attendants bearing gifts from Silva is light and innocuous; it's occasionally cut. But Elvira's cabaletta "Tutto sprezzo che d'Ernani non favella"—*I scorn words that don't speak of Ernani*—makes a worthwhile conclusion to the scene. It's a delicate specimen, brief and shapely, and set to a more refined rhythmic accompaniment than typical at this point in Verdi's career.

Don Carlo, king of Spain, enters, for no particular reason, incognito. He tells Elvira in another gem, "Da quel dì"—*From that day*—of the passion she has inspired in him. Brief but beautiful, this is among the first of many gorgeous moments for baritone Verdi would write. And it's challenging, too, set high up in the singer's range. The most complex character in the opera, Carlo changes before our eyes and ears from a hothead into a mature and judicious ruler.

Here, though, he grabs Elvira, who threatens to kill him then herself with his knife, which she has snatched from him in their struggle—tough, those Spanish noblewomen—when Ernani enters "unexpectedly," according to the libretto, challenging Carlo. A fiery trio ("No, crudeli"—*No, cruel ones*) for the three ensues, which is at a lower plane than what it follows, though Verdi effectively sets Carlo's introductory lines, "Tu se' Ernani"—*You are Ernani*—in which he scornfully recognizes his rival. Verdi instructs that Carlo's words are "*declamato*"—declaimed. This type of singing, suggesting speech, is to be delivered quickly and with fire, as opposed to long-held notes sung in full voice, called *cantabile*—songful.

Now, the fourth principal, Silva, enters the room, also "unexpectedly," though why so is uncertain, since it is his castle. Naturally, he's appalled to find two young men in his fiancée's room, and sings a short but affecting aria ("Infelice"—*Unhappy man!*) bewailing his age and present dishonor. As Carlo's identity is revealed to Silva, the big ensemble that ends the act gets under way. At first it's slow and grandiose, to record the astonishment of Silva and his household. After the impressive opening section, Verdi accelerates continually, beginning with Silva's tense apology to Carlo, followed by Ernani's angry "Io tuo fido?"—*I, loyal to you?*—on to a breathless stretta (the quick-tempo conclusion) for the principals and chorus set to a wild jump beat, that once again shows Verdi's astonishing rhythmic forcefulness.

Verdi opens the second act ("The Guest") with a mild-mannered chorus celebrating Elvira's impending marriage to Silva. But the musical and dramatic temperatures rise as Ernani, disguised as a pilgrim, enters. His proclamation that he has brought the price on his head as a wedding gift ("Oro, quant'oro ogn'avido"—*As much gold as can satisfy*) kicks off an exciting and unusual sequence of trio and duet between Elvira, Ernani, and Silva. Verdi takes pains to characterize the principals' vocal parts here, with Ernani's in particular reflecting the hotheaded pride that keeps him in trouble. As soon as Silva goes out, Ernani, believing that Elvira is marrying Silva willingly, accuses her of faithlessness. She replies in a grandly soaring phrase that she will kill herself before yielding to Silva. Ernani now sings in ringing tones of his undying love in a great duet. "Ah, morir, potessi adesso"—*Ah, if I could die now*—is marked by delicate writing for the woodwinds and a central section that features a weeping figure for flutes and oboes. The vocal lines intertwine beautifully, but Verdi gives Ernani the brighter side of the two-part harmony. The tune Silva hurls at the lovers when he reenters ("No, vendetta"—*No, revenge*), with its repeated notes, concisely captures the unyielding nature of this angry old man. As with Ernani, Verdi's music brings a two-dimensional character like Silva to life.

An angry Carlo enters, showing another side: a feudal ruler, sure of his prerogatives. His duet with Silva ("Cugino, a che munito il tuo castel ritrovo?"—*Cousin, why is your castle armed?*) is brilliant in its portrayal of tension between the strong young king and the wily yet dignified vassal. The driving rhythm of the accompaniment, into which Verdi sets an insistent harmonic tug, captures the unease between the two. This is an early specimen in a long line of great Verdian duets for baritone and bass. Duels between men of power are a Verdian specialty, and this one holds its own as a masterful early example. The composer plays off their voices in a different way in the brief lines that follow. Silva's lament ("Io l'amo"—*I love her*) captures the old man's pitiful weakness when it comes to Elvira, even though he knows she hates him; yet it's very impressive when sung by a great bass. Carlo's seductive "Vieni meco, sol di rose intrecciar" (CD Track 2)—*Come with me, I want your life to be surrounded with roses*—sung to Elvira, whom he still desires, is a glorious tune that shows off the baritone voice in its most flattering register.

The big duet for Ernani and Silva that concludes the act includes Ernani's absurd oath, made genuinely ominous by the backdrop of Verdi's trembling strings and brass. The theme that we heard in the prelude to act 1 resonates on its return. The equally ridiculous oath the two make to avenge themselves on Carlo is an exciting, again rather coarse, example of vows between men that would ring down curtains in Verdi until the greatest oath duet of them all, in *Otello*. This one, "In arcione, cavalieri"—*Into your saddles, knights*—is set to a bounding theme of high rhythmic profile, though, and the music is exciting. The composer ratchets the rhythm to fever pitch, throwing in an exciting harmonic jolt and thundering brass as the male chorus joins in.

The third act ("The Pardon") set at the tombs of the Holy Roman Emperors at Aix-la-Chapelle, stands apart from the rest of *Ernani* in its display of Verdi's skills as an orchestrator, and as a musical dramatist of the keenest instincts. Here, Carlo, on the day of his election as emperor, transcends the petty politics of his Spanish dominions and masters his personal desires. He dominates this act, the last in *Ernani* in which he appears. The prelude is a minor masterpiece of orchestral writing, a somber passage for winds, dominated by the bass clarinet. The mood—at once gloomy and exalted—will return in the opening moments of act 4 of *Il trovatore* and in the San Yuste monastery scenes of *Don Carlo*, both of which claim this as an ancestor.

As Carlo prepares to hide in the chapel that contains the tomb of Charlemagne, he sings a brief but profound aria, considering the conspirators and their hatred of him, then the responsibilities of the office to which he hopes to be elected. Accompanied by a chamber-size ensemble led by a solo cello, Carlo reflects on the illusions of youth and the greater glories he now aspires to. Known by the first line in which the cello joins the baritone, "Oh, de' verd'anni miei"—*Dreams and shadows of my green* [verdi] *youth*—cello and baritone voice twine like noble brothers. As Carlo sings of his high aspirations, the vocal line rises and expands majestically—Verdi marks it "*grandioso*" in the score. The full orchestra joins the swelling of Carlo's promise to himself. Cellos and baritones will pair off again in King Philip's aria "Ella giammai m'amò" in *Don Carlo*, and while that great meditation displays a wisdom achieved only by maturity, this aria is a flawless example of Verdi's early manner, striking precisely the correct note. The conspirators enter to spooky music, filled with soft brass and pizzicato strings as they call passwords across the crypt. Verdi's musical ideas here are conventional, but so well executed that the scene is fun to listen to. Note the trills for bassoon and tuba.

Silva and Ernani draw lots for the honor of assassinating Carlo. Ernani wins, crowing triumphantly about his anticipated revenge. Silva asks Ernani to yield the right. But of course the hero declines, and Silva warns Ernani that "T'aspetta la più orribile vendetta"—*A terrible revenge awaits you*. All this takes place to an extended version of the conspirators' stalking themes. The conspirators then launch into an energetic but crude chorus to Spain and their revenge, "Si ridesti il Leon di Castiglia"—*Let the Lion of Castile awaken*. Although thunderous, this is the weakest moment musically in this otherwise brilliant scene. (The chorus was likely a coded signal to nationalists during this early phase of the Risorgimento.[4]) Three cannon shots signal Carlo's election, as he emerges from the tomb where he has been hiding, calling the conspirators traitors. They think he's Charlemagne's ghost, anticipating another dramatic twist in *Don Carlo*. Soldiers, electors, and Elvira, whom Carlo holds as a hostage, swarm onstage, thwarting the conspirators' plans. Ernani reveals his true noble identity and offers Carlo his head for his role in the conspiracy. Again, Verdi captures Ernani's contempt in tense music that reflects his instinctual pride; Elvira pleads for him in a long, lyrical melodic phrase.

With the solemn aria for Carlo ("O sommo Carlo"—*Mighty Charles*— referring here to Charlemagne) and the ensemble that fills in around it, his character reaches its apogee. Carlo broods grandly on the greatness of his predecessor, whom he now seeks to emulate. He pardons the conspirators and, sacrificing his own desires, grants Ernani and Elvira the right to marry, conciliating everyone but Silva, who mutters wrathfully below the ensemble offering praise to the new emperor. The depth of Verdi's characterizations in the later opera is extraordinary but hardly a surprise. What is remarkable is the superb way in which he captures the ascent of Carlo's character in this youthful masterpiece.

The last act ("The Mask"), the shortest of the four, is tight dramatically and musically, opening with dance music to celebrate the marriage of Ernani and Elvira. Almost at once, though, Silva stalks into the background. The chorus, as wedding guests, comment uneasily on the evil look in the eye of the masked old man in black ("Ha per occhi brage ardenti"—*His eyes are glowing coals*); the audience, at least, knows what to expect. Ernani and Elvira enter to the broad love theme from the prelude, and begin what would be a great love duet ("Cessaro i suoni"—*The sounds have stopped*). But the sound of a horn in the distance rattles Ernani's nerves, expressed convincingly in brief lines of high agitation. Silva enters, reminding Ernani—as if it were necessary—of his pledge to kill himself. The music, of course, is the same as in the second scene of act 2, and in the prelude. Ernani appeals for pity in a ringing aria, "Solingo, errante e misero"—*Solitary, a wanderer, and miserable*—but Silva is implacable.

Elvira returns, beginning the passionate trio that forms the climax to the opera: "Quale d'averno demone"—*What hellish demon*—with Elvira and Ernani pleading, and Silva replying stubbornly below. It reaches a climax on a phrase of extravagant despair that is Italian opera at its purest, as Ernani, enslaved by his honor, stabs himself. A drumroll leads to a beautiful closing melody for Ernani ("Vivi, d'amarmi e vivere"—*Live, I command you, dear*) beneath a shimmering string accompaniment; Silva gloats horribly. The orchestra thunders its brief commentary as the curtain falls, ending *Ernani* at the same headlong pace that characterizes the entire opera.

## Macbeth

Set in eleventh-century Scotland, the opera remains close to the Shakespearean original.

The Teatro della Pergola in Florence commissioned *Macbeth*. The idea of composing to a Shakespearean play had excited Verdi for a while, as it would for the rest of his career. He approached the project with a sense of profound responsibility about the English dramatist, though, ironically, the lack of a decent tenor at the time was one impetus that pushed the composer toward the subject. Once on it, though, Verdi's imagination carried him away. The libretto by Francesco Maria Piave revised by Andrea Maffei adheres closely to the play, with interpolations as dictated by operatic convention. Verdi complained even more than usual to Piave about the quality of the text. The opera was hailed as a masterwork at its premiere, and has always been the most prestigious of Verdi's early period; it was a favorite of the composer's as well. He then insisted on singers for the lead roles who were not pretty to look at, and who could express vocally the evil and ambition of their characters.

In one letter to Piave early in the process, Verdi wrote, "I've got the general character and the color of the work in my head just as if the opera were already written."[5] Indeed, *Macbeth* has a distinct atmosphere and musical tint all its own, despite the fact that the version we invariably hear is a revision from 1865 for the Théâtre-Lyrique in Paris. That coexistence of early and middle styles is not always an easy one: the more sophisticated music from 1865 makes even the best of the earlier work sound a bit primitive. For example, Lady Macbeth's sweeping act 2 aria "La luce langue," added in 1865, places the earlier material that follows it at a disadvantage; and even the best moments from the 1847 version—the duet for Macbeth and his wife and his monologue in act 1, and even her sleep-walking scene—seem stiff next to the later material.[6] This is a shame, because these stand as some of the finest moments in Verdi's early style. Listen for the freedom of the later material, next to which the 1847 sections sound rigid in rhythm and phrasing, and predictably simple in harmony and orchestration. The 1865 additions are better than the material they replace, and the consistency of the earlier version doesn't outweigh its weaknesses. One just has to get used to the mix of styles in the revised version, which in the end isn't all that difficult; *Macbeth* has a sincerity that shines through, helping to overcome the awkward moments.

The first act consists almost entirely of material from the original version of the opera. A brief orchestral prelude sets the atmosphere, opening with themes associated with the witches, then material from Lady Macbeth's sleepwalking scene. A boisterous chorus for the witches—three groups of eight women—will get into your memory immediately. Its catchiness is balanced by a triviality—a vulgarity, even—that's intentional on Verdi's part. Macbeth and Banquo enter, receive their prophecies ("Salve!"—*Hail!*), then embark on a noble duet ("Due vaticini"—*Two of the prophecies*) in which the two reflect, together but separately, on the witches' predictions. This magnificent duet displays their disparate personalities, as well as the greatness of Verdi's dramatic imagination even early on. Note when you listen to the flawless expression of their different reactions, as well as the grandeur of the blending of the two bass-baritone voices. A second chorus for the witches, "S'allontanarono"—*They have left*—again trivial but attractive, rounds out the scene.

Lady Macbeth (referred to as "Lady" by Verdi) is introduced in the second scene in which her ferocity and ambition, often exceeding her husband's, are exposed, even in the driving force and twisting lines of the orchestral introduction. Other early Verdian heroines are introduced by gentle or yearning arias, but Lady Macbeth's is the alarming "Vieni! t'affretta"—*Come! hurry*—in which she lays out her ambition with a leaping vocal line almost as challenging as the music for Abigaille in *Nabucco*. After a servant announces that Macbeth and Duncan are about to arrive together, the cabaletta that follows her aria ("Or tutti sorgete, ministri infernali"—*Arise, ministers of hell*) turns the aria–arrival of news–reflection–resolution structure on its head. Here Verdi finds new content for the well-used formula, with good news begetting evil in his female protagonist. The composer's instructions to his singers here are exceptionally detailed: he tells the singers to deliver their parts "in low, hollow, voice," "stretched out," and "in a suffocated voice."

Macbeth enters; the entire scene that follows, as she persuades him to act and Duncan arrives is pretty impressive, though the jaunty little march that accompanies the pantomime of the king's arrival (Duncan's part is silent) is for most listeners out of place at this intense moment of the drama. But what follows, Macbeth's monologue "Mi si affaccia un pugnal?"—*Is this a dagger?*—stands as one of the boldest moments in Verdi's early operas. Listen for the absolute freedom of the vocal line, as well as its fidelity to the text. (The composer made small but significant changes to this scene in 1865.[7])

The spectral duet between Macbeth and Lady, with its dark and nervous orchestral accompaniment, keeps up the intensity; Verdi marries Italian opera fruitfully to its Shakespearean source in his solemn but emphatic setting of the great line "Non v'è che vigilia Caudore, per te"—*You shall sleep no more*. And he drives the drama ahead with flawless instinct as Lady returns to Duncan's chamber with the dagger and Macbeth sings of his shattered nerves ("Ogni rumore mi spaventa"—*Every sound terrifies me*), while Banquo and Macduff bang on the gate of his castle. This is all as good as it can be, as is Banquo's monologue on the gloom of the night ("O, qual orrenda notte"—*What a horrendous night!*) and Macduff's horror as he reports Duncan's murder. The big ensemble that ends the act, "Schiudi, inferno, la bocca"—*Open wide, hell, your gaping maw*—is thunderously impressive and can be seen as a forerunner of the Requiem in the force of its choral writing. The foursquare regularity of the phrasing seems a fair example of the composer's less sophisticated early manner. But as usual, Verdi moves things along swiftly to an exciting, quick-tempo ending.

The greatest disparities between the original and revised versions of *Macbeth* are to be found in the second act, which contains Lady's great aria from 1865 and the old-fashioned *brindisi*—drinking song—of the final scene, to which Verdi made subtle improvements in the revision. The act opens with a brief instrumental prelude quoting a theme from the duet in act 1, setting a mood of unease. The dialogue between Macbeth, now king, and his wife, plotting the murder of Banquo, is old material, but very free, and well done. Note the snarling trills for the low strings that underpin the royal couple's machinations.

As Macbeth goes off to put their plan into effect, Lady sings the majestic aria "La luce langue"—*Light thickens*—that epitomizes the greatness of the 1865 material. You won't be able to miss the grandeur of Verdi's mature style marked by the richness of the orchestration and harmony, and his brilliant creation of a triumphant closing passage "O voluttà del soglio"—*The joy of the throne*—in the spirit of a cabaletta, but with none of that form's exasperating rigidity. Although the orchestra carries the rocking vocal line with a completely different, almost tidal sweep, Lady Macbeth's part here is quite difficult, surging to a couple of high Bs before the end. But these are so embedded in the melodic undulations that it's impossible to hear them as anything but part of its flow. Verdi wrote these lines himself for the revision to replace a clattery 1847 cabaletta for Lady.

The chorus of murderers that follows, "Chi v'impose unirvi a noi?"—*Who bid you join us?*—takes us back to Verdi's naive early style, reminding us of choruses of conspirators from *Ernani* and other early works. Anything but menacing, it's rather funny. But it does show the composer's rhythmic wit, and his use of the timpani to accompany it is worth listening for. Banquo's final monologue ("Come dal ciel"—*How darkness falls from heaven*) before his murder carries considerable weight and might come across better were it not been preceded by "La luce langue." Verdi's scoring, set to muttering of the low brass, is powerful and, as usual for Verdi, the piece surges ahead, leading directly to Banquo's offstage murder.

Some may find the presence of a *brindisi*, the Italian operatic convention, in an eleventh-century Scottish court hard to digest. Luckily, Verdi is a master of the form, reaching higher peaks than here with Alfredo's in act 1 of *Traviata* and Iago's in the first act of *Otello*. To set the mood of Macbeth's glittering court (which, again, a hard-bitten realist might question) Verdi created a brilliant theme, that's restless in both melody and harmony, and slightly uneasy in affect. At her husband's request, Lady M sings an old-fashioned operatic tune of great regularity, "Si colmi il calice"—*Fill up the cup*—to which the chorus replies. Drinking songs, like this, are typically brisk and lilting, with a note of vulgarity. The restless opening theme is interrupted by the appearance of the recently murdered Banquo's ghost, wounds and all, which only Macbeth sees. This music, from the revised version, expresses Macbeth's terror ("Di voi chi ciò fece"—*Which of you have done this?*) with vivid power, the horns braying fearfully. Lady Macbeth's attempts to calm him and the crowd, while keeping cool herself, are brilliantly rendered in sotto voce interjections ("E un uomo voi siete?"—*Are you a man?*). The return of the *brindisi* theme again displays its intentional triviality; the reappearance of the ghost sends Macbeth into spasms of terror, portrayed by his free, powerful vocal line, underpinned by shuddering strings. Macbeth's closing aria "Sangue a me"—*The phantom will have blood*—dates to the original version, as does the big ensemble it initiates. Verdi's work is detailed and relatively transparent in its expression of the characters' different points of view, and it moves forward with his typical urgency. But its old-fashioned idiom is hard to mistake.

Act 3 is relatively brief but powerful, unless its two ballets are included; the first and longer of the two belongs to the 1865 Paris production; you'll be struck by Verdi's amazing skill with the orchestra, and perhaps, by how much it reminds you of Tchaikovsky. The second ballet, which follows Macbeth's fainting spell at the end of his big scene with the witches, comes from the original production, and contains a chorus. Both can be heard on the 1976 recording led by Claudio Abbado; live productions typically omit one or both.

The act opens with a chorus for the witches, who now sound fierce as they sing the whining theme heard at the very opening of the prelude ("Tre volte miagola la gatta"—*Thrice the cat has mewed*). They take on a solemn tone as they greet Macbeth and begin to reply to his questions, which are marked for thunderous chords for the full orchestra. Here, Verdi captures Shakespeare's gloomy atmosphere masterfully, as the spirits makes their replies to strangely harmonized chords, brilliantly orchestrated. Strings mysteriously underpin the vision of the eight kings, also set to bizarre harmonies. For a moment, on hearing that no man born of woman can kill him, Macbeth shows a twinge of humanity, pardoning Macduff, then furiously changes his mind ("O Macduffo, tua vita perdono"—*Then live, Macduff*). The fast-moving shifting of the protagonist's consciousness is captured with all the power and immediacy music can summon.

The strange sonority of a clarinet-heavy wind band offstage is one of the most striking moments of the whole score, interspersed by regal, stalking figures for the strings as Macbeth declaims grandly above ("Fuggi, regal fantasima"—*Begone, royal phantom*). Again, Verdi paints the grandeur, terrible as it is, of Macbeth's possessed character. The final scene consists of a rich and potent duet for Macbeth and his wife in which he tells her of the witches' predictions and they swear, for the last time, to best their growing list of foes ("Ora di morte e di vendetta"—*Hour of death and vengeance*). If you've been paying attention you'll know right away from its freedom and breadth that it's from the revised score. The scene ends on ferocious cries for blood, vengeance, and death from the pair; Lady's part ends on an exciting high C—a note that's the equivalent of a home run for opera fans.

The fourth act of *Macbeth* contains disparate elements, mostly of high quality, from both versions. The opening chorus "Patria oppressa!"— *Downtrodden homeland!*—was intended by Verdi as a dark sibling to "Va, pensiero," but it's filled with despair and musically it's of a complexity that surpasses the *Nabucco* chorus's early style. The sad recitative and aria for Macduff that follow ("Ah, la paterna mano"—*Alas, a father's hand*) are old and, while touching, show their conventionality next to the great opening chorus. The chorus for warring exiled Scots that follows has vulgar energy but little more.

Verdi pulled out all the stops for Lady Macbeth's sleepwalking scene, the "Gran Scena del Sonnambulisma," as it's titled in the score. If you've never heard it, you'll first notice its spaciousness—here the composer takes his time building his effects—as well as its low volume and delicate orchestration. Verdi accomplishes everything with only the chilly sound of muted strings, clarinet, and English horn. Neither the orchestra nor the singers have any thumping, screeching, or conventional operatic histrionics to do; Verdi accomplishes all at two gentle tempos. There are three main thematic ideas: the five-note mincing figure for violins that suggests Lady's attempt to rub the blood from her hands; a shuddering figure ending with a moan for the English horn that accompanies her murderous recollections; and the sweeping, melancholy melody first heard in the prelude to the opera. A lady-in-waiting and a doctor comment in horror as Lady Macbeth, in a trancelike state, reviews her bloody career; she sings ("Una macchia è qui tuttora"—*Yet here's a spot*) with no coloratura distractions in an ever-rising wave over bravely shifting harmonies toward a high note (a rare D-flat on "Andiam, Macbetto"—*Come, Macbeth*) at the end, suggested by Verdi to be sung with a "*fil di voce*"—at an eerie whisper. It is very difficult, and often botched or omitted in performance. Nevertheless, this scene represents perhaps the highest point of Verdi's early style—you'll want to listen and listen again—it is a perfect portrait of a tormented mind. This nearly perfect scene is also remarkably daring for its time and place.

Verdi gives Macbeth one last, elegiac aria, "Pietà, rispetto, amore"— *Compassion, honor, love*—in which the character looks back on his life and ahead at very little; it's a solid, old-fashioned tune that a great baritone can lift above its class. Told of his wife's death, Macbeth replies with one of Shakespeare's darkest and most familiar lines ("Life's . . . a tale/ Told by an idiot, full of sound and fury/Signifying nothing"), rendered by Verdi in trills and harsh harmonies that anticipate Iago's monologue from *Otello*. He responds bravely to his final battle call; the composer depicts the conflict with a fugue. Stabbed by Macduff, Macbeth sings a brief but effective monologue, "Mal per me"—*So must I suffer*—from the 1847 version that's strong enough to stand, even though the composer dropped it from the revised version. *Macbeth* ends with a spirited, quick-time march ("Vittoria"—*Victory!*) for Macduff; the new king, Malcolm; and the chorus.

# The "Galley" Operas

I n this chapter, we'll look at eleven of Verdi's "lesser" operas, obscure and unfamiliar to many, even in the opera-going crowd. These include his first and second operas, *Oberto* and *Un giorno di regno*, the second notorious as his only comedy before *Falstaff*, and as the biggest failure of his career. We'll look at *I Lombardi*, his fourth opera, and his twelfth, *Jérusalem*, a revision of *Lombardi* in French for Paris. We'll study two other operas usually grouped with these lesser works in chapter 5. Although clearly atypical in many ways, *Stiffelio* is a significant but underappreciated opera; and it makes sense to look at *Aroldo*, an 1857 revision of *Stiffelio*, in context, right after the source work, as well as in its place chronologically, as Verdi wrote these eleven operas between 1839 and 1849.

"Sixteen years in the galleys!"[1] So, Verdi, in a letter written in 1858, poignantly described his workload once he had found popular success with *Nabucco*. To the composer, everything between that and *Aroldo* were from his "galley" period. This would, of course, include his artistic triumphs of the early 1850s—*Rigoletto*, *Il trovatore*, and *La traviata*—as well as *Luisa Miller* and *Stiffelio*, major works that showed a swift ripening of his style, and his appetite for difficult subjects, too. The "galley" period, to Verdi, included *I vespri siciliani*, a commission from the Paris Opéra to the by-then-renowned master; the first version of *Simon Boccanegra*, and, as noted, *Aroldo*. Verdi must have seen everything from ground level, with the works themselves tied to the circumstances of their creation. Certainly no one would argue that that the production of fourteen operas (these plus *Nabucco*, *Ernani*, and *Macbeth*) in ten years is anything but the heaviest lifting. History has regarded these years and the operas Verdi wrote in them more judgmentally, with the works from *Luisa Miller* on rising above most of what preceded them. But a look at these eleven operas reveals that although variable in quality, they display a steady development—an upward movement—that's clear if you look at them as a group, and fairly consistent from one to the next.

In years after *Nabucco*, Verdi went from being one of several promising and productive artists to the undisputed master of the genre. The eleven operas we'll look at in this chapter represent the material on which he mastered his art. Three areas in particular will prove revealing: first, Verdi's simplifies his vocal writing, making it more directly expressive, and less reliant on coloratura and other decorative techniques. Alongside this, his orchestration goes from common and even coarse in *Oberto*, to genuinely refined in *I due Foscari*, reaching what can fairly be described as masterful in *I masnadieri*, *Il corsaro*, and *La battaglia di Legnano*. But perhaps most significant is Verdi's ever more purposeful focus on pushing the drama ahead. His pressing the music and story on is, as we've already seen, one of his greatest qualities: and in the early operas as in the late he keeps things moving. But if you listen to (or watch live or on DVD) *Oberto* and then *La battaglia*, you'll see how great a distance the composer traveled in those ten years. The old-fashioned arias that stop the proceedings in *Oberto* can hardly be found in the later, sadly neglected, opera. Instead, Verdi weaves short solo passages that begin like arias but dissolve into the action that follows. The smaller ensembles between characters are similarly compressed: the *duetto* of the early works is now more frequently a *duettino*, if, indeed, it's picked out at all. The big ensembles retain their spacious grandeur, but are assembled with ever more subtle skill.

In one sense, it's misleading to take these eleven operas out of the context of Verdi's development from one to the next. Remember that the writing of *Nabucco*, *Ernani*, and *Macbeth* affected these operas, just as these eleven helped him in the creation of those more famous and successful works. So, please don't get the impression that these belong in the dumb class, or aren't that good. Indeed, they are often very good, with much to enjoy and admire.

## Oberto, Conte di San Bonifacio

As the master's first opera, *Oberto* should hold a place of honor, but it's no masterpiece. It's among of the least performed and recorded of his works, of interest chiefly to the hardest of hard-core Verdians. If you want to acquaint yourself with *Oberto*, try watching it on DVD, more fun than listening to a CD while trying to follow the trite libretto, or listening online, which invites distraction.

Nevertheless, *Oberto* has its moments. The brief overture presents some interesting ideas from the opera, ending with an excited theme on the flute over a percussive accompaniment, which you'll hear a few minutes later as the cabaletta to Riccardo's opening aria, anticipating the opening scene of *La traviata*, and already showing the strength and consistency of Verdi's style. Leonora's aria describing her and her father's plight has merit, as does the delicate woodwind writing of the orchestral introduction preceding Oberto's entrance. Verdi handles his monologue well, and the dialogue in recitative between Oberto and Leonora gives an impressive foretaste of his career-long excellence at father-daughter (and baritone-soprano) duets. One can really see these characters growing into Rigoletto and Gilda. The first part of the big trio for Oberto, Leonora, and Cuniza ("Son io stesso"—*It is I*) is appropriately tense, displaying characters' different affects. The final ensemble of act 1 turns convincingly somber when Oberto joins ("A quell' aspetto un fremito"—*I shudder at that look*), as the composer's familiar voice comes through unmistakably; it's probably the best passage in the opera. And the racing closing section of the ensemble shows typical Verdian energy, here in its rawest state.

The second act contains a big aria for Oberto ("L'orror del tradimento"—*The horror of betrayal*), which is fair at best, but his cabaletta ("Ma tu, superbo giovine"—*But you, proud youth*) is energetic, and presages better ones for low male voice. The duet in which Oberto provokes Riccardo is fiery. Riccardo's aria after killing Oberto ("Ciel! Chi feci?"—*Heaven! What have I done?*) expresses Riccardo's torment reasonably well. Unfortunately, little from this point to the end is memorable.

The overall effect of listening to or watching *Oberto* is positive, though, because Verdi never takes his foot off the gas, keeping the drama moving; and his energy—expressed in vigorous rhythmic patterns—is unmistakable. *Oberto*'s problem is how far its creator grew beyond it.

## *Un giorno di regno*

Verdi's second opera is an opera buffa, a comedy in the old-fashioned style best recognized in the popular masterpieces by Rossini (*Il barbiere di Siviglia* and *La Cenerentola*) and Donizetti (*L'elisir d'amore* and *Don Pasquale*). Plots of buffa works are larded with even more disguises, reversals, and misunderstandings than operatic tragedies.

The worst disaster in Verdi's career, *Un giorno di regno*—King for a Day—flopped in a big way at its premiere. There were a number of reasons, including (speculatively) Verdi's humorless character, his difficulty in writing a comedy while grieving for his wife, his inexperience at writing comedy, and a poor cast. Also, as Budden has shown,[2] the long passages of dialogue in recitative stopped the inexperienced composer from pushing the plot along, his greatest asset in the early operas.

As with *Oberto*, no one claims *Un giorno di regno* is a sleeper among Verdi's operas: it is weak next to later work, especially *Falstaff*, with which it does not bear comparison. But hearing the opera is not unpleasant. The overture, for example, features grotesque contrasts between the strings and oddly paired high and low winds and brass. The first scene contains a chorus that chugs along pleasantly, and Belfiore's aria "Compagnoni di Parigi"—*My Parisian comrades*—is set to an interesting tune with an even more interesting, swinging gait. Verdi assembles the big sextet ("Cara Giulia, alfin ti vedo"—*I see you at last, dear Julia*) carefully enough: the buffo manner requires individuation of the parts, and he meets that challenge, at least. The busy ensemble that ends the act ("In qual punto il re ci ha côlto!"—*What a time for the king to surprise us!*) is unoriginal but moves with assurance, and writing a fast-moving ensemble number like this one must have been a salutary experience for the ambitious young composer.

The second act holds together better than the first, partly by virtue of being about twenty minutes shorter. High points such as they are include a breathless buffo duet for Baron Kelbar and his treasurer, "Tutti l'arme si può prendere"—*You may use all the weapons*—in which Verdi copies Rossini's style well, except for the older composer's elegance. The scene for Belfiore and the Marchesa has its moments, notably a charming closing section ("Perché dunque non vien?"—*Why hasn't he come?*) in waltz tempo. And the big finale holds together pretty well.

*Un giorno di regno* is known by another title, *Il finto Stanislao*—The False Stanislaus—which was used for a revival in Venice in 1854, then in Naples five years later. No one was more surprised that these productions took place than Verdi himself.[3]

## I Lombardi alla prima crociata

Although there's no whiff of realism in the plot, Verdi does what he can with the preposterous situations and wordy libretto by Temistocle Solera. One of best moments in the first act is the tense ensemble for five principals and chorus ("T'assale un tremito"—*A tremor assails me*) in which Verdi separates their different points of view musically. It's also full of his explosive rhythmic energy. Pagano's aria ("Sciagurata, hai tu creduto"—*Wretched woman, did you believe*) features a jumpy accompaniment for low strings that also express his fury; it's also admirably brief. Finally, Giselda's aria "Salve Maria"—*Hail Mary*—addressed to the Virgin, is delicately and beautifully scored for a small orchestra of winds and strings. It's very difficult—like Giselda's entire role—but also effective. Note, when you listen, the strange harmonies the composer introduces into the accompaniment.

Typically for early Verdi, the action-packed second act features moments of high inspiration, banality, and everything in between. The excellent moments include Oronte's pretty aria apostrophizing Giselda, "La mia letizia infondere"—*My happiness instills*—to which Verdi appends a cabaletta that's delicate rather than coarse. Also fine are the Hermit's short aria "Ma quando un suon terribile"—*But when a terrible sound*—as well as his noble dialogue with Arvino. Giselda's big aria ("Se vano è il pregare"—*My prayer is in vain*) in the third scene, which looks back to Bellini in its lyricism, is also draped in considerable technical difficulty. Finally, her despairing cry on hearing the false report of Oronte's death is unusual, carefully put together, and persuasive. Conventional piety often elicited conventional music from Verdi, but Giselda's challenge to divine justice clearly stimulated him.

From a structural standpoint, act 3 of *I Lombardi* represents a step up. Verdi unifies its final scenes with a violin solo that runs through the entire sequence, lasting about fifteen minutes. With the exception of the second scene, set in Arvino's tent, the composer achieves a higher musical plane, beginning with the beautiful, leisurely Pilgrim's Chorus ("Gerusalem! Gerusalem!") set to a heart-easing tune over a flowing solo cello. The urgent duet for Giselda and Oronte looks ahead to the master's middle period style. But the chief development for Verdi is the structural experiment of the final scenes, beginning with a concerto-like passage for the solo violin, then the short duet for the now wounded Oronte and Giselda, and carrying through to his baptism by the Hermit, a trio ("Qual voluttà trascorrere"—*What wondrous pleasure I feel*) for the three, and finally Oronte's very tenorial death, singing a high A. The violin accompanies the action throughout; and, there's no question that Verdi's handling of form, at least, shows a new level of mastery. There's real grandeur and breadth in the melodic phrasing of the scene, and the violin pulls everything together over a comparably broad period of the drama. The fourth act, unfortunately, has less to recommend it. Oronte appears in a dream to Giselda, where he sings a sugary aria ("In cielo benedetto"—*In heaven blessed*) that instructs the thirsty Crusaders to a nearby pool. Giselda's cabaletta ("Non fu sogno"—*It was not a dream*) possesses raw energy; and Pagano's brief, agonized dying monologue also holds together well. With the chorus "O Signore, dal tetto natio"—*Lord, to our native hearths*—Verdi tries to re-create the success of "Va, pensiero" from *Nabucco*. But some silly decoration for flutes keeps this chorus on a lower plane.

*I Lombardi* premiered in 1843, after *Nabucco*, by which time the composer was a popular figure. It was a big success in Italy, where the idea of Italians coming together for a noble cause appealed to the Risorgimento spirit of the time.

## Jérusalem

When asked by the Paris Opéra to adapt an earlier work, Verdi naturally jumped at the chance, eventually selecting *I Lombardi*. The result is *Jérusalem*, perhaps the most obscure of all his operas. It's a shame, too, as the new work is quite different from its source, and because the master's style had developed considerably in three and a half years between the composition and recomposition of the two. Parisian operatic taste was more refined than Milanese, forcing Verdi to purge the work of most of its vulgar moments.

Sung in French to a new libretto by Alphonse Royer and Gustave Vaëz, *Jérusalem* transplants *I Lombardi*'s themes of jealousy, revenge, repentance, and redemption to Toulouse, France, and makes its Count, an actual leader of the First Crusade, a protagonist. If you do listen to *Jérusalem*, notice the difference between how an Italian opera sounds when sung in French, without the typical breadth of Italian vowels. From the start, differences are striking: a powerful funeral march takes the place of the disorderly *Lombardi* prelude; the little duet ("Adieu, mon bien-aimé"—*Farewell, my beloved*) for Gaston and Hélène is brief, beautiful, and decorated by an exquisite horn solo; her "Ave Maria" works at least as well in its new setting. A remarkable orchestral passage portraying dawn is new and looks ahead in its brilliance to the one in *Simon Boccanegra*. (And there's another musical portrayal of dawn in *Attila*.) The act 1 quintet from *Lombardi* one of the best numbers in that score, is transformed here to a sextet here, "Je tremble"—*I tremble*—that's no less superb with parts redistributed. Verdi transforms Pagano's furious aria "Sciagurata!" to Roger's quieter, but more focused "Oh, dans l'ombre"—*In the shadow*.

The new second act include Hélène's yearning interrogation of Gaston's squire, followed by a slightly toned-down version of the cabaletta from act 4 of *Lombardi*, apparently a sure-fire hit in Paris, as in Milan, once she learns he's alive. (To some it may still sound intrusive.) The Pilgrim's Chorus, here transferred to the French, sounds a bit peculiar in its unmistakably Italian melodic idiom. The second scene, between the Emir of Ramla, Gaston, and Hélène, features a spacious and beautifully scored duet ("Dans la honte et l'épouvante"—*You cannot share in the horror and shame*) for the lovers, based on their act 2 duet from *Lombardi*.

The third act of *Jérusalem* consists of two scenes. The first, set in the harem of the Emir of Ramla, is taken up with a long ballet, expected by the Parisian audience. But the second scene contains some more forward-looking material. Gaston's aria "O, mes amis, mes frères d'armes"—*My friends, my brothers-in-arms*—is mature in style, anticipating fine middle-period solo numbers in its urgent yet subtle expression of the character's shifting moods of sorrow and despair. And the big scene in which Gaston's sword, shield, and helmet are broken very clearly anticipate the dramatic and musical structures of trial scene in *Aida*,[4] though of course the latter, written twenty-five years later, packs an infinitely greater punch.

The best numbers in the fourth act are transfers from act 3 of *I Lombardi*: the pilgrim's chorus, and the trio with the long violin solo that ended that act. Verdi adds a melancholy oboe solo to the chorus, which otherwise sounds lovely and spacious, as before. He changes the trio completely, however, removing the violin obbligato, while condensing the scene. You may find that the tighter, less fussy handling here is an improvement over the better-known original.

## I due Foscari

The Foscari were a noble family of Venice, about whom Byron wrote a play, purportedly based on an historical incident. The two Foscari in the story were a father, Francesco, and his son, Jacopo. The brief prelude sets an ominous tone, alternating agitated ideas against a sorrow-laden tune associated with Jacopo Foscari. (Verdi experiments here with themes to identify important characters and groups.) With the chorus of senators that opens the drama ("Silenzio!") Verdi sets a mood of mystery; note when you listen the fine orchestration, including an important role for the timpani and flute, as well as the interesting and unusual harmonic background. Jacopo's aria "Dal più remoto esiglio"—*From distant exile*—set to the melody already heard in the prelude, is in the usual two parts. The pithy and effective cavatina, delicately scored for flute and winds, is a gem. In the next scene, his wife, Lucrezia, enters to an agitated theme associated with her throughout the opera, anticipating later, greater, desperate heroines, notably Amelia in *Ballo* and Leonora in *Forza*. Verdi captures her imperious character well in majestic recitatives that frame her prayer "Tu al cui sguardo onnipossente"—*Beneath your almighty glance*. Again, this is a fine, coloratura-laden version of another theme from the prelude, carefully scored and succinct. The third scene, in the Doge's room, opens with an introduction for a small ensemble of violas and cellos that sketches Francesco's reflective character, followed by the Doge's excellent *romanza* "O vecchio cor"—*Ancient heart that beats in my breast*—in which the old ruler pours out his sorrow over his son's situation. Again, its brevity and beautiful scoring make us appreciate Verdi's sense of proportion. Lucrezia enters, and she and the Doge begin an impressive, multipart duet, "Tu pur lo sai, che giudice"—*You sat as a judge among them*—that ends the act.

Note, when you listen, the urgency she consistently expresses and the heavy coloratura difficulties of her role.

A prelude for solo viola and cello, this one stark and strange, opens act 2; an imprisoned Jacopo awakes to nightmarish fantasies, brilliantly if brutally rendered, then launches into a frantic prayer ("Non maledirmi, o prode"—*Don't curse me, mighty warrior*) that captures his hallucination with a disturbing vividness. Lucrezia enters, bringing Jacopo more bad news, and the two sing a tender, unusual duet ("No, non morrai"—*No, you are not to die*) that deserves to be better known. The Doge, who is Jacopo's father, enters, and the three characters begin a trio that anticipates the famous quartet from the last act of *Rigoletto*. The final scene, in which Jacopo is sentenced back into exile, once more captures the anguish of the Foscari and Lucrezia, as well as the cruelty of their nemesis, Jacopo Loredano. The first scene of the third act, set in the Piazzetta of San Marco, provides a moment of contrast in this gloomy indoor tale, as the public, watching a gondola race, sings a barcarolle. But the good mood ends as Jacopo is led to the ship that will return him to exile. His farewell, "All'infelice veglio conforta"—*Comfort the sorrow*—is a moving chain of solos and duetlike exchanges, building into a big ensemble, as a mostly sympathetic crowd looks on. The melodic phrases swell grandly as the ensemble moves quickly to its climax. The opera's final scene, set in the Doge's apartment, works intermittently: old Foscari is introduced by his noble theme, as in act 1. Lucrezia reports Jacopo's death in a cabaletta laden with embellished, showy writing that sounds inconsistent with the sorrow she's supposed to feel. But Foscari's somber arias as he's pushed from power ("Questa dunque"—*This is the unjust reward*) and hears the bell announcing his successor's election ("Quel bronzo ferale"—*That fatal knell*) hit the mark.

The weaknesses of *I due Foscari* include a plot that lacks variety, as well as obedience to operatic conventions, as in act 3, that blunt the edges of some characters' affective expression. And Verdi's attempt to use recurring themes, rather like Wagnerian leitmotivs, to identify and describe the main characters adds little dramatically, interesting as it may be as a stylistic experiment. (By 1844, Wagner had completed *Der fliegende Holländer*, where the use of repeating themes—they can hardly be called leitmotivs—is appealing but hardly more sophisticated.) But Verdi's consistency is notable in evoking moods of pathos and sorrow in this tight, well-crafted opera. The music is generally excellent, with his deployment of the orchestra displaying considerable refinement, as in the unusual prelude to the second act. The master also addresses skillfully and with insight one of his favorite themes, that of public responsibility trumping personal desires, when old Foscari is forced to act as Doge against his paternal instincts.

## Giovanna d'Arco

The plot of Verdi's seventh opera, to a libretto by Temistocle Solera, plays fast and loose with the life and death of Joan of Arc. The three acts of *Giovanna d'Arco* are preceded with a prologue that's long enough to stand as another act. And Verdi opens with a seven-minute overture here called a *sinfonia*, in the manner of Rossini that's good (though not performed apart from the opera), alternating stormy sections with long passages, beautifully written for the woodwinds, in a pastoral mode. High points of the prologue include the grandly conceived opening scene for Carlo and the chorus, where the young king expresses self-doubt, in dialogue with the chorus, which speaks as the voice of the French people. He describes a dream in a delicate aria, "Sotto una quercia"—*Beneath an oak*—in which the chorus continues its participation in a quieter mode that works along with the melancholy tone of Carlo's narrative. The cabaletta that follows, "Pondo è letal"—*A deadly burden*—is a polished example of the form. The second part of the prologue, set at a shrine in the forest nearby, is mostly weaker. But in the stormy, exciting, if rum-tum-tum music for Giovanna's father, Giacomo, we may hear hints of the last act of *Rigoletto*; and the adagio a cappella—unaccompanied—trio for Giovanna, Carlo, and Giacomo, she ending on a *pianissimo* high C that comes in the middle of it all, is a bold stroke. The choruses of evil spirits and angels are trite, though, and both unfortunately recur throughout the opera.

An exciting chorus ("Ai lari!"—*Let's return home*) for English soldiers recently defeated in battle by the newly inspired French army gets act 1 off to a fine start, which, like the prologue, is a mixed affair. Giovanna's *romanza* "O fatidica foresta"—*Prophetic forest*—in the second scene is another high point: woodwinds, imitating birdsong, twine prettily with her exquisite melody; the great "O sombre fôret" from Rossini's *Guillaume*

*Tell* surely inspired the reflective mood of Verdi's take-off, if not its details. Giovanna's duet with Carlo ("Dunque, o cruda"—*And so, cruel one*) is also well put together. The delineation of Giovanna's torment and Carlo's puzzlement and solicitous concern for her stand as one of the best moments in the opera, at least until the chorus of demons, accompanied by the *banda*, enters the scene.

There's little to recommend in the second act. In the big ensemble that ends the act, Verdi expresses the bewilderment of the crowd well, with edgy, off-the-beat interjections, but then wraps everything up conventionally. The third and last act has some good material, though, including the opening, in which Giovanna, now a prisoner of the English, is roused by the sound of battle. Her scene with Giacomo, "Amai, ma un solo istante"—*I loved, but only for a moment*—is a good father-daughter duet in Verdi's early style, ending with a sweeping falling tune in a sharply accented rhythm for both. Carlo's sad *romanza* ("Quale più fido amico"—*Which of my truest friends?*) on hearing that she has been killed also works well, with a weeping English horn over a flowing solo cello. What with the commentary of the regular chorus as well as angels and demons piled on top of Giovanna's dying vision, the final scene is very busy and a bit corny. But alongside the holy busyness, Verdi takes care to delineate Carlo's and Giacomo's grief.

## Alzira

Set in sixteenth-century Peru, *Alzira* turns a play by the rationalist skeptic Voltaire into a standard Italian operatic plot. The opera begins with a three-part overture that's quite entertaining. The opening section features colorful woodwind writing to set an exotic mood; the closing part has a version of one of Verdi's signature tunes, an excited, trill-laden idea for flutes over a chugging accompaniment. (The theme goes back to *Oberto*, reaching full fruition in act 1 of *Traviata*.) Here it's the Spaniard's march in act 1. A short prologue sets up the drama. It features a rollicking chorus for *"selvaggi"*—savages—that, like much in the work, quickly turns coarse. Verdi depicts Zamoro's innate nobility in fiery recitatives and an aria ("Un Inca") that describes his hatred for Gusman, and the cabaletta-like passage that follows ("Risorto fra le tenebre"—*Raised from the dead*) is fine.

The first act opens with Spaniards in Lima, singing a chorus ("Giunse or or"—*A message has arrived*) to Verdi's signature tune. You'll note in the first scene the preponderance of low male voices, with Alvaro, Gusman, and Ataliba onstage. The second scene, which opens with Alzira's dream, is more interesting as shimmering strings paint her yearning as she dreams of Zamoro. "Udite. Da Gusman"—*Listen. Of Gusman*—her big aria, sweeps along with impressive momentum, though here the musical ideas are not particularly memorable. The duet for Alzira and Zamoro ("Anima mia!"—*My soul!*) is one of the better moments in the score, as they greet each other with passion and swear their love tenderly. "Nella polve"—*In the dust*—the big ensemble that ends the act, is interrupted by an Incan march that amusingly resembles the "Turkish" music of Mozart's era.

The rapidly moving second act works better. The opening scene, with its chorus of drunk, victorious Spanish soldiers, is interrupted effectively—quite movingly, in fact—by the entrance of Incan prisoners, rendered as a trudging funeral march. The soldiers continue to drink and sing brokenly, but the effect is chilling. The duet between Alzira and Gusman that follows ("Il pianto, l'angoscia"—*The tears, the anguish*) seem to echo the scenes between Elvira and Carlo in *Ernani*, she desperate, he alternately threatening and seductive. And the vocal parts for both leads are notably difficult. The second scene opens with a somber introduction that's unusually interesting music: "Irne lungi ancor"—*Must I go again*—Zamoro's aria of self-doubt, is impressive, starting quietly, then swelling grandly. The cabaletta that follows ("Non di codarde lagrime"—*This is not the time for cowardly tears*) is rough but exciting. The final scene opens with a chorus for Incan maidens ("Tergi del pianto, America"—*Dry your tears, America*) of some charm. Gusman's aria "È dolce la tromba"—*Sweet is the trumpet's sound*—is rendered with such richness and warmth that Verdi turns him into a sympathetic character. The big final ensemble, for the stricken Gusman and the rest, is impressive, too. Listen for the Foscari-like outburst of grief from Alvaro for his dying son.

*Alzira*, about which Verdi later commented, "Quella è propria brutta"—*That one is really ugly*[5]—has the reputation as his worst opera, whatever that may mean, and however it might be measured. You can even take the comment of the composer, for whom dissatisfaction with early works was the norm, with a grain of salt. *Alzira* is an exciting, propulsive work whose worst fault is a tendency to coarseness. With a playing time of around ninety minutes, it's very short, too. But *Alzira* is never dull, and though it is undoubtedly weaker, the master can be observed tightening up, stripping down, and pressing on.

## *Attila*

Set in fifth-century Italy, *Attila* tells the tale of the Huns' invasion, but with a strong Risorgimento subtext. Cast in three acts and a prologue that's as long as an act, *Attila* begins promisingly, with an orchestral prelude that's solemn, simple, and impressive. The curtain rises on barbarians' celebrating their conquest of Italy, with Rome in their sights. It will amuse Wagnerians to hear them praising their supposed god "Wodano, in Valalla"—Wotan in Valhalla. Attila's entrance depicts his character in regal mode. Odabella's entrance, as a prisoner, is remarkable: this character spits fire in a very challenging vocal part that stands in terms of difficulty close to Lady Macbeth and Abigaille, from *Nabucco*. Her vocal line, marked by a ferocious coloratura, tells us much about her resolute, and in fact unappealing character. Her cavatina "Allor che i forti"—*Thus do the strong*—is crowned by a line in which she tells Attila that, unlike others, Italian women are ready to fight. The duet between Attila and Ezio, who somehow are old acquaintances, contains the line for the Roman Ezio that worked up the audiences of the day: "Avrai tu l'universo, resti l'Italia a me"—*You may have the universe, but leave Italy to me.* Verdi sets this so emphatically that there can be no doubt about the nature of its message to an Italian audience of 1846. The second scene, set in the Venetian lagoon, is remarkable for several reasons, the first being a lengthy, violent storm, depicted by the orchestra, followed by a chorus of hermits, then a long, passage for orchestra depicting the dawn, which starts quietly, then builds thunderously. One of several such passages in Verdi's career, this is likely the least familiar. We're introduced to Foresto, the young hero, who sings, "Qui, qui sostiamo"—*Here we'll sustain ourselves*—set to an interesting, folk-like tune. He then sighs for Odabella, more conventionally, in the cavatina "Ella, in poter del barbaro"—*She in the power of the barbarian*—followed by a pounding cabaletta that's yet another hymn to Italian unity.

Odabella's recitative and *romanza* that open act 1 form the best sequence in the opera. The recitative "Liberamente or piangi"—*Freedom or tears*—is a freely conceived passage, richly expressive of the her sorrow; the aria "Oh, nel fulgente nuvolo"—*In a glowing cloud*—is astonishing, a gorgeous conversation among solo cello, harp, English horn, flute, and voice, a magical bit of tone painting that's very difficult for the singer. The second scene, in Attila's tent, starts with an uneasy orchestral introduction that portrays the Hun's nightmare ("Mentre gonfiarsi l'anima"—*As my soul seemed to swell*) which he then relates to his lieutenant. Spooky enough, this is a type of narrative Verdi would get much better at, as in *Il trovatore*, and, consummately, in *Otello* and *Falstaff*. In the final scene of the act, the barbarians' war chant (another brassy prayer to "Wodano") is interrupted by a choir, accompanying who but the pope onstage. While the component parts seem corny and are certainly undistinguished musically, the dramatic effect works. And the big ensemble that ends the act ("No, non è sogno"—*It was not a dream*) show Verdi's growing skill at assembling these passages so that individual vocal lines and characterizations emerge clearly.

The second act opens with a scene for Ezio that shows Verdi as classicist: the recitative ("Tregua è cogl'Unni"—*There's a truce with the Huns*) sounds like a page from Mozart's *La clemenza di Tito*, so pure is its expression of Ezio's scorn and desire for glory. And the arching melody of the aria it introduces, "Dagli immortali vertici"—*To immortal summits*—is also classical in form and feeling. The big finale of the act begins with a chorus and dance for priestesses that looks ahead to light-footed passages in *Traviata*, *Ballo*, and *Aida*, but which seems incongruous in this rugged tale of Romans and Huns. The short third act contains bewildering plot twists, which the composer dispatches in urgent dialogues. But the trio for Odabella, Foresto, and Ezio ("Te sol, quest'anima"—*The sun, that spirit*) is quite beautiful, as is the improbable final quartet ("Nella tenda"—*In the tent*), introduced by Attila's suspicious questions, accompanied by convincingly stern strings.

The Risorgimento subtext of *Attila* made the work popular in its day, although of course that aspect of its appeal has passed. Nevertheless, it boasts Odabella's "Oh, nel fulgente nuvolo," perhaps the most purely beautiful passage Verdi had composed to this point.

## I masnadieri

The German poet and playwright Friedrich Schiller was a seminal figure in nineteenth-century European literature, with an influence that spread well beyond German readers and the dramatic stage. By using *"An die Freude"*—the Ode to Joy—as the text for the choral finale of his Ninth Symphony, Beethoven provided Schiller's verse with its widest exposure. Dostoyevsky used the plot and key characters of Schiller's tragedy *Die Räuber*—The Robbers—as a framework for his last novel, *The Brothers Karamazov*. Verdi used adaptations of Schiller's plays for the librettos of three and part of a fourth (*Forza*) of his operas, including *I masnadieri*, also based on *Die Räuber*. The Italian word shades toward "bandit" or "brigand"; you might remember that in act 1 of *Ernani*, Carlo calls the title character *un masnadiero*, which is usually translated as "bandit." The libretto, by Verdi's friend Andrea Maffei, employs a wider vocabulary than those by Piave, Cammarano, and Solera, giving it a more literary quality. Which is not to say that it's better. In some respects, the text anticipates those by Boito, without displaying that writer's dramatic and musical acuity, and Verdi may have found it unwieldy. The composer's own growing fame is demonstrated by the fact that *I masnadieri* was written in England, on a commission from Her Majesty's Theatre in London.

This tragedy of Biblical resonance concerns the family Moor: a gentle old father, Massimiliano, and his two sons, the handsome Carlo, and his younger brother Francesco, whose life is ruled by his envy of Carlo.

The work opens with a short orchestral introduction, featuring passages for the solo cello over a pulsing accompaniment that sets an impressively somber tone for the drama. The curtain rises to show Carlo, reading and reflecting on his home, family, and love, Amalia. Verdi captures Carlo's youthful impetuous yet sensitive character well, in his monologue and exchanges with the male chorus. His aria "O mio castel paterno"—*Castle of my fathers*—sets a lilting melody over pizzicato strings and carefully scored woodwinds, that underlines his appeal. The composer dispatches his reading of Francesco's letter effectively, in moments, and the cabaletta with the chorus, "Nell'argilla maledetta"—*Let my wrath plunge these swords*—moves along briskly, making a better impression than others of the species.

If you've sensed that Verdi's skill at depicting Carlo's motivation is acute, then you're right; and his characterization of Francesco is even better. The most interesting character in *Masnadieri*, this proto-Iago receives bold musical treatment, starting with a snarling orchestral introduction that depicts him vividly before he sings a note. As he reflects on the father he despises and the brother he hates ("Vecchio! spiccai da te"—*Old man, I have plucked from you that hated first-born*), Verdi's music follows his thoughts with unsparing clarity. One must appreciate the composer's focus on the moral motivations of the brothers, here shown in a sharpening of his dramatic skills as the composer, no longer satisfied by the portrayal of standard operatic affects, probes more deeply into human nature. It almost seems a shame that he had to force Francesco's next lines into the straitjacket of an aria ("La sua lampada vitale"—*The lamp of his life burns low*) and cabaletta ("Tremate, o miseri"—*Tremble, you wretches*), though the aria itself, set to a grating rhythmic figure that captures Francesco's obsessive hate, works well enough. The scene for Amalia and Massimiliano that follows is, like the characters themselves, less interesting. What makes Amalia's aria "Lo sguardo avea degli angeli"—*His face had the smile of the angels*—intriguing is the fact that Verdi wrote it for the soprano Jenny Lind, nicknamed the "Swedish Nightingale," who was revered for her trills and other coloratura. So, this aria (as, in fact, Amalia's entire role) is full of trills and turns. Verdi even makes a spot for an improvised cadenza up to a high C, showing the master's singular regard for Lind's vocal skills and taste.[6] Although illustrative of the conditions under which Verdi worked during the early phase of his career, the role of Amalia, who's too good to be true, can't benefit from the kind of vigorous characterizations that makes the brothers Moor live and breathe. But the aria is carefully scored, especially for winds, hinting at the heights Verdi would reach when composing for Gilda in *Rigoletto* four years later. A duet of weepy affect for Amalia and Massimiliano is followed by a powerful quartet, in which Francesco and his retainer Arminio join. This swiftly moving ensemble "Sul capo mio colpevole"—*May the wrath of heaven fall*—is tight, sharp in its musical depictions of the characters' varied affects, with Francesco's aggression and Amalia's saintliness effectively contrasted. It's also harmonically interesting, as Verdi moves boldly to great dramatic effect. And there's an effective strettalike speedup at the end, as Amalia and Francesco react to the false news that Massimiliano is dead.

The first scene of the second act is Amalia's. After a sorrow-laden prelude, she laments her lonely existence; then an offstage a cappella chorus portraying revelers in the castle that's now Francesco's can be heard having a great time. Verdi contrasts her desolation with their mindless pleasure in a way that looks ahead to the dying Violetta hearing the Lenten carnival outside in the last act of *La traviata*. Amalia's aria ("Tu del mio Carlo al seno"—*Blessed spirit, you have flown to the bosom of my Carlo*) may be old-fashioned but it's a real beauty, its swelling melody carried ahead with a fine flow provided by the harp and woodwinds. When she learns from Arminio that Carlo and Massimiliano are both still alive, her cabaletta ("Carlo vive?"—*Carlo lives?*), while musically and dramatically a letdown, is striking for its difficulty. Listen for the quick jumps and trills on the word "*accento*" Verdi wrote in for Lind, whose skills shaped the role. Francesco enters and tries to win her over with a suave tune ("Io t'amo, Amalia!"—*I love you, Amalia!*). She resists; soon they're calling each other names ("Tyrant!" "Whore!") and struggling over his knife, which Amalia grabs. (The plot here is very similar to that of the first act of *Ernani*.) The second scene, which takes place in the bandits' camp in the Bohemian Forest, is interesting for being almost entirely written for the chorus. News of a raid on Prague is transmitted from group to group across the stage, and the choral part writing is exceptionally difficult and interesting. Listen for the contrast between the frozen chords for terrified women, against which are set the leaping lines for the bandits. Carlo enters, brooding briefly but poignantly ("Di ladroni attorniato"—*Surrounded by robbers*) over the mess he's made of things. But soon the bandit groups coalesce into a quick final chorus ("Su, fratelli, corriamo alla pugna"—*Up, brothers, hasten to the fight*) that sounds much like a cancan.

Act 3 opens once more with a scene for a lost and bewildered Amalia, who now presents a vocal persona that's rather more grand, in sweeping lines that add interest to her character. Reunited with Carlo, the lovers express their rapture in a lilting duet ("Qual mare, qual terra"—*What sea, what land*) that is touching and beautiful, as they exchange cries of delight in their breathless dialogue. The cabaletta for two that follows ("Lassù risplendere"—*We shall see the star of our love*) is filled with detached notes and phrases most singers find difficult. It's tough to sing in a way that's atypical for Verdi, who normally wrote in a more regular, stepwise fashion. (Clearly Lind was better than most at leaps like these.)

The virtuoso exercise for bandits, "Le rube, gli stupri. gl'incendi"—
*Pillage, rape, arson*—more cheerful than the text suggests—is another
remarkable study for the chorus. The varied rhythms and colors almost
act as a choreographic interlude; the high level of the choral writing here
anticipates the virtuosic choruses in *Forza*, and perhaps even *Aida*. In
the final scene, the ever-conflicted Carlo considers suicide ("Ti delusi,
Amalia!"—*I deceived you, Amalia*) when Arminio and Massimiliano enter.
The old man recounts Francesco's treachery in a substantial narrative ("Un
ignoto"—*An unknown*). Enraged, Carlo summons his men to help him
avenge his father in a surging solo accompanied by the male chorus ("Giuri
ognun"—*Each of you swear*) that anticipates the finest of the composer's
thunderous oaths to come.

The last act opens with some of the opera's best music. Francesco,
guilty but as yet unrepentant, suffers from nightmares brought on by his
misdeeds. Here Verdi engages in some fine tone painting, as Francesco
recounts his dream in horror to Arminio ("Pareami che sorto"—*I fancied
that*). These passages do not possess the force of the Requiem of 1874, but
it's hard not to hear in some of them anticipations of that great work, and
particularly of the Dies irae. Slippery chromatic harmony and orchestration of exceptional clarity mark the growing freedom of the composer's
imagination. And Francesco's dialogue with the minister Moser follows
in the same brilliant vein, as a now desperate Francesco flings his pleas for
mercy against Moser's rocklike vocal line: it's impressive stuff. The final
scene comprises a trio for Carlo, Amalia, and Massimiliano; father and son
are reconciled, but now Carlo cannot reconcile with himself. The now-
demonic accompaniment of the chorus of brigands demands their leader's
loyalty. Carlo's solo "Caduto è il reprobo"—*The evildoer is fallen*—opens
another substantial but fast-moving ensemble that ends *I masnadieri* convincingly on a musical level even if the dramatic situation is improbable.

*I masnadieri* falls short of greatness, but the opera has innumerable
qualities, making its acquaintance essential. Verdi bravely tackles a difficult topic here—what Melville would call "natural depravity: a depravity
according to nature" (*Billy Budd*, chapter 11)—with considerable success,
drawing in the brothers Moor two of his richest early characters. Each
of the four acts seems better than the previous one. On a more practical
level, Verdi grabbed the opportunity offered by a great chorus to write
some of the best choral material in his output thus far. And he continues

in *Masnadieri* to refine his technique, with the orchestral writing showing perhaps its highest point yet, that for woodwinds being particularly fine. The opera's chief flaws are that it's uneven and that its heroine is a bore in every way other than vocally; but its probing quality must have been stimulated by the writing of *Macbeth*, its immediate predecessor.

## Il corsaro

Based, like *I due Foscari*, on a verse drama by Byron, *Il corsaro* tells the story of a Byronic antihero, Corrado, a pirate captain on the Aegean in the early years of the nineteenth century.

A short but well-made orchestral prelude kicks the opera off: a slashing, fiercely dissonant racket for the full orchestra is followed by a long sighing passage, then a sad melody, here sung by the clarinet that we won't hear again until act 3, and finally a surging sequence that suggests the movement and open feeling of the sea. The curtain rises to a chorus of pirates singing lustily of the joys of their piratical life: "Come liberi volano i venti"—*As the winds fly freely*. Corrado enters, heroically proclaiming a bland line of dialogue, just barely hinting at Otello's great entrance of thirty-five years later. He tells the audience that he's unhappy and then launches into an aria ("Tutto parea sorridere"—*Everything seemed to smile*) that presents the singer and orchestra in an intimate relationship. The accompaniment is a polished mix of pizzicato strings and delicately scored winds, and in contrast with his brash entrance, Corrado's line is sensitive to the text and never showy. News is brought of an opportunity to attack the Turks, and Corrado and the chorus launch into an aggressive cabaletta "Si, de'Corsari il fulmine"—*The pirates' thunderbolt*. The second scene presents the sad heroine, Medora. Her *romanza* "Non so le tetre immagini"—*I cannot banish dark imaginings*—displays further refinement of Verdi's style. Set to a rocking folklike melody over a simple accompaniment, at first for harp and flute, later joined by a few strings and winds, it's easy to hear Leonora's aria "Tacea la notte placida" from *Trovatore* anticipated here. In the second verse, her melodic line is heavily ornamented. The duet for Medora and Corrado ("No, tu non sai comprendere"—*No, you cannot understand*) opens with a piercing tune with a sharply accented profile that rises and falls gently. In the stretta, Corrado tries to reassure Medora, but fails to relieve her agitation: "Tornerai, ma forse spenta"—*You'll return, but perhaps this sorrowing heart will then have ceased to beat*—is another affecting moment as the two voices join in an arching melody over an urgent, throbbing accompaniment in the strings.

The second act seems a bit weaker than the first, overall. It starts with a self-consciously "Oriental" scene, set in the harem of Pasha Seid. Dated but still charming, this short chorus introduces Gulnara, the real heroine, whom Corrado will rescue. She comments to her harem-mates that she hates Seid, before singing a delicious cavatina ("Vola talor dal carcere"—*At times, far from my prison, my thoughts soar freely*) that's folklike in character and marked by a profusion of turns on the vocal side. Soon the high winds join as a burbling accompaniment. The cabaletta that follows, "Ah, conforto è sol la speme"—*My only comfort is the hope*—is old-fashioned, and difficult, filled with leaps. After a chorus for Turkish soldiers ("Sol grida di festa"—*Let only festive shouts*), leading into Pasha Seid's big number "Salve, Allah"—*Save, Allah*. This aria with chorus, accompanied by thumping brass and drums, is purposely pompous, with a heavy sound all its own that you may or may not like. The finale begins, with Corrado, disguised (as a "dervish"), brought in to distract and misinform Seid. The action here seems too busy for Verdi to keep to a consistent tone. The dialogue between Corrado and Seid, for example, should sound tense, but its speed makes it unintentionally comic. With the big ensemble ("Audace cotanto"—*Can you yet show yourself so bold?*) things begin to coalesce, however. Seid's lunging melody expresses his anger very well, and Verdi sets the stretta ("Sì, morrai"—*Yes, you will die*) with unusual thematic and harmonic sophistication.

Act 3, the longest and best in *Il corsaro*, begins with an angry monologue for Seid, "Alfin questo corsaro è mio prigione"—*At last this corsair is my prisoner*—in which the lovesick character reflects on his situation. His aria "Cento leggiadre vergini"—*A hundred charming maidens*—presents another excellent example of Verdi's classical bent, sounding chastely like Haydn or Beethoven, at least until the orchestra erupts on the word "fulmini"—*thunderbolts*. His cabaletta ("S'avvicina il tuo momento"—*Your moment approaches*) is ugly, the weakest passage in this otherwise fascinating act. His duet with Gulnara ("Eccola . . . fingasi"—*Here she comes . . . let me pretend*) showing the two characters playing cat and mouse, is very strong: the lower strings portray the tension that underpins the characters' dialogue, starting out blandly but soon growing agitated. Finally, Seid accuses Gulnara of loving Corrado, as Verdi captures the tone between master and slave, he blustering, she alarmed, wary, and set unusually low in the soprano range. A worthy step on the composer's path to continuous musical drama, this duet is remarkable, and deserves to be better known.

The next scene, set in Seid's dungeon, continues in the same ambitious vein, though it follows a more structured "rescue opera" pattern. There are obvious parallels between the chained Florestan in act 2 of Beethoven's *Fidelio* and Corrado, in the same situation here, but the two masters take different approaches, Verdi's being lower keyed. The scene opens with a long, sad melody for strings, after which Corrado's monologue ("Eccomi prigioniero"—*Behold me, a prisoner*) sadly reflects on Medora. Gulnara enters, and, in a long dialogue, tries to persuade Corrado to let her rescue him. They debate, urgently but quietly, to a succession of repeating melodic ideas and accompaniments, but the overall sense is of freedom and truthful representation of the characters' words. Corrado erupts grandly once: "Cessa, o Gulnara, lasciami"—*Cease, leave me*—to which she replies in high agitation, "Non sai tu che sulla testa"—*Don't you know what tempest rages above our heads?* Taking matters into her own hands, Gulnara goes upstairs, carrying a knife. As we wait tensely with Corrado, Verdi brings back the stormy music that opened the prelude to act 1 to depict Gulnara's murder of Seid, a remarkably effective dramatic device. Once she returns, the music of their duet "La terra, il ciel m'aborrino"—*Let earth and heaven abhor me*—sounds more conventional. But one has to be impressed by the sureness of Verdi's hand in finding a new path through this long scene in dialogue.

The final scene, set back at the corsair's island, opens with a stern orchestral prelude into which a sad oboe melody is woven, followed by the clarinet tune from the prelude to act 1, which, as we'll soon hear is that of Medora's lament for Corrado, who she believes to be dead ("Il mio Corrado"). Short but still beautiful, the tune is interrupted by the excitement of Corrado's return with Gulnara; seeing Medora is failing, he launches into "Per me infelice"—*you see her, unhappy*—set to a plain, folklike melody that anticipates in feeling those in *Il trovatore*. "O mio Corrado, appressati"—*Corrado, come close to me*—the closing ensemble, for Corrado, Medora, Gulnara, and chorus has a delicacy that sets it apart from others by Verdi; and the swift, shocking ending looks ahead, again, to that of *Trovatore*.

*Il corsaro* shows the master polishing his technique further. The coarse moments, such as Seid's cabaletta near the beginning of act 3, now obtrude into a score that's otherwise of notable refinement. And the composer's flexibility in handling the drama by bringing the stormy opening of the prelude back later for a real dramatic purpose, not to mention his skillful handling of the long passages in dialogue in the third act, make this a "galley" opera that's worth knowing.

## La battaglia di Legnano

Verdi's most overtly patriotic opera, *La battaglia di Legnano* is set in northern Italy in 1176, during the war of the Lombard League against the Frederick Barbarossa, the German Holy Roman Emperor. Salvatore Cammarano, the librettist, had to work into the story situations designed to stoke the fires of Risorgimento sentiment, then (1849) at fever pitch, alongside the standard romantic and dramatic reversals that still form the bulk of the plot. But once again Verdi took the opportunity to move ahead in this interesting, though certainly flawed work. You'll note similarities of plot with *Lombardi* and *Giovanna d'Arco*, where the hero/heroine dies in triumph; as well as with *Attila*, where the villain dies, and the cause for good triumphs. Otherwise, the plot's as congested with coincidences and reversals as any.

Verdi begins the opera with a long, complex overture, here called a *sinfonia*, built from themes taken from the work. It opens with the brass stating a marchlike theme from act 1 that turns hymnlike, then a slow and songful tune, given by the flute and clarinet, to an elaborate accompaniment, first of pizzicato strings, then, even more floridly, by the other woodwinds. Finally, the opening theme returns, subjected by the composer to a powerful and exciting symphonic development. You can feel Verdi's stretching his musical intellect with an almost Beethoven-like sense of purpose in this marvelous prelude. (The great *Luisa Miller* overture is its fitting successor.) As the curtain rises, soldiers from cities of the Lombard League gather near the wall of Milan. Getting straight to patriotic business, the soldiers, later joined by women, sing an unaccompanied hymn, "Viva Italia," that starts quietly but soon builds grandly. Arrigo enters, singing a beautiful cavatina ("La pia materna mano"—*A mother's kindly hand*), actually in tribute to Lida, for whom he believes he has survived. A complex backing of plucked strings and delicately scored winds accompany the irregular melody, marked in the middle section by a sighing figure for winds. Rolando enters, then sings a brief but warm aria ("Ah, m'abbraccia"—*Come to my arms*) in a three short sections, the outer accompanied by winds, the middle by pizzicato strings. Next, the men, backed by the chorus, sing an oath to defend Italy, "Tutti giuriam difenderla"—*Let us all swear to defend her*. This thunderous passage gets the blood boiling, just as Verdi intended. Lida's aria "Quante volte come un dono"—*How many times have I prayed for death, as a gift*—is as beautiful as Arrigo's in the opening scene, and more complex musically. Listen for the restless shifts of harmony—the tonic underpinning—in the accompaniment that express the sorrow that grips Lida every bit as vividly as the twisting ornamentation of the vocal line. Her joy on learning that Arrigo is alive is swiftly and powerfully caught. Her cabaletta "A frenarti, o cor, nel petto"—*My heart, I no longer have the power*—is a polished and restrained specimen. Another fascinating example of a long scene in dialogue, "È ver, sei d'altri?"—*Is is true that you're another's?*— shows a sarcastic Arrigo attacking Lida for her faithlessness, as he sees it, of course. The music carries the dialogue along effortlessly, as the singers' parts finally overlap in an exciting, angry ending.

At only twenty minutes or so, the second act seems disproportionately short. But it does contain a strong duet for Arrigo and Rolando ("Ah, ben vi scorgo"—*I clearly see in your features*) as they appeal passionately to the fellow sprit of the uncooperative council of Como for aid. Suddenly, Barbarossa himself enters, opening an impressive trio with the protagonists, including Frederick's terrifying cry "Il destino d'Italia son io"—*I am Italy's destiny*. The emperor roars out his line over a surging accompaniment by the strings as Arrigo and Rolando spit defiance and the Como chorus comments that a pitiless war is inevitable.

*La battaglia di Legnano* is without doubt top-heavy with oath scenes, but the one for Arrigo and the Knights of Death that opens act 3 ("Campioni della Morte"—*Champions of death*) is probably the most impressive. Framed by a rather long, very somber introduction for the orchestra, and a postlude of similar material, the oldest member of the Knights yields its leadership to Arrigo's fiery commitment. And finally the group sings its oath "Giuriam d'Italia por fine ai danni"—*We swear to end Italy's wrongs*—as thunderously as you might expect, with Arrigo joining in, his tenor voice showing the one bright line in this dark musical canvas. While there's nothing unexpected here, Verdi puts it all together very well. The second scene, a long chain of duets, mostly in dialogue, between Lida and her maid Imelda; Rolando, and finally Arrigo displays Verdi's growing skill with such passages. He captures Lida's anxiety in a brief, aria-like passage ("Questo foglio"—*This letter*). With their child present, Rolando asks Lida to raise him to honor his fatherland of Italy ("Digli ch'è sangue italico"—*Tell him he's of Italian blood*), one of Verdi's unfailingly smooth tunes for baritone, though this one is laden with sadness. Lida joins him in a closing section, "Sperda ogni triste augurio"—*May the hand that guides our destiny*—in which their voices blend and soar over shimmering strings and harp, one of the most remarkable moments in this score. The dialogue between Arrigo and Rolando that follows is very fine, too, with Rolando given another gorgeous tune ("Se al nuovo dì pugnardo"—*If, when we fight tomorrow*), to which Arrigo comments, uneasily as befits his ambivalence, to himself. After Arrigo has sworn—quietly this time—to watch over Lida and their son, Rolando enters on another dialogue, this one swift, in which the villainous Marcovaldo shows him a letter he's intercepted from Lida to Arrigo, mentioning their old love. A brief cabaletta-like duet, "Ah, scellerate"—*The scoundrels*—punctuated by violent chords, reinforced by the timpani, captures Rolando's rage and Marcovaldo's bitterness with devastating accuracy. The wild final scene of act 3 begins with Arrigo and Lida quietly confessing an enduring mutual love, as Rolando breaks in, waving Lida's letter. A trio ("Ah, d'un consorte, o perfidi"—*Wretches, you've made mockery of a husband*) begun by Rolando begins; Arrigo, with his usual reckless courage, asks his old friend to kill him. But instead, Rolando tears into a fierce solo, "Vendetta d'un momento"—*Revenge of an instant*—in which the timpani underline the characters' agitation with a powerful, pulselike throbbing. He locks Lida and Arrigo into her room; but Arrigo, hearing the trumpets of the Knights of Death outside, leaps from Lida's balcony, to a frantic, dissonant orchestral accompaniment that captures his desperation.

The short fourth act has less to offer. In its opening passage, an offstage chorus is heard praying, to which a still anxious Lida adds her personal prayer for the safety of those she loves, creating an interesting effect. In the next passage, news of the death of Barbarossa at Arrigo's hands is transmitted, with trumpets chattering and a new choral outburst. Arrigo is brought in, mortally wounded. He sings a brief, sorrow-laden aria, "Per la salvata Italia"—*By Italy's salvation*—that turns into a trio as Lida (whom Arrigo has exonerated) and Rolando join him. Again, the chorus comes in, and Arrigo dies, after kissing the Italian battle flag and singing a juicy high A.

The chief flaw of *La battaglia* is its patriotic purpose, expressed in an abundance of oaths, prayers, and business for the chorus. But that should not blind the newbie to its virtues: the arias for the three principals are, without exception, beautiful, and Verdi exercises great care in weaving them into the flow of the musical drama, always subsuming them to its current. And, particularly in the first and third acts, he continues to get better and better at rendering the dialogues that carry the story.

IN CASE YOU'RE THINKING OF SKIMMING THE TOP OF THESE "GALLEY YEARS" operas, then the four likeliest to satisfy are probably *I due Foscari, I masnadieri, Il corsaro,* and *La battaglia di Legnano,* the most tightly woven and predictive of the master's mature style. Since the likelihood of catching these in live performances—unless you live in Italy or close to an important music school somewhere else—is slim, then DVDs will be the best way to see and enjoy these works. Opera is theater, and meant to be experienced and enjoyed in performance, not dully following along in a little booklet as you listen to a compact disc. And, fortunately, there are good—or at least adequate—performances of all of them on DVD.

Again, the second-class citizenship that placement in this chapter imposes on these works, each one worthwhile in its way, is worrisome. As I worked, for example, I learned that while I still don't love *Giovanna d'Arco,* there's more strong material than I noticed before; and that even though the luxuriant mess that is *I Lombardi* will probably never contend to be in my top ten Verdi operas, that it, too, holds more gems than I realized. So, if Verdi appeals to you, please keep an open mind, and get to these eleven at some point. The composer's own attitude is worth noting, then setting aside: he preferred not to look back. If he revised an earlier work, he felt it aesthetically merited that very considerable effort. The heights he reaches in his greatest works inevitably throw these into the shade. But we have—and we should take—the luxury of acquainting ourselves with these eleven, as well. Verdi is never boring, even when he isn't great.

# The Transition to the Middle Period

## Luisa Miller and Stiffelio; Aroldo

### Luisa Miller

The operas we'll look at in this chapter stand as crucial turning points from Verdi's early style to the full glory of his middle period. The first, *Luisa Miller*, composed in 1849, has long been appreciated for its display of the master's swiftly ripening style. But *Stiffelio*, composed in the following year, was lost to history for more than a century, subsumed in *Aroldo*, an obscure revision Verdi made in 1857. Rediscovered in the 1960s, *Stiffelio* is rarely produced and remains shamefully little known.

*Luisa Miller*'s greatness and importance are beyond debate. After an overture that's one of the best to open any opera, we witness a composer whose skill seems to grow geometrically from one act to the next, with the third and last a monument to his musical and dramatic evolution. In the first and second acts we see Verdi's early style brought to new peaks in a drama that, echoing Bellini's *La sonnambula*, opens with an innocent girl about to be brought down by a society that only looks ideal. At once intimate, grand, and dramatically tight, the last act of *Luisa Miller* shows the composer's skills at a new level and his insights into the human condition ever deepening.

Based on Schiller's drama *Kabale und Liebe* ("Intrigue and Love"), *Luisa Miller* is set in a small Tyrolean town in the early seventeenth century.

What sound like typical operatic twists and turns in a plot summary are far less trite than they may appear; the opera's story line is clear and direct. And with only a few lapses along the way, Verdi's music reaches a new level of excellence. *Luisa Miller* marks an important turning point in his style, more spacious than in any previous opera except perhaps *Macbeth*. The composer seems less worried here about pushing the story ahead, and more comfortable in allowing it to unfold at a natural, unhurried pace. It's also an important turn for Verdi toward portraying humble characters in modest settings, which continues with the domestic drama of *Stiffelio*, then reaches maturity in *Rigoletto* and *La traviata*. Some scholars think this shift in focus began with Verdi's exposure to dramas and fiction about the middle class that he saw and read in Paris, where he had begun to spend more time.[1] Another reason that the master turned away from political subjects may have been the setbacks in the movement for Italian unification.[2] And perhaps as he got older it became easier for Verdi to deal with matters of the heart—filial and marital—and, in *Don Carlo*, friendship.

The overture, which Verdi calls a *sinfonia*, is along with that to *Forza*, one of his greatest. Based on a single theme in two phrases, this is a masterpiece of taut musical logic and dramatic tension. The theme is a purely instrumental conception, with no reappearances in an aria, though it is brought back in altered form, and to powerful effect, at the opening of the third act. Rather than referring to incidents in the opera, it sets a mood of agitation and conflict. The unforgettable opening tune is built on a series of sinuous phrases in a long-short-short-long rhythm, ending in long-held notes and striking silences; the second portion of the theme is frantic and violent. Verdi passes the theme from one instrumental group to another, but the clarinet, which takes it up at around one minute, twenty seconds into its five-and-a-half-minute length maintains a role as the most important woodwind. Note the chattering incarnation of the theme for strings, followed by a spooky, chromatic one. There are immensely long and dramatic pauses and a wildly exciting climax and coda. With this astonishing instrumental essay, Verdi joins the ranks of the great musical intellects.

Salvatore Cammarano, the librettist, liked to name the acts of his librettos, and so the first is titled "Love." The opening scene reveals a rustic paradise that's about to be lost. A flourish for the clarinet introduces the chorus of peasants "Ti desta, Luisa"—*Awake, Luisa*—gently set and scored, in which all is sweet, consonant, and pretty. Miller and Luisa come out of their home, and he warns her about her boyfriend, whom no one knows but who arrived at the same time as the sinister new Count. But Luisa tells her father it was love at first sight, in a playful cantabile,

"Lo vidi, e'l primo palpito"—*I saw him, and my heart felt its first thrill of love.* Marked by burbling triplets, this cheerful aria brilliantly captures Luisa's naïveté. As Rodolfo enters, Miller expresses his unease in muttered asides. The two lovers sing a glittering, cabaletta-like refrain, "T'amo d'amor ch'esprimere"—*I love you with a love that words can poorly express.* The church bells chime, as Verdi contrives an artful fade-down to allow the chorus and lovers to exit, leaving Miller alone onstage. Wurm, the Count's evil retainer, enters to a snarling commentary for strings of the sort Verdi now favors as an orchestral companion to his villains. The two engage in an intense discussion about Luisa's plans, when Miller launches into an old-fashioned aria ("Sacra la scelta è d'un consorte"—*The choice of a husband is sacred*) over a rustling accompaniment, to a tune that's notable for its nobility. Its second verse, "In terra un padre"—*On earth a father*—is set to a different, surging melody. Miller's cabaletta "Ah, fu giusto il mio sospetto!"—*Ah, my suspicion was right!*—displays an evolved, almost refined style for this athletic form, with subtle touches of orchestration and some powerful harmonic jolts. It's with Miller that a new species, the Verdi baritone, emerges. Demanding a slightly higher tessitura—a higher range—and a demanding a rich, burnished sound in the ideal, these roles, from Rigoletto to Renato in *Ballo* to Amonasro of *Aida*, Iago, and Ford, are all juicy from a vocal standpoint.

The second scene begins with a brief dialogue for Wurm and Count Walter, backed by biting strings. An impressive monologue ("Il mio sangue"—*I would give my blood*) for Count Walter follows. In it, the Count laments Rodolfo's unwillingness to take advantage of the course he has risked everything for. The grandiose vocal line, accompanied by muttering strings and occasional outbursts for the full orchestra, paints a formidable character. Verdi's growth is evident in the skill with which he depicts Walter not as appealing; rather, as believable: an old but still headstrong man we might know. A middle section, accompanied by paired clarinets, contrasts with a slightly softer musical impression, though the lyric remains stern: "Di dolcezze l'affetto"—*Paternal love is not a source of sweetness.* Rodolfo enters; father and son have a quick, tense dialogue in which Walter tells Rodolfo that he's to marry the Duchess Federica, and the son murmurs in despair. A rather trivial fanfare and chorus introduce the Duchess, widowed but young, a woman of strong character herself. She opens their discussion with a suave melody ("Dall'aule raggianti"—*From glittering halls*) of a folklike cast, over an exceptionally beautiful accompaniment of strings, some plucked, others quietly held. Naively assuming that his old friend will understand his love for Luisa, Rodolfo pours out his heart to Federica, who responds first in shock, but soon in anger. Verdi captures all in a dramatic dialogue at nearly real-time pacing and great musical fidelity to the text.

The last scene of the act, set in Miller's cottage, opens with a hunting chorus, heard in the distance, which frames the action. Miller tells his daughter that the young man she knows as Carlo is actually Rodolfo, son of the Count, who then enters. Preceded and followed by an impassioned comment by the clarinet, Rodolfo kneels and declares in a soaring phrase that Luisa is "his wife." In mysterious tones, he assures Miller that he can persuade his own father to go along with their marriage, because he knows a dark secret; the orchestra writhes menacingly behind Rodolfo's words. The pace of the drama accelerates as Count Walter enters to a sharply profiled melody for the strings, accusing Luisa of being a seductress. She falls to her knees, pleading. Miller insists she not humble herself before Walter in an unusual cantabile ("Fra' mortali ancora oppressa"—*Among mortals innocence is not yet so oppressed*) in which he spits out his contempt for the Count, backed by growling low winds and strings. The various conversations and comments soon come together into a quartet, over which Luisa's line soars radiantly. But the words are all set with great sensitivity, and the big climax of the ensemble features a powerful change of key.

Act 2, titled "Intrigue," opens, once again, inside Miller's house. To a tumbling accompaniment, the chorus relates that Miller has been seized, over which Luisa bewails in fairly predictable phrases. Wurm enters. To ticking pizzicato strings, he dictates a letter claiming she really loves Wurm, which, he insists, is the only means of saving her father. Verdi characterizes her agony by a pleading phrase for the clarinet, which as you have gathered by now, plays a leading role in the sound of *Luisa Miller*. She sings a grandly expressive cantabile ("Tu puniscimi, o Signore"—*You punish me, o Lord*) over shuddering strings, her vocal line persistently doubled, again by the clarinet. After Luisa signs the letter, Wurm gloats, and Luisa launches into a rather refined and melancholy cabaletta, "A brani, o perfido"—*Perfidious wretch*—marked by a pleading middle section. In the next scene, Walter and Wurm discuss the murder of the old count, done by Wurm at Walter's instigation, but discovered, accidentally, by Rodolfo

("L'alto retaggio non ho bramato"—*The noble inheritance of my cousin*). This superb scene shows Verdi's hard-won skill at narrative passages. This one clarifies something we knew only from Rodolfo's intimations, without delaying the drama, while deepening the two characters involved, as well. We have a better feel for Walter's determination, and for Wurm, who's wicked *and* cowardly. Verdi accelerates its pace as it proceeds. The remainder of the scene, in which Luisa is forced to perform for Federica, coached and threatened by Walter and Wurm, is fine, if not up to the grandeur of what it follows. It leads into a remarkable a cappella quartet for the four characters, "Come celar le smanie"—*How can I hide the crav-ings*—that sounds great in studio recordings of the opera, where perfection can be achieved in increments, but is so treacherous that it's usually shortened in live performances. The final scene of the act contains one of the highlights of the opera, and a culmination of the master's early style, Rodolfo's majestic aria "Quando le sere al placido" (CD Track 3)—*When in the evening, in the tranquil glimmer of a starry sky*. Having received and read Luisa's false letter, Rodolfo pours out his despair over the betrayal in a noble melody over a delicate accompaniment that includes a swiftly rippling clarinet arpeggio. The greatness of this showpiece (a favorite of tenors) will be obvious to even a first-time listener, but it's worth noting that the immense melody is repeated twice, without a contrasting section, and with increasing intensity of expression. Verdi marks the singer's part with an exceptional instruction, "*appassionatissimo*"—as passionately as possible. The emphasis is always put on the incandescent phrase "Ah! mia tradia"—*Ah, she betrayed me*—which the performer is to sing "*con espressione*," "*con molto espressione*," and finally "*con disperazione*." There's a tranquility to Rodolfo's great melody, too, as the composer takes his cue from the opening line, with which the cry of despair is contrasted, yet within which it's also contained, encasing memory and despair in a vessel of purest lyricism. Verdi takes Bellini's melodic grandeur and amplifies it to a new level in this monument to the cantabile style. The remainder of the act, in which Rodolfo challenges the frightened Wurm, then agrees to marry Federica, works well, but can only feel like a letdown after the ecstasy of Rodolfo's aria.

The third act, titled "Poison," is cast in three scenes, all set in Miller's cottage, that are so closely interwoven musically and dramatically that they read as one. The curtain rises to reveal a melancholy Luisa, kept company by friends who form a chorus. The music combines the powerful theme from the overture, here recast in a coiling rhythm, into which Verdi weaves a pair of flutes, playing a desolate reminiscence of the act 1 duet for Luisa and Rodolfo, "T'amo d'amor ch'esprimere." The theme from the overture captures Luisa's despondence, punctuating the entire scene. The girls sing an exquisite chorus with a folklike lilt ("Come in un giorno solo"—*How, in a single day*) bewailing the shocking change they see in their friend. Miller, freed by Luisa's letter, enters joyfully, but finds his daughter depressed and writing another letter. Their duet is usually identified by Luisa's line "La tomba è un letto"—*The grave is a bed*—in which she tells her shocked father that her letter is to Rodolfo, proposing a suicide pact. Her melody, again with a profound feeling of folk song, simple on its surface at least, reflects her longing for the release of death. Miller's reply ("Di rughe il volto, mira, ho solcato"—*See, my face is furrowed with wrinkles*) is at once tender, tortured, and beautiful; it persuades her to tear up her letter and agree to leave their town forever. It's easy to hear Rigoletto and Gilda anticipated by their rejoicing, in yet another great Verdian father-daughter scene. Their mild, sweet duet "Andrem, raminghi e poveri"—*We will go, roaming and poor*—has Miller singing the melody, to which Luisa adds a high and dreamy descant. (It is much in the same spirit as act 5 scene 3 of *King Lear*, in which the old King wishes "so we'll live, /and pray, and sing, and tell old tales, and laugh/at gilded butterflies..."—making us regret bitterly that Verdi never set that grandest father-daughter tragedy.)

The final scene begins with an organ heard from the church across the road; its plain chords have an oddly unsetting effect. Luisa sings a piercing farewell to her town ("Ah, l'ultima preghiera"—*Ah, the last prayer*). Rodolfo enters, crazed, and the menace implied in the organ music becomes ironically clear. He notes that she's praying, as well she should, he says to himself, and to us. Their dialogue, in which he questions her about her letter and she maintains its lie, is very tense and powerful, with stern orchestral interjections. Writing this must have provided invaluable precedent for Verdi in composing the fearful fourth act of *Otello*, so similar in many ways, and clearly its descendant. He drinks from the poisoned cup he's brought and then has Luisa drink. Still unaware of the truth, Rodolfo insults Luisa, and then weeps. The orchestral accompaniment to Rodolfo's lines turns chromatically dizzy, suggesting the poison that's starting to work, anticipating the poisoned Simon Boccanegra. This turns into a brief duet that's at once furious and soaring. Once Luisa learns that she's dying, she tells Rodolfo everything. His frantic response "Ah, maledetto, il dì ch'io nacqui"—*Cursed be the day I was born!*—is pure, patented Verdi, brilliantly capturing Rodolfo's shock and horror. Their uproar brings Miller onto the scene for the final trio "Padre, ricevi l'estremo addio"—*Father, receive my last farewell*—which, though brief, is so intense as to form the lyrical climax of the third act. The final melodramatic actions after Luisa dies—Rodolfo's killing of Wurm before dying—take but a few, thunderous moments. Verdi was good at these fast, shocking endings, but the glory of the soaring twined voices in the trio is what will stick with you.

## Stiffelio

The history of *Stiffelio*, perhaps Verdi's most unusual opera, is not a happy one. Already thinking about what would become *Rigoletto*, Verdi composed the work to fulfill a contract with the Teatro Grande in Trieste. Its subject, a Protestant minister and his straying wife, enraged censors and puzzled Italian audiences, though it was not a flop in its initial run in Trieste.[3] But the difficult subject made staging in a preunified Italy unlikely, as censors in each of the individual Italian states would take a swing at it. Recognizing this reality, but still finding merit in the opera, Verdi rewrote it in 1857 as *Aroldo*, which work, though musically fine, turns the modern minister into a medieval Crusader, weakening the ethical twist that makes the story so intriguing. Thinking that *Stiffelio* was done with, the composer used much of his handwritten score for *Aroldo*, and had other copies of *Stiffelio* destroyed. It's only by luck that *Stiffelio* survived at all. In the 1960s, copyists' scores of *Stiffelio* were discovered, and the opera was published, as well as recorded and staged. But performances have been few: "Considering that it was composed between *Luisa Miller* and *Rigoletto*, the comparative lack of interest shown for *Stiffelio* is extraordinary."[4] Part of the problem may still be the opera's intimate subject, and part may stem from its mood and color—its *tinta*—which seems austere and stern for Verdi. But though neglected, *Stiffelio* is a work of beauty and power, every bit as important a link in the chain of his creativity as the operas it follows and precedes.

*Stiffelio* begins unpromisingly, with a rambling *sinfonia* that seems poorly matched to this somber and impressive drama. At ten minutes' playing time, it's also too long, considering the triviality of some of its material. It opens with a simple theme for strings, gently interrupted by winds, that sets a prayerlike mood, then a vocally styled melody for trumpet, which Verdi gives an accompaniment that's intricate, and even busy. These develop into a thunderous climax. The opening sections of the overture at least capture some of the opera's rugged grandeur; but the remainder unfortunately does not. Yet another version of the high-strung theme that obsessed the composer, finally reaching its pinnacle in the opening scene of *La traviata*, is presented. The last theme to enter is a bland tune for the chorus from the end of act 1. The rest of the overture repeats everything from the *Traviata*-like theme on a second time, generating little in the way of expectation or dramatic sparks. And curiously, Verdi saw fit to retain the overture, with a few modifications, in *Aroldo*.

Quality rises with the curtain, as Jorg, an elderly minister in Stiffelio's sect, praises the Bible, then relates in majestic tones that their leader has returned ("Oh santo libro"—*Oh, holy book*). Stiffelio enters with Lina, his wife; her father, Stankar; and Raffaele, her still-secret lover. The plot is quickly kicked into motion as Stiffelio pitches into the fire a letter that has turned up under the most suspicious circumstances. It was dropped into the water by a frantic man who leapt from a high window, in which a terrified woman was also spotted. It will turn out that the window was Stiffelio's and the guilty couple Lina and Raffaele. Opening with a beautiful cantabile for Stiffelio in barcarolle rhythm describing the boat-man who found the letter and gave it to him, "Di qua varcando sul primo albore"—*As he put out from here at dawn's first light*—Verdi shows great skill in blending a wide range of emotions, from Stiffelio's nobility, to Stankar's suspicion, to Lina's and Raffaele's anxiety, in a quick-moving, lightly scored, short ensemble that's remarkable for its quality and for its unusual placement so early in the opera. Soon, Lina and Stiffelio are left alone, he eager to talk, she deeply uneasy, as he notices immediately: "Non ha per me un accento"—*She has not a word for me*. Their fast-moving dialogue is caught in music that shows Verdi's remarkable progress in rendering such scenes believably in terms of pacing, here so quick; his musical and psychological depth is very impressive, too. Stiffelio tells of the corrupt world he's seen, including women who have "broken the bonds of conjugal affection," upsetting Lina again. Finally, Stiffelio notices that his mother's ring is missing from his wife's hand, which she cannot excuse or explain, and he launches into a furious aria, "Ah, v'appare in fronte scritto"—*Clearly written on your brow*—capturing the very human anger of a man who wants to be saintly, but who, like many of us, can't control himself. Lina's occasional interjections capture her terror and anguish. These two great roles offer skilled singers so much dramatically and vocally that it's hard to believe the opera isn't better known. Stiffelio himself is not a young man, but like Otello, he can't hide his emotions, and his vocal part is set thrillingly high. And Lina, though guilty, is portrayed throughout the opera with great dignity and depth; it's impossible not to sympathize with her. And her vocal part is equally rich and exciting.

Stankar enters; a still-angry Stiffelio exits. Father and daughter—this pair out of sympathy and in conflict—have a wonderful scene together. At first alone, Lina, looking for a way out of her predicament, thinks of confessing to Stiffelio in a letter. (The plot of *Stiffelio* turns on five letters.) Stankar enters and then berates her furiously ("Dite che il fallo a tergere"—*Tell him that your heart lacks the strength*) in a hybrid that displays a cabaletta-like energy. This is followed (not as is usual preceded) by a cantabile, "Ed io pure in faccia agl'uomini"—*Before the face of mankind*—in which he reviles a helpless Lina, showing that his real motivation is fear of being dishonored. As you listen to their duet you'll hear clearly that *Rigoletto* is in the offing. Stankar, another high, "paternal" baritone, is also a great role.

In a quick scene, Raffaele, spotted by Jorg, inserts the opera's third important letter, a request to meet Lina, into a book. The final scene of the act opens with the bland tune from the overture, here set in waltz rhythm, which accompanies a chorus praising Stiffelio. Jorg tells Stiffelio about the book but his suspicion for some reason falls on someone other than Raffaele. When Raffaele boldly asks Stiffelio what theme he will preach on, the minister furiously replies, "On those guilty of betrayal," kicking off a big, complex ensemble that ends the act. Eventually, the letter is found, but this time Stankar snatches it. The ensemble, begun by Stiffelio's line "Oh, qual m'invade ed agita"—*What dreadful thought possesses and troubles me*—shows advances in Verdi's harmonic sophistication and in other technical ways, but you'll be struck by its beauty and, again, by the accuracy of its musical characterizations.

Except for one lapse, act 2 is tight, fast moving, and really fine from a dramatic standpoint. Set in the church graveyard, a short but somber and altogether impressive orchestral prelude sets the mood of dread. Lina enters, reading her own guilt on every tombstone. Finding her mother's grave, she sings a cantabile, "Ah, dalli scanni eterei"—*From among the ethereal thrones where, blessed, you sit*—in which she implores her mother's spirit for forgiveness. Although brief, the aria is remarkable for the soaring beauty of its vocal line and for the delicacy of its orchestral accompaniment, a carefully reduced contingent of strings, some playing muted. Raffaele enters, and in a scherzolike exchange Lina tells him she has never loved him. (The scherzolike trio led by Iago in act 3 of *Otello* may have its roots in this passage.) Lina then launches into "Perder dunque voi volete questa misera tradita"—*Then you wish to destroy this unhappy betrayed wretch*—an old-fashioned cabaletta, with the verse repeated, that neither advances the drama nor fits its mood.

Stankar enters, and immediately tries to provoke Raffaele into a duel. The younger man refuses to fight the elder. But Stankar's brisk insults finally hit home. This is another brilliantly drawn scene, in which the singers spit out their lines ferociously, backed by an orchestra that seems ready to explode. The two sing a brief, fiery, oathlike duet ("Nessun demone, niun Dio"—*No demon, no god*), then start to fight. Drawn by the racket, Lina and Stiffelio enter. Much as Otello will, Stiffelio commands them to lower their weapons. He then nobly tries to reconcile the two, at which point Stankar reveals that Raffaele is Lina's lover. A quartet for the four that is extraordinarily fine and exceptionally dark follows. "Ah, era vero? Ah, no, è impossibile!"—*It was true! No, it can't be!*—is a swiftly moving and complex harmonic structure, with sharply drawn vocal characterizations.

Stiffelio, now enraged, wants to fight Raffaele, in one of the great moral paradoxes illuminated in the opera: The man who preaches peace and forgiveness is shown as human in both his injured pride and his murderous anger. He advocates forgiveness, and needs forgiveness himself, but cannot yet bring himself to forgive. Verdi gives Stiffelio's vocal line here the expression mark "*con voce terribile*" (in a terrifying voice) as his line is broken into treacherous wide leaps painting his fury in music: "Non odi in suon terribile"—*Do you not hear a terrible cry arising from these tombs?*

Raffaele refuses to fight the man of God, when, in a striking coup de théâtre, the sound of worshippers singing a hymn is heard from offstage. Jorg enters, trying to bring Stiffelio back to himself, but the minister clings to his rage: "Me disperato abbruciano ira"—*Anger and hellish fury consume my being.* In the grand tableau that closes the act, Stiffelio cries out that he cannot forgive Lina.

The third act opens with a huge, three-part scene for Stankar. Having intercepted an important letter (number four) from Raffaele to Lina suggesting they run off together, he curses the seducer. He then bewails the lost honor with which he's obsessed; Verdi shrewdly has him repeat the word "disonorato." After contemplating suicide, Stankar's thoughts turn to Lina, "La mia colpevol figlia!"—*My guilty daughter!* In his cantabile "Lina pensai che un angelo"—*Lina, I thought that in you an angel brought me heavenly bliss*—he again laments the dishonor she's brought on him. The difficult vocal line is set high in the baritone range, and enriched by rhythmic devices that make it interesting and beautiful. When Jorg interrupts with news that at Stiffelio's request Raffaele is about to arrive, Stankar tears into a new kind of cabaletta, "Oh gioia inesprimibile"—*Oh inexpressible joy*—quick like most, but light-footed and low in volume. This is also quite difficult, and again Verdi captures the character's disturbed state with a vocal line broken into detached notes that sound like panting; apparently it was carefully tailored for the capacities of the first performer to sing the role.[5] The aria also ends on a rare and difficult high G.

A short but important scene between Stiffelio and a wary Raffaele follows. In a stirring phrase that reflects the passion Stiffelio is straining to control, the minister asks the younger man what he would do if Lina were free: "Saper s'è a voi più cara, colpevol libertade"—*To find which is dearer to you, a guilty freedom.* Stiffelio sends Raffaele into the next room so he may overhear his discussion with Lina. He tells her their paths must diverge ("Opposto è il calle"—*Opposite are the paths that our lives must follow*) in a regret-laden melody over a rocking string accompaniment. The oboe adds its plangent tone to the second verse. He explains that they can divorce because she married him when he was under an alias, Rodolfo Müller, to protect himself from religious persecution. He has signed the divorce agreement (letter number five), which she must now do. In high agitation, Lina protests ("Ah! Fatal colpo attendermi, Rodolfo"—*Rodolfo, I knew that a fatal blow awaited me*) that she loves him. He answers tartly, a dry pizzicato accompaniment capturing his stubborn bitterness ("Speraste che per lagrime"—*Do you hope with these tears to blunt my grief?*). Unexpectedly, Lina signs the bill of divorce. Then, in a powerful, pulsating phrase, "Non allo sposo volgomi"—*I turn not to the husband*—she places herself as a sinner before him as a man of God. Then she majestically demands that as her minister, he hear her confession: "Ministro, ministro, confessatemi!"

Lina then sings another of the great, patented Verdian laments by a desperate heroine, "Egli un patto proponea"—*He proposed to me a pact*—in the same line and of the same quality level as those for Luisa Miller, Gilda, the Leonoras from *Trovatore* and *Forza*, Violetta, Amelia, and others, the only difference being that this one's unknown. As its sorrowful melody is murmured over a rocking accompaniment led by the English horn, Lina reveals that she was "betrayed" into sin. This is the weakest aspect of *Stiffelio*'s plot, raising two questions, neither of which is answered: What does she mean by *betrayed*; and if Raffaele betrayed her, why does she continue the sinful relationship? Don't blink, because now things happen quickly: Shocked, Stiffelio concludes that he has the right to kill Raffaele, but Stankar enters the room, carrying the bloody sword with which he has just performed that very deed. A furious, exciting duet for Stiffelio and Lina follows, both dazed with horror, and she with guilt, too ("Ah, sì, voliamo al tempio"—*Yes, let's flee to the church*). Verdi gives to Stiffelio's lines a churning and violent accompaniment, but Lina's is almost soothing. From a vocal standpoint, both are very difficult, with Lina having to enter at one point on a high A.

The final scene set inside the church, though brief, is remarkable, providing an uplifting conclusion to the drama. Verdi displays his compositional range by opening the scene with a prelude for organ in flawless four-part counterpoint. Worshippers, including Stankar and Lina—who's veiled—file in. They sing the hymn heard from offstage at the end of act 2, to which Stankar adds his personal plea for mercy for having "punished him who betrayed me." Lina's prayer, a simpler one for divine pity, is expressed in murmured notes followed by a high jump, in some cases a full and treacherous octave from middle to high A. Its effect is of lyrical embroidery to the hymn.

At its conclusion, a dazed Stiffelio enters, accompanied by Jorg. He notices Lina but does not recognize her until she raises her veil. Her presence disturbs him, but Jorg keeps up a steady murmur of encouragement. Underneath all, the orchestra intones two simple motifs, one rhythmical for the trumpet, the other a falling pattern for strings. Stiffelio mounts the pulpit, opens the Bible, and reads from the page he has chosen at random. It's the parable of the wife taken in adultery (John 8) and forgiven by Jesus. Stiffelio seems to choke on the word "perdonata"—*forgiven*—but as he repeats it a second, third, and fourth time, each time more powerfully, we are made to witness the character's internal transformation, as he finally discovers forgiveness for his wife, grasping it with his own spirit. There's one final, thunderous iteration of the hymn and Lina cries, "Gran Dio!" on a high C as the curtain falls. This mighty moment, toward which Verdi builds over the entire span of the drama, may well choke you up. If you've heard *Le nozze di Figaro*, you'll recall how just before the end of that opera the Countess forgives her philandering husband. Mozart's handling, where the Countess sings in simple phrases but to music expressing the same message: To forgive is a sacred act. Although different in detail, Verdi's treatment is similar in its outlines, with the music pared down to a rare stillness, so that a depth of feeling may be evoked without distraction or compromise. No less than Mozart, Verdi knew what he was doing.

## *Aroldo*

*Aroldo*, Verdi's 1857 recasting of *Stiffelio*, is even less known than its parent, with perhaps only *Jérusalem* having a lower profile among Verdi's operas. Justifiably uneasy about censorship and angry about an unauthorized revision, *Guglielmo Wellingrode*, in which the protagonist is transformed into a minister of state, Verdi and his librettist Piave moved the time and setting from recent Austria to a remote England, ca. 1200. Stiffelio is transformed to Aroldo, a Crusader, recently returned from Palestine. Lina becomes Mina; Stankar is transformed to Egberto; Raffaele has become Godvino. The biggest change to the dramatis personae is the addition of Briano, a "pious hermit," who takes on much of Jorg's role as the protagonist's conscience. The most significant change to the plot and structure of *Stiffelio* is the addition of a fourth act, set in Scotland, where

Aroldo and Briano have fled. A storm casts who but Mina and Egberto there. At first horrified at the interruption of his prayerful peace, and still enraged at her betrayal, Aroldo refuses to forgive Mina. Briano reminds Aroldo of Christ forgiving the woman taken in adultery, and Aroldo forgives Mina.

Leaving aside minor inconsistencies, such as drawing rooms in thirteenth-century castles, *Aroldo*'s chief problem is that of the title character's motivation. Among the great strengths of *Stiffelio* are the believability of its circumstances and the characters' behavior. Here, it's difficult to see why a professional warrior from a more violent era would scruple to kill his wife's seducer. You won't be surprised to learn, however, that where Verdi changed the music, it was mostly for the better.

With a few significant exceptions, the first act of *Aroldo* tracks *Stiffelio* closely. The overture is the same rather mediocre one, but Verdi employs the trumpet tune that's probably the best element in it in one of Aroldo's cantabiles; a good idea, because the trumpet melody goes unused in *Stiffelio*. Since Jorg no longer sings in this opera, Verdi replaced his impressive opening recitative with an undistinguished a cappella chorus for the men, "Tocchiamo! A gaudio insolito"—*Let's toast! Let each heart be open.* An agitated Mina then enters, singing a dramatic recitative of great force, "Ciel! Ch'io respiri"—*Heavens! Let me breathe!*—that leads to a short, prayerful cantabile establishing immediately her presence and stature. Accompanied by Briano, Aroldo joins her, noticing that she's unhappy. Here, the two operas follow the same path, but Aroldo tells her in his cantabile "Sotto il sol di Siria ardente"—*Under the burning sun of Syria*—that his thoughts while away on the Crusade were only for her. This is set to the trumpet tune from the overture, a reference that tightens the opera's structure to good effect. When Aroldo notices his mother's ring is missing from Mina's hand, he launches into a reproachful tirade ("Non sai che la sua perdita"—*Don't you realize that to lose it would be fatal for us?*) that's set ironically in a very gentle, late style of Verdian cabaletta. Mina's scene with Egberto is the same as Lina's and Stankar's. The waltz theme that dominated the finale of act 1 of *Stiffelio* is reorchestrated to give it a giddier, disembodied quality. The other new and very good addition to the scene is Aroldo's tense cantabile "Vi fu in Palestina"—*There was in Palestine*—in which he prepares to accuse someone of betrayal. This, of course, parallels Stiffelio's anger in the same spot, but adapted to the new protagonist's circumstances.

Act 2 of *Aroldo* hews even more closely to its source. It's opened by the same, excellent prelude, and Mina's recitative and cantabile are the same as Lina's. Verdi expands the brief, quick duet for Lina and Raffaele into a big scene for Mina, opened by a somber passage, "Ah, dal sen di quella tomba"—*From the depths of that tomb*—in which she pours out her contempt to the man who led her astray—the crucial question of his betrayal remaining unanswered—over pulsing strings. She then sings a big-boned cabaletta ("Ah, fuggite! Il mio spavento"—*Ah, flee! My terror is redoubled in your presence*) that looks backward in its aggressive style. The remainder of the act is the same, with Briano taking on what was Jorg's material. The third act, too, is almost exactly the same as in *Stiffelio*. The chief differences are that it ends with the first scene, here the murder of Godvino by Egberto and the quick horrified duet of Aroldo and Mina. Egberto has a poison ring he plays with instead of a pistol (there were none in 1200, of course) and Mina asks Aroldo not to hear her confession, but to "judge" her.

The fourth act is new, however. Verdi begins it with a bit of charming tone painting to set a rustic mood from thematic fragments that come together, then gently break apart. A chorus, consisting of shepherds, huntsmen, and reapers, interjects sweetly. Aroldo, accompanied by Briano, comments that the singing may be sweet, but "Io l'inferno ho in core"—*Hell rages in my heart*. This is followed by an a cappella prayer for the two men and chorus, "Angiol di Dio"—*Angel of God*—that's meant to suggest the roughness of its outdoor setting but is assembled with high musical sophistication.

The storm that casts Mina and Egberto also on these shores is brilliantly done, with moaning wind and pattering raindrops rendered with marvelous poetry. In the final scene an exhausted Mina recognizes Aroldo's voice. He's anything but happy to see her, as he tells her emphatically ("Ah, da me fuggi"—*Ah, fly from me*). In grandiose tones, Briano reminds him that Christ forgave sinners, and the four characters enter into a short but beautifully wrought quartet, led by Mina's mournful line "Allora che gl'anni avran domo il core"—*When the weight of years has crushed my heart*. Before long, and rather out of nowhere, Aroldo changes his mind, forgiving her.

Here, again, the question of his motivation intrudes, lovely though the music of the final quartet undoubtedly is.

With Verdi, later is invariably better; but if you do listen and compare *Stiffelio* and *Aroldo* in their strengths and weaknesses, you may find that, warts and all, the older work has a greater unity. The closing scene of *Stiffelio* is so strong and striking that its absence hurts *Aroldo*, even though the later opera is more polished and balanced somewhat by fine material not in *Stiffelio*.

# The Big Three of the Middle Period

## Rigoletto, Il trovatore, and La traviata

long with *Aida*, this is the trio of Verdi's operas that has long stood at the pinnacle of popularity and esteem. In the first half of the twentieth century, only *Nabucco*, *Ernani*, *Macbeth*, and, occasionally, *Luisa Miller* among the early works were performed. Of course, now we understand that the three we're looking at here did not spring without warning from a mass of mostly undistinguished early operas, and that Verdi honed his craft painstakingly in the creations of the "galley years." Happily for us, all have come into a new perspective, in which *Luisa Miller* and *Stiffelio* particularly can be grouped with these beloved works of 1851 to 1853 as part of an important phase of the master's development. What makes these three so popular is the composer's increasing skill in all aspects of his craft, from an evolved musical sophistication, to profound characterization, especially in *Rigoletto* and *Traviata*, to his matchless pacing, where dullness is banished from the scene: "Let him keep in view the demands of the public which always likes brevity . . . ,"[1] Verdi asked a Neapolitan friend to communicate to Salvatore Cammarano, the librettist for *Trovatore*. This can be regarded as Verdi's golden rule, from which we all benefit.

## Rigoletto

Victor Hugo's controversial 1832 play *Le roi s'amuse* had long been on Verdi's list of potential operatic treatments. Its subject, the destructive effect of an affair of the sixteenth-century French king Francis I, caused the play to be banned in France. But the hunchbacked jester who is its vivid protagonist as well as its worldly point of view drew Verdi irresistibly. Francesco Maria Piave, his librettist, believed (or told the composer he believed) that the civil authorities in Venice, for which the opera was written, would give the creative team no difficulties about the subject. But this was not the case; the king had to be demoted to a duke, and the story moved from France to the Italian duchy of Mantua. After much negotiation, the opera as we know it was cleared. *Rigoletto* has remained in the repertory since its 1851 premiere at La Fenice.

Piave deserves credit for the tight, tough libretto, his best for Verdi. And, while its qualities are many and obvious, the popularity of the music drama, which is uncompromisingly dark from start to finish, may be more difficult to explain. Obviously, much of its appeal stems from Verdi's extraordinary score and from its many gems for the voice, including that ultimate operatic chestnut "La donna è mobile." But even a quick review of the events and dialogue shows the characters' actions leading to catastrophe, with all except Gilda behaving with selfishness, indifference, or outright malice. And Gilda's pointless self-sacrifice has a cost, in this case, to her father. There isn't room in this book to list the appalling deeds that the characters in *Rigoletto* suggest or actually perform, but if you read the libretto you'll see that the low road is nearly always the one proposed and taken.

In addition to Verdi's music, great characters are what make this music drama live, from the remarkable protagonist, so repellent in his actions yet believable in his idealization of his not-so-innocent daughter; and the brilliant portraits of the heedless Duke, his vicious court, and of Sparafucile, the murderer with a moral code. Like its predecessors *Stiffelio* and *Luisa Miller*, this is a drama of characters, not plot. Verdi and Piave (Hugo, too) insisted that Monterone's curse was the event from which all else flows, but they did so to reassure a clergy-heavy mid-nineteenth century power structure that a moral authority governed this supremely amoral tale. As one commentator has shown, the plot of *Rigoletto* can be told without even mentioning Monterone or his curse.[2] The superstitious Rigoletto wants to believe that the curse is behind his woes, but we should make no mistake: his character and actions are what destroy him.

The opening scene, set in the palace of the Duke of Mantua, begins the opera with a complex and brilliant structure. The short but weighty prelude sets the mood for this dark-hued work with a statement of what's known as the "curse" motive, though it's actually the somber music that accompanies Rigoletto's reflections on the curse, stated by low brass and timpani. This swells into a fierce chordal climax, leading into a wailing figure for strings and high woodwinds. The "curse" theme returns, interrupted by menacing rumbles from the timpani. The curtain rises on a ball in the Duke's palace, set to jaunty music for an offstage *banda* that breaks completely with the mood of the prelude, the darkness of which lingers over the opening scene. A creature of pure sexual drive, the Duke is in the middle of a conversation with a member of his court, telling of the young beauty he's been flirting with in church. The Duke's attention is drawn by the beautiful wife of the Count Ceprano; soon he launches into "Questa o quella"—*This woman or that*—the *ballata* (an aria form Verdi borrowed from French opera, where it's called a *ballade*) in which he rejoices in his indifference to women as individuals, admiring all for their various charms. The good-humored elegance of the piece captures the character of this lucky young man, whom one simply cannot hate. This familiar little aria is easy to grasp, but note Verdi's light but sure touch in capturing the Duke's heedlessness with slight, unexpected shifts in its melodic and harmonic trajectories. A group of string players on the stage breaks into a new dance, as the Duke besieges the Countess Ceprano with flattery as Rigoletto continues to mock her infuriated husband. Verdi handles his three instrumental groups (one offstage, one on, and the orchestra in the pit) with consummate skill, cutting from one to the other with a proto-cinematic rapidity. His example for this scene could only have been the one that closes of act 1 of Mozart's *Don Giovanni*, in which three small orchestra play onstage along with the regular one. Mozart builds tremendous tension in his scene, whereas Verdi, earlier his narrative, evokes the excitement of the ball and sets up the plot. Verdi's study of this remarkable moment in Mozart's music drama results in the best kind of imitation: one that's just a good as the original.

Marullo, another courtier, enters with gossip about Rigoletto that astonishes this cynical crowd: the ugly old hunchback has a beautiful young mistress. In a swift dialogue, Rigoletto continues his nasty teasing of Ceprano, even suggesting to the Duke that he be exiled, imprisoned, or beheaded to get him out of the way. The Duke's halfhearted rejections of Rigoletto's outrageous proposals show he'd consider them if only he could. Finally provoked into drawing his sword, Ceprano swears vengeance on

Rigoletto, as do others in the court, all of whom the jester has at one time or another antagonized. This builds into a quick, light-footed ensemble in which the courtiers mutter against Rigoletto and the Duke tells him, "Ah, sempre tu spingi lo scherzo all'estremo, quell'ira che sfidi colpirti potrà"—*You always carry a joke too far; the anger you arouse may return to haunt you.*

Suddenly, over majestic, stalking figures for the strings, the Count Monterone enters, seeking the Duke, who has seduced and dishonored his daughter. Rigoletto mocks him, too. Monterone curses the Duke and Rigoletto, whom he addresses as "Serpente, tu che d'un padre ridi al dolore"—*Snake, who mocks a father's grief.* Rigoletto is horrified. Monterone is arrested; a jaunty chorus ends the scene.

The next scene, set in three large parts, opens with Rigoletto standing in front of his house on a quiet back alley, still brooding about the old man's curse ("Quel vecchio maledivami"—*The old man cursed me*) as the "curse" motif sounds. A man wearing a sword enters, to a strange, restless melody stated by a solo cello and bass, accompanied by a carefully reduced ensemble of lower winds and strings. This is Sparafucile, a freelance assassin, looking for business. The duet between Rigoletto and Sparafucile is remarkable for its hair-raising music, as the two low-voiced singers talk, accompanied only by lower-pitched instruments playing the unnerving melody. Sparafucile offers his services to a jumpy Rigoletto, who takes him at first for a thief. Sparafucile guesses that Rigoletto fears a romantic rival, grasping that "La vostra donna è là"—*Your lady lives here*—meaning in this quiet part of town. Since all the nobles hate him, Rigoletto asks, "E quanto spendere per un signor dovrei?"—*How much for a nobleman?*—with no idea he'll soon be plotting to kill the Duke. They discuss price, payment terms, and method as under his breath Rigoletto mutters, "Demonio!"—*Demon!* Sparafucile explains that he runs an inn on the edge of town, where his beautiful sister lures his victims. So, when the third act begins, we know who the characters are, allowing us to focus on the drama and anticipate its dreadful events.

Sparafucile walks off, as Rigoletto reflects on the similarities between himself, who wounds with his tongue, and the killer, who works with his blade ("Pari siamo!"—*We are alike!*). This famous monologue, Shakespearean in its ambition, presents a different side of this character, whom we've only witnessed in loathsome words and actions. He reflects that man and nature have conspired to make him a villain, with his ugly hump and cutting wit leaving him no options but to be a jester. He then compares himself with the Duke, "Giovin, giocondo, sì possente, bello"— *Young, gay, powerful, handsome*—who expects Rigoletto only to make him laugh. To forceful chords for the full orchestra he curses the courtiers that sneer at him. And once more, he broods on Monterone's curse. This magnificent monologue, moving nearly at the speed of thought, and just as flexibly, forces us to see Rigoletto as a suffering fellow human, even if we can't love him.

In the third part of the scene Verdi shows the jester in yet warmer colors. As he enters his courtyard, Gilda, Rigoletto's daughter, rushes out. The composer describes her (and them) with a big, agitated melody set high in the winds and strings. Strangely moving, this trill-laden tune captures Gilda's youthful warmth, as well as the overwrought relationship between her and Rigoletto, of which we now get a taste. After they exchange greetings, she asks, clearly not for the first time, about her family and his name, which he has not told her; later in the scene we learn that Gilda has been in Mantua for only three months. When she asks about her mother, Rigoletto sings a suave little arioso, "Deh, non parlare al misero"—*Don't speak of her*—then thanking God for leaving him with Gilda. She joins him in a duet in which she again asks his real name; when she inquires about his country or friends, he replies: "Culto, famiglia, la patria, il mio universo è in te!"—*Religion, family, country—my whole world is you!* In this duet, Rigoletto's droning melody and Gilda's embroidery join to form a piercing and unforgettable lyric structure. Gilda now asks whether she might now be permitted to see the city, to which Rigoletto answers, "Never," then shouts for Giovanna, Gilda's paid guardian, whom he grills about the security of his home.

But events Rigoletto knows nothing about have already taken place. As Rigoletto goes offstage for a moment, the Duke, dressed in ordinary garb, slips into the garden of the girl he's been flirting with in church, who is actually Gilda. He notices with mild surprise that it's Rigoletto's house, and tosses a purse to Giovanna, who has spotted him, to buy her collusion, another example of the bleak accuracy of this opera's worldview. Rigoletto and Gilda part, to the high-strung tune.

After Gilda discusses with Giovanna the handsome young man in church, saying that she hopes he's poor, like her ("Signor nè principe io

lo vorrei"—*I'd have neither nobleman nor prince*—is her ironic line), and
which he overhears, he's there with her, singing passionately of his love
("È il sol dell'anima"—*Love is the sunshine of the soul*) and she joins, falling for him immediately and hard. Their lovely duet is accompanied by
high strings, and ends on a melting cadenza for the two voices. Giovanna,
hearing Ceprano and the other kidnappers outside, breaks things up, and
two sing a passionate stretta of farewell ("Addio!").

Left alone, Gilda moons over her lover, "Gualtier Maldè," the false
name the Duke gave her. Her great aria, "Caro nome"—*Dearest name*—
may be a fond look back at the bel canto style, with its trills, grace notes,
runs and delicate pauses. No mere vocal display, however, it's heartfelt
and dreamy affects wonderfully depict a young woman's sexual awakening.
Gilda's erotic awareness underlies the dreaminess of the music, showing
the new level of psychological accuracy the composer has reached. Verdi
sets its very sweet melody to a mincing rhythm, accompanied by some
of his most exquisite writing for a pared down group of woodwinds and
a murmuring solo violin. The composer works some delicate shifts of
harmony in at the end. This remarkable aria portrays a young woman in
love with love, as well as with her lover.

The sound of lightly struck timpani portends trouble, as Ceprano
and others mount their raid. Night having fallen, Rigoletto returns in
the middle of it all, barking at the unknown invaders, but as soon as the
courtiers identify themselves and misinform him that they're kidnapping
Ceprano's wife, he gladly joins in the enterprise. Relieved they're not
going after Gilda, Rigoletto shows a shameful joy at another's apparent
misfortune, and adding another item to the long list of behavior in the
opera that's not admirable, but true. Since they're all wearing masks,
Rigoletto wants one, too, and the others manage to blindfold him while
putting it on. In a quick, quiet, chorus ("Zitti, zitti"—*Softly, softly*)
notable for just two small crescendos, they abduct Gilda as the blindfolded
Rigoletto holds the ladder. He soon realizes that something's wrong, pulls
off the blindfold, hears Gilda's cries, figures out what's happened, and,
over a thundering orchestra, bewails Monterone's curse.

The Haydnesque purity of the tiny introduction for stings that opens
act 2 is a wonderful example of Verdi's classical bent, and one of the small
pleasures in this great score. The curtain rises on a Duke frustrated by
the loss of Gilda. Here, he speaks in the tones of an utterly conventional

operatic lover, even telling himself, "Colei sì pura, al cui modesto sguardo quasi spinto a virtù talor mi credo!"—*She so pure, that before her modest gaze I feel myself overcome with virtue.* Having watched his behavior, the audience knows how absurd these words are coming from the character, who opened the opera with "Questa o quella," yet Verdi and Piave perceptively show him idealizing the woman he thinks he's lost. His aria "Parmi veder le lagrime"—*I seem to see the tears*—is the exquisite cantabile in which he relates his "love" for Gilda, in conventional words and beautifully wrought music. When the courtiers enter with news of their successful adventure, some note a change in the Duke: "Come cangiò d'umor"—*How his mood has changed.* The Duke's crowing cabaletta ("Possente amor mi chiama"—*Mighty love calls me*) shows his true sentiments as he prepares to enjoy his prize. This rather nasty cabaletta used to be omitted, with even such respected recordings as the 1955 with Gobbi, Callas, and di Stefano leaving it out, but its role in defining the Duke's personality is crucial. It has returned to performance practice; formally it balances his cantabile, too.

Rigoletto briefly feigns calm as he looks for evidence of Gilda's whereabouts, while the courtiers, who know his true state of mind but pretend not to, coolly and cruelly savor his misery. He enters, singing "La rà, la rà . . ." as though he's just doing his job. But the minor-key inflections and the underlying tension of the music show his real affect. Count Ceprano, his enemy, asks, "Ch'hai di nuovo, buffon?"—*What's new, buffoon?*—although he knows perfectly well what's new. At first, Rigoletto gamely tries to parry Ceprano's question with an insult, but when the courtiers answer a page evasively about the Duke's whereabouts, Rigoletto figures out that Gilda is with the Duke in his bedroom. He then reveals, in a tremendous phrase accompanied by an explosion from the orchestra, that she's his daughter, and begs for their help, throwing himself at the bedroom door. But the courtiers block his way. He then launches into his great and powerful condemnation "Cortigiani, vil razza dannata"—*Courtiers, you vile, accursed race.* Furiously declaimed over a surging string accompaniment, and building quickly to a tremendous climax for voice and the full orchestra, as Rigoletto cuts loose with "Quella porta, assassini, m'aprite"—*Open that door, you murderers.* He hurls himself at the door again, and is again repulsed. Knowing they're united against him, he pleads with them, not without dignity, to a mournful accompaniment led by a solo cello and

English horn. Verdi seems to find every nuance of consciousness and feeling in this extraordinary scene's interlocking layers of irony while moving things along in his most characteristic and exciting manner.

The door finally opens, and Gilda runs out. Rigoletto is relieved, of course, but his daughter's teary demeanor tells him that she has bad news: "Ah, l'onta, padre mio!"—*My shame, father!* Rigoletto fiercely shoos the gawking courtiers, so Gilda can recount her story. In her aria "Tutte le feste al tempio"—*Every Sunday in church*—she tells of her flirtation with the "fatally handsome young man" who misled her about his identity. Its main melody, folklike and irresistibly memorable, is sounded first by the oboe. The pulse of the melody intensifies twice (the first time at the line "Se i labbri nostri tacquero"—*Though our lips were silent*—then again as Gilda relates her kidnapping). Rigoletto's comments to himself that his hopes for Gilda are gone ("Solo per me l'infamia"—*Infamy, for myself alone*) are set to a declaimed line over a rich accompaniment that seems to recall that of "Cortigiani," but here in a more resigned mood. Tenderly, he encourages Gilda to cry ("Piangi, piangi") as the violins take up a seven-note weeping figure and the voices of father and daughter twine briefly but beautifully.

Monterone is brought through on his way to prison. Apostrophizing a portrait of the Duke, he comments bitterly that his curse was in vain. But Rigoletto sings that he's wrong, he will indeed be avenged. Rigoletto then tears into a cabaletta, "Sì, vendetta"—*Yes, vengeance*—that gives the old-fashioned form a new ferocity and force, foreshadowing some of the great Verdian oaths to come. Gilda, still smitten with the Duke, pleads for Rigoletto to forgive him; Rigoletto makes it clear that he has no such intention.

The final act of *Rigoletto* reaches new levels of musical and dramatic brilliance. It opens with a grave introduction for strings; outside Sparafucile's inn, Rigoletto asks Gilda whether she still loves the Duke, and she replies that she does. Through a crack in the wall of the ramshackle building, the two watch as the Duke, once again in disguise, enters, calling for a room and wine. He then sings, "La donna è mobile" (CD Track 4)—*Women are wayward*—the most famous music from this opera, and perhaps from any opera. If you've never heard it in context, well sung and conducted, you'll find that it's no cliché, and you may even be electrified by the elemental tune. What's most important to remember is that "La donna è mobile" is ironic, because the Duke is depicted singing a popular ditty, not his own "aria." (Not that the irony that this most wayward of men is singing a song calling women wayward should be ignored.) Its simplicity and popular nature are the result of careful calculation. A sketchbook shows that Verdi worked hard to sculpt this most primal of his melodies,[3] and once satisfied with it, swore all the singers and musicians in the Venetian premiere not to sing or play it before opening night, because he knew just how catchy it was.

Sparafucile summons his sister, Maddalena, from upstairs, then slips outside to talk to Rigoletto. Gilda and her father watch, transfixed, as the Duke plies his charms on Maddalena. He begins his seduction with an elegant, rising melody ("Un dì, se ben rammentomi, o bella, t'incontrai"—*We've met, if I recall rightly, o fair one, haven't we*) accompanied by nervous strings that suggest his predatory excitement. Within a minute, he suggests marriage. Maddalena, who's been around this block before, fends him off, but soon can't resist his looks and charms for long, as her own banter shows, the music bubbling along with a playful urgency at virtually real-time speed. Outside, an appalled Gilda learns the truth ("Iniquo!"—*Wretch!*) as Rigoletto observes what he already knows with bitter satisfaction.

This leads directly into another famous and revered passage, the quartet for Gilda and Rigoletto outside the inn, and the Duke and Maddalena within, known by the Duke's insinuating opening line "Bella figlia dell'amore" (CD Track 5)—*Fair daughter of pleasure*. The four pour out their feelings, Gilda and Rigoletto honestly, the other two not, in an ensemble that starts gently but soon soars ecstatically, Gilda's famous broken line ("In-fe-li-ce cor tra-di-to"—*I've heard the traitor speak words of love*) floating climactically above the rest. To allow the singers the dominant role, the orchestral underpinning is kept very light. Rigoletto instructs Gilda to disguise herself as a boy and then head to Verona, where he will soon follow.

A strange sound of droning string chords with the oboe sounding one piercing note above make clear that this is outdoor music with an ominous tone. Rigoletto and the intelligent Sparafucile continue their negotiations. When Sparafucile asks who the victim is, Rigoletto answers impressively, "Egli è *Delitto, Punizion* son io"—*He is* Crime, *and I am* Punishment. Maddalena, now infatuated with the Duke, warns him not to spend the night, which he has decided to do. In the background, Verdi is pulling together one of his most tremendous orchestral storms to depict the oncoming dramatic climax. He does this by piling other orchestral effects onto the droning figure that opened the scene, including other strings, these shuddering, as well as flutes and piccolos suggesting faraway lightning. But his most inspired idea is to have the offstage male chorus hum wordlessly, with their mouths closed, to depict the moaning wind, creating an extraordinary sound that shows his imagination at high tide. With this as an intensifying background, Maddalena begins to think out loud what a shame it would be to kill this fine young man; the Duke, from his bed, sings a drunk and drowsy verse of "La donna è mobile."

Gilda returns, dressed as a boy but definitely not on her way to Verona. She overhears Maddalena suggest that Sparafucile kill "Il gobbo"—*The hunchback*—instead; in a bit of darkest humor, Sparafucile retorts, "What do you take me for, a thief?" But Maddalena is now desperate to save her new love. She persuades Sparafucile to agree to kill anyone else who might come by for shelter, though Maddalena frets that that's unlikely, because "È buia la notte"—*It's too rough a night.* Verdi has set the dialogue between Maddalena and Sparafucile in heavy, pulsing triplets (three notes in the space of two), and mostly to repeated notes as the oncoming storm builds in the orchestra. Gilda decides to sacrifice herself for her faithless lover, and in a brief but intense concerted passage (opened by Sparafucile's "Se pria ch'abbia il mezzo la notte"—*If anyone else should come before midnight*) voice their thoughts, with Gilda's part soaring high above. To the surprise of Sparafucile and his sister, someone knocks on the door. When they ask who's there, Gilda says she's a beggar; they open the door to her. The storm that accompanies Gilda's murder is one of the fiercest in music, not outdone by others by Beethoven or Wagner.

The storm recedes gradually over course of the final scene. Rigoletto reflects on the events of the night, ending by saying with a grandiosity that will soon prove bitterly ironic, "Oh, come invero qui grande mi sento!"—*How great I feel now!* The outdoor feeling pervades Rigoletto's quick exchanges with Sparafucile, who passes him the sack; again, he takes joy in the victory he's about to learn is false. The reversal is a devastating but brilliant coup: Rigoletto sings triumphantly, "All'onda"—*To the water*—as he prepares to drag the sack to the river, but suddenly the voice of the Duke is heard, singing "La donna è mobile." Stunned, Rigoletto tears open the sack, as lightning reveals Gilda, alive but fatally wounded. In weak tones, she tells her father she deceived him ("V'ho ingannato, colpevole fui"—*It's my own fault*) as she sings briefly but radiantly of the mother she'll join in heaven ("Lassù in cielo"—*Bless your daughter, o father, in heaven*). Rigoletto begs her not to leave him in a phrase that's at once noble and pitiable, "Non morir, mio tesoro, pietade"—*Do not die, my treasure*. But die she must, as to an orchestral cataclysm Rigoletto bewails Monterone's curse.

## Il trovatore

If you look at the five operas from *Luisa Miller* to *La traviata*, then *Il trovatore*, with its stock characters and plot laden with wild twists and turns, is an outlier, a look backward to the older style of Italian opera Verdi had struggled to put behind him, and as a retreat after the frank depictions of character and society displayed in *Luisa Miller*, *Stiffelio*, and *Rigoletto*, as well as in *La traviata*, which follows. Its form is more traditional, too, with aria-like set pieces and ensembles dominating. Of the four main characters, only Azucena has three dimensions, and she not all the time. The Spanish setting and hot-tempered personalities of Manrico and the Count di Luna are straight from the playbook. Leonora, the least realistic character, is nothing more than a catalog of womanly virtues.

What makes *Il trovatore* work is, unsurprisingly, Verdi's music. By turns passionately lyrical and headlong in his best manner, the score has a density of feeling and sound, as well as a distinctive *tinta*—color—all its own, and a mood which one might stretch a bit to call melancholy exaltation. Hugely popular since its premiere, *Trovatore* does supremely well what Italian opera does best: expressing joys and passions such as we feel, amplifying and dramatizing these elemental but familiar states with music of rare concentration and beauty. Three of the four principals are given cantabile outpourings of great magnificence, while the half-mad Azucena is musically characterized by a style reminiscent of folk song, known as the *canzone* (song).[4] Perhaps Azucena touches us the most, Verdi depicting her obsession masterfully, giving her tunes of apparent simplicity throughout. He cannily repeats one of these ("Stride la vampa") at crucial moments in the drama, to tremendous effect. We'll never find ourselves in Azucena's, Leonora's, Manrico's, and di Luna's situations, but we can readily understand their passions and agonies as expressed by Verdi in this matchless blend of lyricism and fire.

Only thirty densely packed minutes long, the first act, called "The Duel," opens with drumrolls followed by rolling fanfares for the orchestra, but there's no prelude per se. The booming voice of Ferrando, captain of the guard of the Count di Luna, instructs them to be on watch for the mysterious troubadour who has been singing in the garden, enraging the Count. The chorus of soldiers asks Ferrando to tell the tale of Garcia ("Garzia" in Italian), Luna's younger brother. Ferrando launches into a long and complex narrative aria with frequent interjections from the chorus as well as changes of speed, key, and melody that keep things lively. The introduction "Di due figli"—*Of two sons*—opens this mythlike story with background about the late Count di Luna's two sons. Then, in "Abbietta zingara"—*A gypsy hag*—the highly articulated main tune, full of fast turns, detached notes, and rests, Ferrando tells of the gypsy woman found hovering over the cradle of Garcia, presumably up to no good. Ferrando then relates that the child sickened: "Ammaliato egli era!"—*He was bewitched*. The witch was captured and burned at the stake, but left behind a daughter—Azucena, though she's not named—who was just as evil. In fact, the sick child disappeared the same day as the mother's execution, and a child's skeleton, presumably Garcia's, was found in the ashes. The father died of grief a few days later, making the present Count swear to search for his missing brother. The chorus suggests that the daughter should join her mother in hell, after which Ferrando narrates in a spectral monotone over a slithering string accompaniment that the mother's soul still haunts the earth. In the quick-tempo passage that follows ("Sull'orlo dei tetti"—*Some have seen her atop the roofs*), the chorus adds a strange, moaning interjection to the recitation.

The second scene presents Leonora, the heroine. Prompted by Ines, her lady-in-waiting, she narrates the story of her mysterious lover, whom she first met when he won a tournament, armored in black. Then, in the cantabile "Tacea la notte placida"—*The peaceful night lay silent*—Leonora tells in a grand and spacious melody of how he has returned as a troubadour, singing beneath her window. The first part of the tune, sung over a pulsing string accompaniment, is solemn and mysterious; the second, beginning with "Dolci s'udiro e flebili"—*The sweet and mournful sound*—rises in a glorious expansion. A second verse allows us to bathe in the melody again. Leonora dismisses Ines's fluttery warnings with a the vocal equivalent of a wave, then launches into "Di tale amor, che dirsi"—*A love that words can scarcely describe*—her cabaletta, where her joy is expressed in brilliant coloratura birdlike trills, detached notes, and leaps. Although old-fashioned, this quick section is admirably light.

The next and last scene in this eventful and musically dense act begins with the Count, who praises Leonora whom he adores ("Tace la notte"—*The night is quiet*). As his anticipation of climbing the stairs to her room rises an offstage harp is heard, then the voice of the tenor lead, Manrico, the troubadour. Manrico sings a simple but noble cantabile, "Deserto sulla terra"—*Alone upon this earth*. The Count is shocked and enraged. Leonora runs down to meet Manrico, but in the darkness mistakes di Luna for him, a traditional plot device that allows all three principals to show surprise, shock, then another affect, different for each. Seeing Leonora with Luna, Manrico chides her, calling her faithless ("Infida!"); Leonora begs him for forgiveness for her mistake ("Ah, dalle tenebre"—*In the darkness I have made an error*) then reassures him passionately that he is her only love. Spurned again, the Count challenges the masked troubadour to identify himself ("Se un vil non sei, discovriti!"—*Identify yourself, if you're not a coward*). Cowardly the Ernani-esque Manrico is not, and a quick-time passage among the three leads to a fast and furious trio, "Di geloso amor sprezzato"—*The fire of jealous love burns in me*—in which a writhing tune limns the fury of the Count; Manrico and Leonora reply in tandem in a leaping melody that pits them together against di Luna. Soon di Luna's line moves to steadier quarter notes, but the tempo remains fast, and the mood fiery. Verdi adds some unanticipated harmonic jolts, ratcheting up the excitement even more. The two men draw swords and prepare to fight as Leonora swoons.

In the opening scene of act 2 (titled "The Gypsy") we meet Azucena, the central character in the opera; she's the gypsy Manrico believes is his mother. It opens with the most famous music in the opera, the "Anvil" chorus. In the unlikely case you've never heard it, this colorful, absurdly memorable tune ("Chi del gitano i giorni abbella? La zingarella!"—*Who brightens the life of the gypsy? The gypsy maiden!*) depicts a group of gypsies in their camp, hammering away with all the rhythmic verve you'd expect. It's followed directly by Azucena's first number, "Stride la vampa"—*The flames are roaring!*—a disturbingly vivid depiction of a woman being burned at the stake amid rejoicing persecutors. The folklike simplicity of the melody and accompaniment serve to conceal great art in this remarkable depiction of Azucena's idée fixe. The tune hovers around one note, returning to it again and again, while the sharp rhythm of the first line suggests dancing flames. When finished, she says, in Manrico's direction, though more to herself, "Mi vendica!"—*Avenge me.* Manrico notes that, once again, she's repeating that mysterious phrase. The gypsies depart, to a fadeout of the famous chorus.

Manrico asks Azucena to relate her story. Her narrative relates in harrowing detail her mother's execution at the stake. Opening with a stabbing figure for strings over which the oboe moans, "Condotta ell'era in ceppi"—*They dragged her in bonds*—we hear the same story told by Ferrando at the opening of act 1, but here from the gypsy's point of view. Without her explaining her mother's presence at the crib, the woman was in any case cruelly punished. Not able to receive her mother's blessing, Azucena could only hear her dying wish: "Mi vendica!" The high tension of the music, darkly colored by comments by the low instruments and a spasmodic vocal line, throws light on the horrifying nature of Azucena's experience, as well as her single-minded motivation. And there's more: telling Manrico that she had stolen the Count's baby, she says she felt pity for the child. And, shockingly, though she had meant to put that child into the fire, in confusion she somehow placed her own. Here, a recollection of the "Stride la vampa" melody is brought back, but used with great freedom, as though this entire passage, in which a Verdi compresses old and new material to parallel Azucena's recount. Verdi sets the final line ("Sul capo mio le chiome sento drizzarsi ancor!"—*My hair still stands on end when I recall*) to a vast and somber phrase, mapping the breadth and sounding the depths of Azucena's memory.

In a fast-moving recitative Manrico, who has been paying attention to Azucena's narrative, now wonders who he is. Recovering her composure, Azucena insists that she is his mother. Was she not the one who nursed him back to health after he was gravely wounded in battle? And, recalling his recent duel with the Count di Luna, she asks why he spared that scoundrel. "Mal reggendo"—*He was helpless under my attack*—Manrico begins his reply proudly, then explaining that a mysterious scruple overcame him before he could strike a fatal blow. (A listener who's alert but ignorant of the plot has probably guessed by now that Manrico is the missing child.) With heavy sarcasm, Azucena replies that Manrico showed a strange kind of pity ("Strana pietà!") toward his enemy, instructing him firmly to show no mercy, should the chance arise again. A messenger arrives with news that Leonora, believing Manrico is dead, is about to enter a convent. Immediately frantic to rush to his love, and despite Azucena's urgent warning ("Perigliarti ancor languente"—*You must not risk your life on this dangerous course*), the young hothead dashes off.

The second scene is set near the convent that Leonora intends to join. Di Luna is there with his men, planning to kidnap, then marry Leonora, whose smile he praises in the great but difficult cantabile "Il balen del suo sorriso"—*The light of her smile*—another big hit, but notorious for its unusually high range (up to an G, with F typically a baritone's highest note) as well as its many turns and grace notes. The melody is a tranquil Bellinian tune as reinterpreted by Verdi. The pulsing second verse ("Ah, l'amore ond'ardo"—*The love that burns in me*) moves with more urgency. A cabaletta, "Per me ora fatale"—*Fatal hour of my life*—is brilliantly inter-woven with light-footed interjections by the chorus of soldiers. A choir of nuns is heard inside the convent, welcoming all to the peace away from the false hopes of the world. Leonora, attended by a sorrowing Ines, enters. A weeping clarinet comments on their conversation, the high point of which is Leonora's passionate arioso "Degg'io volgermi a Quei"—*I must turn to Him.* The Count enters, telling Leonora that she's coming with him; seconds later, Manrico appears, surprising everyone; in a rising phrase of such sharp profile that it's memorable on one or two hearings, Leonora asks, "Sei tu dal ciel disceso?"—*Have you come to me from heaven?* The men argue, Leonora exults, and the various choruses comment in amaze-ment in a big ensemble that's notable for the transparency of its textures. Manrico's men come on the scene to make Leonora's rescue good, as di Luna, foiled again, seethes ("Ho le furie nel cor!"—*Rage is in my heart!*).

Act 3 ("The Gypsy's Son"), opens with two choruses for Luna's guard and other soldiers, "Or co' dadi"—*We play at dice*, then "Squilli, echeggi la tromba guerriera"—*Let the warlike trumpet sound.* While neither is set to tunes of great distinction, Verdi scores both splendidly, invest-ing them with dignity as well as making them ridiculously catchy. The Count enters, fuming with jealousy, as usual. But some of his guards have captured Azucena, found lurking suspiciously around their camp, and he and Ferrando now question her. When asked where she was going, Azucena replies with an evasive insolence that startles the Count and then explains herself in a sequence of free passages, all in her characteristic folklike manner. The first, "Giorni poveri vivea"—*I lived, there, a poor gypsy*—tells of her existence on the road. Then inventing a tale of an ungrateful son for whom she's searching, Azucena's melodic flow warms as she sings, now sincerely, of the love she has for the son ("Qual per esso provo amore"—*The love I feel for him*). But she has aroused her questioners' suspicion. Di Luna provokes Azucena's fear by asking if she knows anything about the son of a count who was stolen from his castle fifteen years earlier. Studying her face and manner, Ferrando quickly realizes that she's the gypsy they've been hunting for all those years. Now accused of the old kidnapping and murder, Azucena begs for mercy ("Deh, rallentate, o barbari"—*Cruel men, loosen these harsh bonds*), her fear made palpable by the tune's rising profile and frantic tone. The Count expresses his pleasure in having finally caught her ("Tua prole, o turpe zingara"—*Your son, o ragged gypsy, is that seducer*) in a melody notable for its battery of repeated notes; he will use her as bait to pry Manrico and Leonora apart, as well as to avenge his brother. This moves into an exciting ensemble for the three principals and the chorus of soldiers.

The second scene is set inside a castle held by Manrico that di Luna and his troops are besieging. The scene opens with dialogue between Manrico and Leonora, who are justifiably worried about their situation. To comfort her, Manrico sings his great aria "Ah, sì, ben mio"—*Ah, yes, my love*—a sad but still radiant tune of classical shape and proportions, against which the winds comment wistfully. The melody turns to a consoling major key as he promises Leonora that if he must die, his last thoughts will be of her. This aristocratic cantabile, a favorite of the tenor repertory, is another lyric peak in a score packed with them. An organ sounds as the two characters sing a tiny duet that's as sweet as at it is short, "L'onda de' suoni mistici"—*The pure wave of holy sound*. But before the lovers have time to marry, Manrico's lieutenant, Ruiz, enters breathlessly with bad news: the gypsy woman has been captured. After reflecting a few seconds in breathless horror, Manrico drops everything to dash off and rescue his mother. His thrilling cabaletta, "Di quella pira"—*Of that horrid pyre*—is so excitingly easy to grasp that little explication is needed, but do listen for the difficult, detached sixteenth notes on which certain words (*pira, foco, fibre*, and so on) are set, expressing Manrico's fury as well as his resolve. You certainly won't be able to miss the electrifying rhythmic jolts, so characteristic of Verdi's style. The chorus joins thrillingly, and all tenors who can manage it make their last note a high C, even though Verdi wrote only a G.

The passionate sweep of the music pulls the fourth act ("The Scaffold") together, making its improbabilities believable and somehow convincing at that gut level where *Il trovatore* works. A dark-hued prelude for clarinets and bassoon introduce Leonora, near the tower where Manrico and Azucena are imprisoned. Her cantabile "D'amor sull'ali rosee"—*On the rosy wings of love*—tells in a fluid melodic line that Verdi contrives, à la Bellini, to make droop and to soar at the same time, of her love for the prisoner in the tower. At the final line, the key changes to a consoling major one and the flute harmonizes with the singer. The closing phrases feature a flute, oboe, and clarinet joining the singer. A quiet offstage chorus sings a grave prayer, the Miserere—*Have mercy*—in which the chorus of invisible monks implores divine mercy. The full orchestra, playing softly, then throbs in an ominous rhythmic device (short-short-long) the shuddering of which suggests a deathly premonition. Leonora sings of her grief and fear ("Quel suon, quelle preci"—*This hymn, these solemn prayers*), and the monks sing another verse of the Miserere. Then, Manrico is heard from the tower, accompanied only by the harp, singing a sad farewell to Leonora, of whose presence he's ignorant: "Non ti scordar di me!"—*Never forget me*—he sings; she replies in a soaring phrase that cuts through her hopeless situation, exalting her voice as an individual over the weighty chanting: "Di te, di te scordarmi!"—*Forget you, ever forget you!* The entire passage is widely and justly revered for its power and beauty; it's also an early example of Verdi's deployment of chanting clergy as a symbol of oppression. Here the monks never appear, and the oppression they represent is only background, relating to Leonora's desperate situation, but in later operas, notably *Don Carlo* and *Aida*, they act more directly to suppress the lives and hopes of protagonists. But in any case, there's no mistaking the breaking out of the spirit made manifest in Leonora's vocal line as it flies heroically above their monolithic chant.

Far less well known is Leonora's cabaletta "Tu vedrai che amore in terra"—*You see how love on earth*—that was almost never performed live until recent years, but can be heard on the 1956 recording of the opera with Maria Callas, Giuseppe di Stefano, Fedora Barbieri, conducted by Herbert von Karajan, as well as on several more recent performances. In this very difficult passage, Leonora pulls herself together, resolving to save Manrico. The Count enters, looking forward to having his revenge on Azucena and Manrico. He's startled when Leonora approaches him. After a quick dialogue, Leonora pleads in the most heroic manner imaginable, commanding more than begging, for Manrico's life ("Mira, di acerbe lagrime"—*See the bitter tears I shed*). Of course, di Luna denies her request, but in a triumphant phrase she insists, "Ma salva il Trovator!"—*But save the Troubadour*. Finally, she offers herself, in yet another exalted phrase, as the reward if the Count will spare Manrico. At first di Luna refuses to believe her, yielding when she swears. But she takes poison hidden in her ring while he runs off to give orders to the soldiers guarding the tower. She and the Count join in a jubilant cabaletta ("Vivrà! Contende il giubilo"—*He shall live! Joy silences my tongue*) marked by its speed, its memorable tune set in a decisive rhythm, and difficult vocal parts for both singers.

Grim and glorious, the final scene opens with soft but oppressively heavy chords for the full orchestra. In prison and feeling death approaching, a broken Azucena makes her foreboding known to Manrico, who can only echo her dread. Soon, she begins to hallucinate the scene of her mother's execution, as Manrico attempts in a brave phrase, "Alcuno, ti rassicura"—*No one, believe me*—to reassure her that she's safe, at least for the moment. But Verdi conjures Azucena's unstoppable terror by recalling the stinging melody of "Stride la vampa," and then in huge phrases ("Mira la terribil vampa!"—*See the terrifying flames!*) set to the accompaniment of powerful stalking figures for the strings. Guiding her to the bed, Manrico begs her to rest; Azucena confirms her weariness in another simple but profound phrase, "Sì, la stanchezza m'opprime" (CD Track 6)—*Yes, weariness weighs upon me*. As Azucena drifts toward sleep, she sings what's undoubtedly her crucial number, and perhaps the most shattering lyrical moment in the opera, "Ai nostri monti ritorneremo"—*Again to our mountains we shall return*. Nostalgic for an idealized peace for mother and son, she sings of the old days, and of how he'll play on his lute once they return; Manrico asks her to sleep while he prays. Azucena's melody is another flawlessly crafted tune, the simplest in structure of all, and the most deeply moving. At the end the strings come in with mincing high decoration, sweetly decorating her dream.

To a majestic phrase like a musical dawn, Leonora enters the cell. She tells Manrico that he must leave immediately, but the moment the Ernani-like hero learns she can't join him he's suspicious of her honor, and of his own ("Balen tremendo! Dal mio rivale! Intendo, intendo!"—*Monstrous idea! From my rival! I understand, I understand!*). Manrico rages in a sweeping phrase ("Ha quest'infame l'amor venduto"—*This wretch has sold her love*) as Leonora pleads with him to flee. Azucena, half-awake, joins in with "Ai nostri monti," in a remarkable concerted passage, into the end of which Verdi works a potent harmonic twist.

It takes some fiery dialogue and Leonora to show effects of the poison for Manrico to grasp that there's more going on than he realized. She tells him what she has done, but it's now too late: di Luna enters the cell to find Leonora dying; in another brief concerted passage, known by Leonora's "Prima che d'altri vivere"—*Rather than live as another's*—the three principals express their varied feelings—Manrico, remorse; the Count, resentment; Leonora, a majestic self-sacrifice—in this short but passionately lyrical ensemble. Leonora dies; the end, though it moves quicker than possible, is devastating: Over surging minor-key chords in the orchestra, di Luna orders his men to take Manrico to the block; Manrico cries out a farewell to his mother, who begs di Luna to wait. The Count, however drags her to the window, where, a moment later, she sees Manrico executed. "Egli era tuo fratello!" she shrieks, ending, unusually for a mezzo, on a high B-flat—*He was your brother!*—and then the clincher, set to sharp chords: "Sei vendicata, o madre!"—*You are avenged, Mother!* The ending, like much of *Trovatore*, looks ridiculous on paper, but don't be surprised when you find yourself shuddering when you hear it.

## La traviata

The opera is based on a play by Alexandre Dumas, *La dame aux camélias*, about Marguerite Gauthier, a real Parisian courtesan of the 1840s, with whom the author had an affair. Verdi (and Piave, whose libretto is decent if not quite as fine as *Rigoletto's*) transform and elevate the tale into myth. Without question, *La traviata* is the most recorded of Verdi's operas; it's probably his most performed, and it seems fair to say that it's the best loved of all his operas. Its popularity stems not only from the beauty of its score, but its trenchancy, as well. Verdi's skill at characterization is remarkable for its fullness of vision: the hero Alfredo, for example, is shown as serious, ardent, and sincere in his love for Violetta, yet when she rejects him, he gives in to adolescent rage. Verdi shows his shifts in fine-grained music, making him believable, a good-hearted but imperfect young man we might know. Germont, his father, destroys their dream, yet we see within moments after his entrance that he's not a bad man, merely a product of his time and place, the prejudices of which he sets forth impartially; he, too, is portrayed with great sympathy, in no sense as the villain. The society that causes Violetta and Alfredo's suffering, consisting of Flora, Baron Douphol, Gaston, and the chorus of partygoers, acts as a fourth principal in the opera, may be regarded as the villain. Its music, hectic and sometimes startlingly noisy in the confines of this otherwise intimate drama, accurately portrays its hedonism, its compulsive need for stimulation, but above all, its indifference, as the crowd celebrating Mardi Gras outside the dying Violetta's window in act 3 represents.

Violetta's nobility might have trapped a lesser composer into music that turned her a into a cardboard cutout, yet, again, the master focuses acutely on her vulnerability and her pain, making her sympathetic and more—she's like us, caught up in crises of illness and of having to fit in. When she's frantic, as in the first scene of act 2, Verdi makes her desperation entirely convincing; we can accept her self-sacrifice, the central rite of the opera, not only because of the great music he conceives for those moments, but because we've liked this bright, warm-hearted, attractive woman from the get-go. Ultimately, it's our sense of familiarity with these modern characters in situations such as we might find ourselves, which probably accounts for much of *Traviata*'s popularity. *Rigoletto* portrays human flaws that are eternal, but its setting in the Mantuan court can be a bit of a barrier; as we've seen, realism plays little role in *Trovatore*, which flies entirely on its passionate music. But Violetta is completely believable: a young woman who's beautiful inside and out, lovably vulnerable, ill, and stuck in a bad job. A woman's sacrificing herself for her lover gives the opera its universality, which our affection for Violetta then focuses. High tragedy and the heroine's personal drama meet in Verdi's music to make *La traviata* intolerably moving.

A short but telling prelude built on two ideas opens the opera. Two of the work's three crucial thematic mottoes are presented. The first, piercing chords in delicately shifting harmonies for high-set strings, depicts Violetta's illness; it will return to dominate the prelude and the opening scene of the last act. The second is a broad, falling melody that Violetta will sing with desperation as she sacrifices herself for Alfredo's sake in act 2. Here the tune sounds blandly pretty, until Verdi decorates it touchingly with dancing figuration for the violins. Two rising scales for the full orchestra thunderously break the reflective mood of the prelude. Then the busy theme that obsessed Verdi since *Oberto* comes back, in its most frantic incarnation, whistled by the high winds over a pounding accompaniment.

The opening scene moves at a pace remarkable even for Verdi. Violetta welcomes late-arriving guests, including a shy and serious Alfredo Germont, who has admired her from afar for more than a year. A fluid theme for the strings, later joined by the oboe, makes a fine background for this swiftly moving scene and the shifting conversations taking place onstage. Alfredo's concern for Violetta's health annoys Baron Douphol, her benefactor. The crowd of revelers demands a toast. Flattering Alfredo, Violetta asks him to lead it. His *brindisi* "Libiamo, ne' lieti calici"—*Let's drink from the joyous chalice*—is set to a free, supremely famous tune in waltz rhythm. As with "La donna è mobile," hearing this familiar melody in its context will prove a revelation. Alfredo pays tribute to wine, love, and pleasure as Violetta replies graciously but with perhaps a bit more than mere politeness; the chorus, here as always the voice of a heedless social world, joins in enthusiastically.

With the toast done, the other guests leave for the other room, where an offstage *banda* strikes up a dance sequence that will form an ironic background to a dialogue between Alfredo and Violetta. She feels faint—again—and Alfredo, who has lingered behind, warns that she must take better care of herself ("Ah, in cotal guisa v'ucciderete"—*The way you're going on you'll kill yourself*). Violetta parries him playfully, but Alfredo, deadly earnest, declares his love in an intense arioso—a short, melodically dense aria—("Un dì felice, eterea"—*One happy day you flashed lightly into my life*), reaching a peak of passion with "Di quell'amor ch'è palpito dell'universo intero"—*Of that unspoken love, the pulse of the world*—on the endless falling melody that is the third major thematic motive in the opera. Again, Violetta tries to banter, as her skittish melodic line ("Ah, se ciò è ver, fuggitemi"—*If that's true, then leave me*) shows, but Alfredo's words have dented her brittle gaiety, and she joins him, echoing his great melody in mixed wonder and surprise. Giving him a flower from her corsage, she invites him to visit her again when the flower has wilted; in other words, tomorrow. Overjoyed, Alfredo again declares his love again, and leaves. Then the other guests depart after a quick but powerful chorus of farewell set to the busy party theme in a stiff rhythm overlaid with powerful syncopation, suggesting the compulsion that underpins their pleasure-driven existence. Listen also for the ferocious gearshifts of melody and harmony, another Verdian stylistic trademark.

The composer focuses on Violetta's reflections in her closing scene, alone onstage. First, she meditates in a fluent accompanied recitative on how Alfredo's words have affected her ("È strano!"—*How strange*). Then, in her famous cantabile "Ah, fors'è lui" (CD Track 7)—*Ah, perhaps this is the man*—Violetta wonders, to one of Verdi's most subtle and beautiful accompaniments, whether Alfredo might be the man she can really love. Her vocal line breaks thoughtfully on the opening phrase, moving with more certainty before reaching Alfredo's great melody ("A quell'amor") that she sings now in ecstasy, accompanied by a single clarinet. Then, trying to shake off her certainty ("Follie"—*It's madness*), Violetta launches into an equally well-known cabaletta "Sempre libera"—*Free and aimless*— in which she mocks her attack of seriousness in glittering coloratura. Verdi makes her voice leap, almost frantically, while adding pauses that break the momentum, suggesting Alfredo's impact on her supposedly carefree life. Suddenly, Alfredo is heard singing his potent refrain from outside; and again, Violetta tells herself she must remain free. We hear Alfredo's voice, offstage, to her aria's brilliant end. But we now understand that the gaiety of her cabaletta is feigned, the cry of a desperate woman.

In act 1, the tragedy is set on its track, whereas act 3 sees its fulfillment. The second act, set in two scenes, is where the drama of *La traviata* is played out. The first scene cuts cinematically to the country house where, for the last three months, Alfredo and Violetta have been living, following her acceptance of his love. Alfredo, thrilled with his new situation, sings of their love in this charming place, where he feels reborn. His cantabile "De'miei bollenti spiriti"—*My passionate spirit, and the fire of youth*—may speak of a newfound mellowness, but both vocal line and busy accompaniment, mostly for plucked strings, betray a youthful energy along with Alfredo's joy. He then learns from Violetta's maid, Annina, that Violetta has been selling assets to pay their household expenses. Violetta didn't want him to know of her actions; his recitatives reveal a fiery temper. A cabaletta, "O mio rimorso! O infamia!"—*Oh, my remorse! Disgrace!*—lays out his self-disgust in conventional phrases that seem ill suited to this inward work. It can be impressive when well sung, however, and, since the trend in Verdi performance is to balance cantabiles with existing cabalettas, it's now generally performed.

Alfredo then rushes off to right the wrong. Violetta enters, commenting to Annina that she'll happily miss tonight's party at her friend Flora Bervoix's. Germont, Alfredo's father, enters, addressing Violetta with open hostility. Her dignified response takes him aback, as does her convincing display of love for Alfredo and her honor (the selling off of her possessions). But even though sympathy springs up quickly between the two, Germont must ask a sacrifice. Violetta responds with words of dread: "Era felice troppo"—*I was too happy.* Germont explains his position in a roundabout way, first describing, in the smooth cantabile "Pura siccome un angelo"—*Pure as an angel*—his daughter, whose upcoming marriage has been jeopardized by Alfredo's notorious mistress. Perhaps in hope rather than realistically, Violetta suggests a temporary separation from Alfredo. But Germont tells her a permanent separation is necessary: "È d'uopo." Violetta feels the grip of circumstance tightening, as she pours out a powerful litany of her love and death: "Non sapete quale affetto"—*You cannot know the kind of passion*—then telling Germont of her illness.

Speaking not unkindly but still relentlessly, Germont points out that the relationship is doomed: Alfredo will tire of her, and, because they're unmarried, society cannot sanction their relationship or any children they may have. This Germont does in a nagging melody ("Un dì, quando le veneri"—*One day, when time has put your charms to flight*) marked by detached notes and a wiggling turn that broadens as he implores her to act as angel for his family. Violetta, already wise in the ways of the world, can only agree: "È ver'"—*It's true*—she says to herself. She expresses her desolation in a high-set phrase ("Così alla misera"—*So, for the wretched woman*) that floats above plucked low strings; finally, she concludes her lament with a broken arioso, "Dite alla giovine"—*Say to your daughter*—that his daughter's happiness has come at a high cost. Although Germont and Violetta are not father and daughter, this glorious, pain-laden passage has to take its place in the line of great Verdian baritone and soprano duets. The composer's obsession, which reaches back to *Oberto*, comes to maturity in *Luisa Miller*, *Rigoletto*, and here, with notable additions in *Boccanegra*, and *Aida*.

They get down to business, in a quick-moving but impassioned dialogue, the gist of which is that Violetta will have to hurt Alfredo to effect the break. Germont asks Violetta what he can do for her, to which she replies, "Morrò! La mia memoria"—*I'll die, and he won't curse my memory*—asking him eventually to tell Alfredo of her sacrifice. There's then a long, bitterly ironic passage of farewell: "Siate felice! Addio!"—*Be happy!*—in which the music paints their misery uncompromisingly.

Violetta sits down to write two letters ("Dammi tu forza o cielo!"—*Heaven, give me strength*). The first is to Douphol, which she dispatches using a shocked Annina as messenger. The second, to Alfredo, is written to the accompaniment of an articulate clarinet. As she's finishing, Alfredo enters, Verdi depicting her frantic confusion flawlessly over throbbing strings. Violetta masters herself. Before she leaves him, in one of the greatest phrases in this or any opera—one of the great things in this world—she asks Alfredo to love her, as she loves him: "Amami, Alfredo! Amami, quant'io t'amo!" The music is the same falling melody from the prelude to act 1, transfigured into Violetta's moment of rapturous surrender to her suffering. It's sung in full voice, in contrast with the panicked fluttering of moments before, over a trembling orchestral background, creating a moment of grandeur and unbearable intensity.

The remainder of the scene records Alfredo's reaction to her note, Germont's attempt to coax him home, and his son's furious rejection of his father's request and expression of his thirst for revenge. Germont's aria "Di Provenza il mar, il suol"—*In Provence the sea and sun*—in which southern France is depicted in an Italianate melody, is harmonized like an Italian folksong. Although a bit old-fashioned, it's effective and perfectly in character for Germont. But Germont's blandishments have no effect on Alfredo, who feels only rage. Most older recordings of *Traviata* omit Germont's cabaletta "No, non udrai rimproveri"—*No, you will not hear reproaches*—but modern ones often include it. This slow, mincing version of the form seems to add little to the drama, which wants to rush to its end on Alfredo's furiously spit out lines and enraged exit.

The second scene of the act, set in Flora Bervoix's town house, opens with a theme that scampers along merrily, setting the mood of the party.

But the sharply accented chords that open each phrase suggest a more violent undertone. Two choruses now slow the drama's headlong flow. The first is for gypsies who sing, dance, and tell the partygoers' fortunes; the second are matadors and picadors from Madrid, who also provide the guests with light, Spanish-flavored entertainment. Charming and beautifully wrought, these are lighter in tone than what has preceded and what will follow, acting to cool the temperature of the work a bit, providing a few moments of distraction, like a ballet in a French opera.

Alfredo enters, alone. When the others ask for Violetta, he replies, "Non ne so"—*I don't know*—with feigned indifference. He sits at the card table and gambles, to an accompaniment of brilliance and power: a wiggling figure in an intense minor key that suggests the shuffling of cards and the tension in the room, without ever descending to literal imitation. It forms a thrilling backdrop to this swift dramatic movement of the scene, as Alfredo wins a few hands, commenting bitterly, "Sfortuna nell'amore, fortuna reca al giuoco"—*Lucky at cards, unlucky at love*. Meanwhile, Violetta and Baron Douphol have arrived. They notice Alfredo, and the Baron warns her not to say a word to her ex-lover. In a soaring, lyrical phrase, she wonders anxiously why she came, imploring God's mercy ("Pietà, gran Dio, pietà di me!"). The Baron sits at the table, as he and Alfredo begin to play, with feigned politeness. Alfredo continues to win, as the music continues to depict the rising tension. Twice again Violetta sings her arching phrase of anxiety. The guests are called to dinner, as Alfredo and Douphol trade veiled threats.

Violetta returns, followed by Alfredo, whom she has summoned to warn off from the angry Baron. Alfredo stiffly asks her, "Mi chiamaste? Che bramate?"—*You called me? What do you want?* Violetta, fearful of the Baron, warns Alfredo to leave. Verdi depicts Alfredo's loss of his self-control with a wound-up short-short-long rhythmic accompaniment, rendered at a very quick clip. After asking why she cares about his life, she begins to explain, again, very hurriedly that she had to leave, but lies, saying that the Baron had the right to summon her, and that she still loves Douphol. Now completely enraged, Alfredo calls the other guests into the room. In ringing *declamato* phrases, he denounces "Questa donna"—*This woman*, for whom he surrendered his honor. He then throws the money he's won at her, as Violetta swoons; the big ensemble that ends the act begins.

Following a huge choral outburst of the guests ("Oh, infamia orribile tu commettesti"—*What you have done is shameful!*), Germont, who has followed his son, condemns Alfredo with the dignity of a Biblical patriarch ("Di sprezzo degno"—*A man who offends a woman, even in anger, merits only scorn*). Alfredo, immediately repentant, pours out his self-loathing in urgent triplets ("Ah, sì! che feci?"—*What have I done?*). Douphol warns Alfredo that the insult will not go unavenged. Finally, Violetta herself joins in, in a pathos-laden melodic line ("Alfredo, di questo core"—*Alfredo, how could you understand the love in my heart?*) that brings a new tone to this complex but crystal-clear ensemble, an early ancestor to the one in act 3 of *Otello*, in which the protagonist humiliates Desdemona to the horror of the crowd.

The third act begins with the same music that opened the opera, but Verdi reduces the orchestral forces; its mood is uncompromisingly desolate. Back in Paris and desperately ill, Violetta is visited by Dr. Grenvil, who tells Annina that her mistress has only a few hours to live. Violetta instructs Annina to give half of the little money she has to the poor, then, in a recitative set to Alfredo's great love theme, she rereads to herself in her speaking voice a letter from Giorgio Germont, in which he informs her of the duel between Alfredo and Baron Douphol, who was wounded but is recovering—"Teneste la promessa" (CD Track 8)—*You kept your promise.* He has told Alfredo of her sacrifice, too. Both are coming to visit her. "È tardi!"—*It's too late!*—she cries, and sings her great lament "Addio del passato"—*Farewell, dreams of happy days*—a mournful but glorious melody accompanied by an oboe solo that practically speaks. The melody turns to the major key and the orchestral backing swells, though delicately, as she sings the clincher: "Della traviata sorridi al desìo, a lei, deh perdona, tu accoglila, o Dio"—*Comfort and sustain an erring soul, and may God pardon and make her his own*—another devastating moment displaying Violetta's profound appeal.

A manic chorus ("Largo al quadrupede"—*Make way for the quadruped*), sung by Mardi Gras revelers bent only on the pleasure and excitement of the moment, is heard from outside. Almost as soon as it ends, Alfredo enters, and the two launch into a feverish love duet. He asks her pardon for himself and his father; soon the duet settles into a wistful section in an easier tempo, "Parigi, o cara"—*We'll leave Paris, my dearest*—as they fantasize about the happy future that can never be. The orchestra adds a dainty, high-set accompaniment. But Alfredo cannot fail to notice how sick Violetta is, and he cries out in despair. And Violetta herself can no longer feign health as she sings, "Gran'Dio! ... morir sì giovane"—*Ah, God! ... to die so young*—a death-haunted fast passage in which Alfredo joins. Germont enters, now ready to welcome Violetta to his family, but she tells him that he's too late, and, in an aside to Dr. Grenvil, that she's dying surrounded by those she loves. Over the quiet shuddering of the orchestra, there's one last, impassioned ensemble led by Violetta ("Prendi, quest'è l'immagine de' miei passati giorni"—*Take this picture of me in happier days gone by*). Suddenly Violetta seems to feel stronger. The music spins dizzily, then thunders as she rises, then falls dead in Alfredo's arms.

# Broadening the Scope
## I vespri siciliani and Un ballo in maschera

Verdi composed the two operas discussed in this chapter in 1854 and 1858, respectively. In between he produced the first version of *Simon Boccanegra* and *Aroldo*, both obscure Verdiana. We've looked at *Aroldo* in chapter 4, and since *Boccanegra* is invariably heard in a revised, superior 1881 revision, we'll examine that in the next chapter. *Vespri* and *Ballo* are quite different from one another, the former relatively little known, the latter deservedly beloved. *Vespri* has qualities but a somewhat awkward plot and bloated format make the work difficult to love. But it's good, and even great in spots, and, as usual, the master tightened and refined his vocal and orchestral styles in this opera. *Ballo* is a triumph from start to finish, as you'll readily see and hear. Both operas reflect Verdi's experience of writing for Paris, usually thought not invariably to their advantage. *Ballo* would hardly be itself without the French elegance of Verdi's characterizations of Riccardo and his court. *Vespri* also displays stylistic refinements, but the rigidity of its format—five acts with a ballet—drags the work out.

## I vespri siciliani

Set in Palermo, Sicily, *I vespri siciliani*—The Sicilian Vespers—merges fiction with historical fact, its final moment depicting a massacre of French soldiers by Sicilians in March 1282. Commissioned by the Paris Opéra, the work's original title is *Les vêpres siciliennes*. Its libretto is by Eugène Scribe and Charles Duveyrier; Scribe was an eminent dramatist of the day. The work met with success at its premiere, but when Verdi wanted to produce an Italian version, he ran into trouble not only with the censors, but with an inept translator, too. The work had to be reset in Portugal, as *Giovanna di Guzman*, to clear censorship. Once Italy was unified, Verdi was able to place it in back in Palermo, as the opera has been produced since. Since there's reason to hear everything the composer wrote, interest in the original French version has grown. Two productions were mounted in 2013, at Covent Garden in London and the Caramoor Festival near New York City, and more are sure to follow.

The chief drawback of *I vespri siciliani* is the sprawling five-act format imposed by the Paris Opéra, which put Verdi into the uncongenial position of having to pad the work, especially in the third and fifth acts. Act 3 suffers far worse because of the half-hour ballet right at its center. The fifth act opens with three numbers that also fail to advance the story, two of which at least are charming arias for Elena and Arrigo that can be enjoyed as such, rather than integral to the action. So, as you explore *Vespri*, remember that the work is thrown off kilter by the ballet, which you can always skip over. Among the opera's strengths are a great overture and ensembles for the principals, particularly the quartet in act 4 and the trio in the last act. In the most interesting of the four principal roles, that of the French governor Monforte, Verdi creates one of his best portraits of a mature man of power: tough but self-aware, with believable weaknesses that round him out. As such, Monforte is a lesser-known forerunner of Philip II of *Don Carlo*.

The opera is opened by one of Verdi's best overtures, drawing music from the entire span of the opera. It begins with a threatening, three-note motive muttered by low instruments, alternating with an eerie seven-note melody of the monks' chant for those about to die from act 4. A broad, falling melody from Elena's act 1 aria alternates with the muttering theme. Once these have played off each other, a drumroll heralds the next theme, wild and violent, that returns to devastating effect for the massacre in the opera's final moments. This is succeeded by a calmer tune stated by the cellos that comes from the act 3 duet for Arrigo and Monforte. A variant of the busy theme Verdi loved makes yet another appearance. The last element is from Elena's farewell to Sicily in the fourth act, here assigned to high, shimmering strings. A final speedup brings this splendid overture, one of Verdi's best, to a rousing ending.

Act 1, set in the main square of Palermo, presents the paired tensions of the Sicilians and the French and the one that underlies the as yet unrevealed kinship of Arrigo and Monforte. All the principals but one, Procida, are introduced. In the opening scene French soldiers drink too much, flirt with unwilling Sicilian women, then unwisely let their guard down. The soldiers open the scene with a chorus, praising themselves and the life of a conqueror ("A te, ciel natio, con dolce desio"—*To you, motherland, my thoughts turn*). The Sicilians, watching resentfully, sing in a different tone, muttering as they watch the French misbehave: "Con empio desio"—*With evil intentions*. Elena, dressed in mourning for her brother, who was executed by Monforte, enters. Although she is of the highest nobility, a drunken French soldier asks her to sing the praises of his army. To everyone's surprise, she calmly agrees, then launching into "In alto mare e battuto dai venti"—*Wind-tossed on the high sea*—a complex and vocally difficult allegory that's really about Sicily in its distress. Opening with a recitative-like passage in a rowing rhythm, it moves into a more lyrical passage ("Ah, Deh, tu calma, o Dio possente"—*Ah, calm, almighty God, the raging sea*) set to a rocking rhythm. Then she sings the intense phrase "Il vostro fato è in vostra man"—*Your fate is in your own hand*—repeating the last words six times, ever more pointedly, scored for the lowest reaches of the soprano voice and requiring an almost threatening delivery. As she sings, the Sicilians gradually surround the unarmed French. Elena's narrative then moves into a stirring cabaletta "Coraggio, su coraggio"—*Arise and be brave*—which excites the Sicilians more, making it look as though an attack on the French is imminent, and in fact the locals pull out their knives. Filled with swooping runs and wide jumps, the cabaletta is a big vocal challenge. The soldiers remain oblivious to the end. They are saved by the appearance of Monforte, their commander and the French governor, whose presence causes everyone but Elena and her two servants flee the square in alarm.

A brief but beautiful and quartet ("D'ira fremo all'aspetto tremendo"—*His sinister presence makes me shudder*) for the two principals and the two minor characters (Elena's servants) follows, in which the Sicilians express their loathing for Monforte, which he welcomes as a mark of his effectiveness. It's nearly a cappella, too, with only an occasional quiet instrumental interjection. Suddenly Arrigo emerges from Monforte's residence. Never having met the governor, he complains about his arrest as Elena and the servants try to quiet him. But Monforte smoothly introduces himself. Arrigo remains defiant, his courage appreciated by Monforte, who sends the others off, then, in the dialogue and duet that concludes the act, questions Arrigo about his background ("Qualè il tuo nome?"—*What is your name?*). Arrigo speaks of Duke Federigo, Elena's brother under whose guidance he flourished ("Ei mi guidò magnanimo"—*Under his generous tutelage I joined the ranks of warriors*). Verdi allows their serious dialogue to move freely in and out of duet passages, setting it to a noble, masculine theme for the violins, playing at the bottom of their range. Again, Monforte expresses appreciation for Arrigo's brashness and bravery, offering the young knight a place in his own troop ("Vien tra mie schiere intrepide"—*Be one of my brave company*). Finally the governor warns him away from Elena, saying, "L'amor ti perderà"—*Love will ruin you*. As before, Arrigo spits defiance at Monforte. In the exciting stretta "Temerario! Qual ardire!"—*Reckless youth! What audacity!*—Arrigo is surprised and disturbed by the ease with which the older man can read his thoughts and heart, while Monforte appreciates in Arrigo behavior he'd never tolerate in another young man. Their mutual sympathy is due, of course, to the kinship neither yet knows of.

The second act introduces the Sicilian patriot Giovanni Procida, who's dropped off at a beach near Palermo as the scene begins. The brief orchestral prelude, in a rowing rhythm, sets the seaside mood, as, after kissing the ground, he sings his great cantabile, "O tu, Palermo, terra adorata"—*Palermo, land I adore*. The slow, broadly rocking tune is introduced by delicately murmuring woodwinds. Cast in three parts, the aria begins with Procida's declaration of love for his much-abused homeland. The middle section turns melancholy for his description of his own unsuccessful efforts to raise support abroad for the Sicilian cause. And the final section is triumphant, as Procida apostrophizes his countrymen over pizzicato strings and more marvelous writing for the winds, to rediscover the old Sicilian valor. This is a fine showpiece for bass and an excellent introduction to the character.

Procida is met by other rebels he sends off to fetch Arrigo and Elena. His cabaletta "Santo amor che in me favelli"—*Sacred love whose voice I hear*—is done mostly at low volume and interwoven with quick, quiet exclamations from the chorus, admonishing silence and looking forward to revenge. This is in much the same manner as the Count di Luna's cabaletta with chorus just before the end of act 2 of *Il trovatore*. This scherzolike hybrid is interesting for its play of dynamics—volume—and for the long silences Verdi writes in. Once everyone has left, Procida gets one big outburst, "Ah, sia salvo il caro suol, poi lieto morirò"—*May the beloved land be freed, then I'll die happy.* Elena and Arrigo enter and the three greet each other warmly. They talk of the Sicilians' fear; Procida tells of his fruitless efforts to raise foreign aid. Mixed with arioso passages of considerable weight is a telling phrase, "E sorga il giorno alfin che di novelli oltraggi"—*May the day come when the French perpetrate such brutality*—that explains the cunning Procida's behavior throughout the opera, as he tries to manipulate the French into provoking a Sicilian rebellion. Always ready to improvise, he proposes a group wedding to take place that evening as another opportunity for provocation, because large crowds will be there and "È forte in massa"—*There's strength in numbers.*

Procida exits, leaving Arrigo and Elena onstage to turn their comradeship into love. Arrigo declares his feelings first to a surprised Elena, who, to his surprise, does not reject him. First, she explains her apparent reluctance, reminding Arrigo of her brother Federigo's death ("Presso alla tomba ch'apresi"—*So near the tomb*), then apostrophizing Federigo, she asks forgiveness for opening her heart to love. Verdi sets her first phrase to somber, falling woodwinds, then swelling delicately as she begs Federigo's pardon. Then, like a true Sicilian, she tells Arrigo that if he avenges her brother, she'll think him "Più nobile d'un re!"—*Nobler than a king.* All this is set against a pretty background, although their double cadenza at the end is fiery enough. French soldiers arrive, with an invitation from Monforte for Arrigo to a ball that evening. He refuses contemptuously, and they drag him off.

A well-mannered tarantella marking the start of the wedding festivities opens the eventful final scene. The French soldiers again admire the Sicilian women as they dance. Procida suggests that, as conquerors, they can take who they want. The French praise war and carry off some of the squawking women as the Sicilian men mutter. Then, to the three-note motto that opens the overture, the men react in frozen rage ("Il rossor mi coprì"—*I'm ashamed!*). Elena and Procida try to stoke their anger and wavering courage. This laconic theme is an odd one to build a large ensemble on, but build it the composer does, amplifying it with additional tensely energetic material, and whipping the chorus of Sicilians into a big climax. Suddenly, from offstage, a lilting chorus of French soldiers and Sicilian women, on a cruise, is heard extolling idle pleasure ("Ah! Del piacer s'avanza l'ora!"—*Pleasure's hour is drawing near*). They are headed to Monforte's ball. Procida decides that the ball will be the time to strike, and to a chorus blending the indolent on the ship with the furious on shore, the act ends.

Act 3 is the longest in the opera because its second scene contains a thirty-minute ballet, as required by the Paris opera. What was right for Paris seems wrong for Verdi, who of course valued swift dramatic and musical motion, and certainly for his modern audiences, which count on the composer to deliver that impetus. While pleasing enough on its own, the ballet stops the drama dead in its tracks. We can listen or watch, wishing it were shorter; or skip over it, understanding that either way it's a major structural flaw.

The opening scene reveals facts about Monforte, and consequently about Arrigo's parentage. A brisk prelude for strings raises the curtain, showing Monforte in his palace, reflecting on his life. "Sì, m'aborriva, ed a ragion!"—*She hated me, and for good reason*—he recalls of the Sicilian beauty he carried off, then fathered a son by. He then damns her for teaching their son—Arrigo—to hate his father. Monforte reads a letter from the mother, dictated recently from her deathbed. She admonishes Monforte to "Risparmia almen quell'innocente capo"—*Spare that innocent head*—should Arrigo fall afoul of him. He then sings warmly of his son: "O figlio!" Monforte then sings his single aria, a fine and flexible structure in three parts, "In braccio alle dovizie"—*Cradled in luxury*—he broods on his pampered life as ruler, and of an emptiness in his heart. Dry strings underline his thoughtful and objective mood. But his tone changes, warming, as he considers what life may offer with Arrigo's companionship. Over a rustling accompaniment featuring a prominent cello line, that instrument ever a companion and second voice to men of power in Verdi, Monforte says, "L'odio invano a me lo toglie"—*Hatred cannot keep him from me*. And the opening refrain returns over a more elaborate accompaniment, to which the cello adds its rich voice. His final reflection on life with his newfound son receives a delicate pulsing accompaniment for violins, giving this leisurely cantabile, which stands among the most beautiful melodies Verdi wrote for baritones, a wistful ending.

Arrigo is brought in, suspicious of the respectful treatment he's receiving from the governor's household. A fine and affecting scene for the newly found father and son follows. Monforte tries to calm the resentful young man, but Arrigo remains bewildered and angry. Monforte again tries to lead the unwilling youth to love him ("Quando al mio sen per te parlava"—*When I was moved by real compassion*), but, given his mother's letter to read, Arrigo is horrified, crying out at once that Elena is now lost to him ("O donna! io t'ho perduto!"—*My lady, I have lost you!*). Monforte tries once more to win his son over, but Arrigo refuses: "Al mio destin mi lascia!"—*Leave me to my own fate!* Two themes from the overture come back, with the second, more urgent one given to the stretta, as Arrigo sings, "Ombra diletta"—*Beloved shade*—appealing to his mother's spirit to aid him in his plight.

(Next follows the ballet, a choreographic fantasy on the four seasons. Not seamlessly joined to the surrounding scenes [though the chorus immediately following does mention it], it functions as part of the ball at Monforte's palace. The music is charming, though, showing Verdi as a professional capable of rolling out colorful dances by the yard. There isn't room here to discuss every one. But do listen for the Tchaikovskian skating dance, the wonderful clarinet solo in the "Spring" portion, and the first dance of "Summer," featuring a melancholy oboe solo over droning strings.)

The final scene shows Arrigo's saving Monforte from the hands of Procida and Elena, who planned to murder him. It opens merrily, with guests praising the ballet in a cheerful chorus. Then the Sicilians, wearing masks, welcome Arrigo as a fellow conspirator: "Arrigo, su te veglia l'amistade"—*Your friends watch over you*. They pin a ribbon, the symbol of the conspiracy, to Arrigo's shirt. The music changes as Monforte enters ("Di tai piacer"—*Are these amusements*), gaining tension to a busy theme reminiscent of the gambling music from act 2 scene 2 of *Traviata*. Arrigo warns his father to leave, giving Monforte joy to know that his son is worried for his safety. Arrigo then reveals the truth about guests' wearing ribbons, and Monforte tears Arrigo's off. When Procida attempts to strike ("Feriam! A noi, Sicilia!"—*Kill! For Sicily!*), Arrigo interposes himself, saving his father. The conspirators (conveniently wearing ribbons) are seized and the huge and impressive ensemble that ends the act begins. The characters and full chorus all sing different lines of text, but you won't miss its beginning, sung by all principals and the chorus to a muttered, two-note phrase. The French thank God for saving Monforte; the shocked Sicilians curse Arrigo's treachery. And poor Arrigo himself doesn't know what came over him: "L'onta rea di tal misfatto fa palese il mio rossor!"—*The shame of this deed surely shows in my livid face!* The Sicilians then sing a hymnlike melody ("Ah, patria adorata"—*Ah, beloved fatherland*) that will carry the ensemble to its climax. Monforte tries to thank Arrigo, who again rejects him ("Mi lascia!"—*Let me go!*). He pleads with the Sicilians to pity him, which they do not; and on an enormous double stretta, the hymnlike melody carries this massive and complex structure to its tidal wave of an ending.

The fourth act, set in the courtyard of the fortress where the conspirators have been imprisoned, is impressive. It opens with an imposing orchestral prelude alternating a stern with yearning elements the latter dominated by woodwind solos. Arrigo enters, telling the guards to bring Elena to him. In a powerful passage blending recitative and arioso ("Voi per me qui gemete"—*Because of me you languish in this grim prison*), he broods over his situation and that of his co-conspirators. This leads into his cantabile "Giorno di pianto"—*Day of tears*—in which he bewails Elena's love, now lost. Remarkable for its sophistication on every level, the melody of this mournful reflection moves unpredictably, as does the harmony below, between major and minor as well as to different tonalities. And the orchestration has a cool, muted sound. Only on the phrase "Il cor piagato tutto perdè"—*My wounded heart lost all*—does his vocal line rise in overt despair. Verdi decorates the reprise of the opening with pizzicato strings beneath and flutes above. As he waits anxiously for Elena, Arrigo sings another passage, "Ah, di terror io tremo!"—*I'm shaking with fear*—notable for its tricky key shifts, which, significantly, takes the place of a cabaletta.[1]

The next scene, between Arrigo and Elena, is remarkable. It begins with Elena's spitting contempt, as we'd expect, but soon Arrigo begins his justification in a lyrical phrase, "Non son reo!"—*I am not guilty*—to a surging melody. As soon as he reveals that Monforte is his father, Elena softens. The two resume the duet to the same tune, but the tone is different, with a moved Elena yielding ("Se sincero è quell'accento, deh, ti muova il suo dolor"—*If he's telling the truth, his grief must arouse compassion*). The final phase of the duet moves in to a new, calm melody, before which is a fiendishly difficult cadenza for Elena, ranging from high C to a low F-sharp, below the staff, but many sopranos sing an easier alternate version. As Elena, freed of her hatred, sings of the love she now feels ("Arrigo! Ah, parli a un core"—*Arrigo, your words fall on a heart*), he replies with relief and gratitude: "È dolce raggio, celeste dono"—*Like a sweet ray of light, a blessing from heaven*. The voices join, twining in a mingling of love and resignation over a diaphanous accompaniment featuring harps and muted violins. Verdi throws in more daring harmonic shifts to emphasize its otherworldliness. Remember that Elena is waiting to be executed, so this is not a moment of conventional passion; one can see in this the ancestry of the duet of the entombed Aida and Radamès that closes *Aida*.

Procida is brought in. Seeing Arrigo, he snarls suspiciously. Monforte enters, telling an aide to fetch the priest and the executioner. When Procida learns that Arrigo is Monforte's son, his voice sinks in despair: "Or compiuto è il nostro fato!"—*Now our fate is truly sealed!* Procida then begins the very beautiful quartet for the four principals, known by his line "Addio mio patria, invendicato"—*Farewell my country, unavenged*— in which the characters express their varied feelings. Elena and Procida have similar points of view but her vocal line soars grandly above, while his holds the bass. Arrigo regrets that he has brought only trouble to the woman he loves. And Monforte gloats that this will put an end to the rebellion. Again, some daring harmonic shifts mark the closing passages of an extraordinary ensemble that merits wider appreciation.

Monks offstage are now heard chanting the prayer for the condemned, "De profundis"—*From the depths*—of which the eerie seven-note phrase first heard in the overture forms a part. As in the penultimate scene of *Il trovatore*, the clergy represent a force indifferent to the sorrows and passions of the characters. There they play a larger role in the structure of the ensemble, while here they're decidedly in the background, adding color and deepening its somber tension. Ready to die, Elena and Procida fall to their knees. Arrigo pleads frantically to Monforte for them to which his father replies, "Chiamami padre, e grazia avran da me!"—*Call me father, and I'll show mercy*. Although Elena begs Arrigo not to yield, the sight of the executioner makes him cry out, "Padre!" An ecstatic Monforte stops the executions, pardoning everyone on the spot, giving his permission to

Arrigo and Elena to marry, a grand gesture toward ending the conflict between France and Sicily.

The big, quick-tempo chorus, "Oh, mia sorpresa, oh giubilo"—*Oh, unexpected jubilation*—seems to turn things around. But underneath the triumph, Procida, plotting as always, warns that another mighty sound will soon be heard. Monforte proclaims that the wedding will take place that very evening, when the day's heat has passed, and "S'udrà squillare il vespero"—*The vesper bell rings out*—setting the stage for the fifth act.

As noted, the first three numbers of act 5 fail to move the story ahead. They certainly repress Verdi's innate urgency, though not nearly as disruptively as the ballet. First comes a cheerful chorus in which clacking castanets are introduced; the second, and best known, is Elena's aria, called a "siciliana" in the score even though it's clearly Spanish in flavor, with recordings of the aria alone calling it a bolero. "Mercè, dilette amiche"—*Thanks, gentle friends*—is so charming that it's difficult to resent the intrusion. It's in three parts, the mock-fiery outer sections, in a bolero rhythm, and a middle part ("O caro sogno, o dolce ebbrezza"—*Cherished dream, sweet ecstasy*) that offers a melting contrast. There's difficult passagework as well as big jumps and a couple of tricky C-sharps for the soprano. Arrigo enters, equally eager and happy, and gets his own unexpected cantabile, "La brezza aleggia intorno"—*The breeze wafts around me*. Arrigo's aria is more delicate than Elena's (and she joins him for one verse) but it's just as difficult, floating up to an exceedingly rare high D in the closing phrase.

The action resumes once Procida enters. He tells a stunned Elena that the bells that announce the wedding will also signal the attack on the French. Procida is surprised by her dismay, questioning her patriotism in an intense passage over a pulsing accompaniment reminiscent of Beethoven ("Più sacra ella ti fia del patrio suolo?"—*Do you hold them more sacred than your country?*). Arrigo enters; noticing at once that something is wrong, he asks Elena to confide in him. "Sì, parla, se tu l'osi"—*Yes, tell him, if you dare*—says Procida, mockingly. Singing to herself, she opens the great trio that is the heart of the act ("Sorte fatal"—*Grim destiny!*). Arrigo begs Elena to share her pain, while Procida reminds her of her murdered brother and her love of Sicily. Although the ensemble starts in fiercely declaimed phrases, Verdi transfigures the lines into a lyrical climax.

Seeing no other way to thwart Procida, Elena tells Arrigo she can't marry him. Now all three are upset, and they rip through a quick concerted passage, dominated by Arrigo ("Oh, mio deluso amor ... dunque addio, beltà fatale"—*Love deluded! ... so farewell, deadly beauty*) to which two accelerations ratchet the tension higher. Monforte enters, to an orchestral groan. Arrigo asks his father what to do; Monforte, taking their hands, tells Elena that she can't deny her heart. The bells begin to ring and the snare drum rattles. The ferocious music from the overture returns but in a new rhythm, with a tidal sweep as the Sicilians attack, crying, "Vendetta!"—*Vengeance!*

## Un ballo in maschera

So brilliant and sure-footed that it's hard to believe the subject wasn't Verdi's first choice, *Un ballo in maschera*—A Masked Ball—stands as one of the composer's best-loved works and undisputed masterpieces. He composed the opera in 1858 to fulfill a contract with the Teatro Apollo in Rome, where it premiered in February of the following year. He tried but failed once again to get a *King Lear* going. Other ideas were kicked around, and ultimately he settled—there's no other word—for the then-familiar story of the assassination of King Gustavus III of Sweden at a ball in 1792. It had been set before, both as opera (Bellini had considered using the story) and ballet. Antonio Somma, a semiprofessional writer with no theatrical experience, was brought on to write the libretto. Verdi had to hold Somma's hand throughout, but the result is mediocre. *Ballo* succeeds because its plot is straightforward and believable, and because Verdi brings the characters to life musically, no matter how trite their words. In another phase of heavy repression, Roman censors threw up major roadblocks for the creative team, asking for absurd changes in the setting and action. Ultimately the story was moved from eighteenth-century Stockholm to Boston in the late 1600s, a setting over which the sense of a glittering royal court in the age of enlightenment hovers uneasily.

Since the majority of recordings and DVDs of the opera are of the version set in Boston, that's how the characters will be named here. Should you come across one set in Sweden, then the role of the tenor protagonist will be Gustavo, with names of the conspirators Tom and Samuel changed to Horn and Ribbing. The names of the other two principals remain as Amelia and Renato. Although the Swedish assassin's name was

Anckarstroem, that spiky mouthful does not fit over broad Italian vowels, so he continues to be Renato. Equally uncongenial to singing is the name given to the sorceress: Mrs. Arvidson, who continues as Ulrica.

*Ballo* marks an immense stylistic advance for Verdi, who clearly warmed to the subject. Interpreting a tale that's varied in incident and, in spite of the libretto's weaknesses, rich in character, the composer responded with a Shakespearean freedom and brilliance. From the opening measure, the work is built on a series of contrasts between light, represented by Riccardo and his page Oscar with their aristocratic playfulness on one side, opposed to most of the other characters, including even the heroine, Amelia, who suffer and rage on the side of darkness, musical as well as existential. Verdi's music seems to capture every nuance of both, and the first-time listener will have no difficulty in appreciating the gaiety that's occasionally forced of Riccardo set against the misery, desperation, and rage of Amelia and Renato on the other, with the passionate yearning of Riccardo and Amelia forming a third important narrative and musical affect. Verdi juggles all with staggering skill, liberally deploying the refined French operatic style in which he was fluent to portray Riccardo, Oscar, the court, and to define the comedy that makes up a significant proportion of *Ballo*. Each act, even the third, where Riccardo is killed, contains long passages of lighthearted material. The dark side shows the composer in his most passionate Italian idiom. Wanting to broaden his reach, Verdi succeeded triumphantly in *Ballo*, perhaps his most purely brilliant opera before *Falstaff*, which it anticipates in many passages. With *Ballo*, we see Verdi on a new and higher trajectory.

A short prelude, like other aspects of the opera, seems deceptively casual. But from the first moment Verdi sets light against dark in the shifting harmonies of the little turns for winds. What follows is the music of the contented hymn of Riccardo's supporters that opens act 1, then in *fugato*—a fuguelike passage—the somewhat comical theme characterizing his grumbling enemies throughout the work. Over pizzicato strings, the winds sound the sculpted, electrifying, and unforgettable tune that describes Riccardo's love for Amelia. Into this, Verdi works the shifting harmony of the woodwind turns. The remainder of this marvelous prelude that's inseparable from the drama it opens ends with the various thematic elements played off against one another. Taking the prelude as a guide, the curtain rises to a chastely consonant hymn, "Posa in pace"—*Rest peacefully, Riccardo*—representing the paradise his enlightened rule is to most of his subjects. Eden to most is tainted for a few, though, who sing the grumbling theme "E sta l'odio, che prepara il fio"—*And hatred prepares its revenge.* The page Oscar, a trouser role (a woman playing a young man, a rich Italian operatic tradition that Verdi uses only in this opera) announces the entrance of Riccardo, to a triumphant fanfare for the full orchestra, unambiguously depicting his radiant personality. Looking over a list of guests to his masked ball, he jokes that he hopes no beautiful woman has been left off. Then seeing Amelia's name, he apostrophizes her, to the glorious love theme "La rivedrà nell'estasi"—*It will be ecstasy to see her again.* As Riccardo spins out his love for Amelia, his friends and enemies join in with their individual points of view represented. Oscar, who plays an important role in *Ballo,* announces Renato, as Riccardo pulls himself together ("Oh, ciel! lo sposo suo!"—*Heaven! her husband!*).

Renato and Riccardo, close friends as well as associates, discuss the plot against the latter, who refuses to take it seriously. In a noble cantabile that reflects his serious nature ("Alla vita che t'arride"—*The life that smiles on you*), Renato reminds Riccardo that the fate of the nation depends on his life and wise government. The Chief Justice enters, asking Riccardo to banish the witch Ulrica. Oscar pipes up amusingly in Ulrica's defense in a *ballata* (the same French form as the Duke of Mantua's opening aria in *Rigoletto*), "Volta la terrea"—*When she turns her dusky face to the stars*—a scampering tune, lightly relating her partnership with the devil, intriguing the restless, pleasure-seeking Riccardo, who decides to visit her den. Renato remarks in consternation that it's not a wise idea: "L'idea non è prudente." Riccardo instructs Oscar to prepare a fisherman's costume, then in his glittering stretta "Ogni cura si doni al diletto"—*Prepare our entertainment carefully*—sings with eager anticipation of the fun the excursion will be. The reactions of Renato and the rest of the court suggest that this is far from their first such adventure, as does the elegant shuffling and slightly hectic quality of Riccardo's melody.

There's no exaggerating the brilliance of the music Verdi sets this great scene to, from the flawless characterizations of Riccardo's restlessness, to the heedless immaturity of Oscar's bouncing, high-set vocal line, to Renato's worry, and even the amusement of the conspirators at Renato's worry. In addition to noting the sharpness of the musical depiction, you certainly won't be able to miss the stunning speed at which it all flies by.

Here the master has introduced a buffo—comic—element to the musical language that forms so crucial a part of the sound and *tinta*—the singular musical atmosphere of each Verdi opera—of *Ballo* from start almost to its finish. This will come to full fruition more than thirty years later in *Falstaff*, but Verdi's mastery of comedy is astonishing for a composer who wrote only one flop in the genre eighteen years earlier. There are hints of it in the party scenes of *Rigoletto* and *Traviata*, but nothing to suggest the fully evolved comic style Verdi displays here. Note, too, the orchestral accompaniment that sounds like a cancan, but one that packs a punch, especially in the explosive chords, each preceded by a huge windup. That explosive orchestral sound is pure Verdi and a key part of his skill as a tragedian, but it also makes sense when wed—with Verdian skill—to comedy. It, too, will return in a big way in *Falstaff*; in fact, from that opera's opening two chords.

We have little room for technical matters, but the prelude and Ulrica's "Invocazione" show Verdi's compositional skills so clearly that it's worth pointing out that he uses a standard, spooky sounding chord in ways that are original and evocative, breaking it up rhythmically and harmonically, as well as spreading it around the orchestra, to create an atmosphere of awe and terror. The master's ability to make so much of basic musical material will remind you more of Haydn and Beethoven than his Italian predecessors. The extent of his development in depicting the supernatural (or at any rate, the eerie) from the charming witches of *Macbeth*, eleven years before, to this scene is also impressive.

Ulrica's dwelling is crowded with men, women, and young girls, eager to watch the famous witch at work. And she puts on quite a show for them, summoning Lucifer with the most solemn, dark tone ("Re dell'abisso, affrettati"—*Lord of the abyss, hasten to me*), then disappearing and reappearing in a puff of smoke. A sailor, Silvano (Cristiano in the Swedish version), pushes through the crowd, to ask whether his fifteen years of loyal service to the Governor (or His Majesty) will be rewarded. Verdi makes his brief presentation count: the straightforward Silvano's musical characterization makes him so likable that Riccardo, who has arrived early, makes Ulrica's prediction of a promotion come true, scribbling a commission and slipping it into the sailor's pocket on the sly. A servant of Amelia's, whom Riccardo recognizes, enters, telling Ulrica that her mistress needs a private consultation; the witch sends the spectators out, but Riccardo hides and remains. Amelia enters, *"agitatissima,"* to one of Verdi's great themes depicting a troubled heroine, a scrambling, intense figure for the strings. An earlier example was heard in *I due Foscari*, and another famous one belongs, unforgettably, to Leonora, in *La forza del destino*. Amelia confesses to Ulrica—and to Riccardo's surprise—a secret love. To a soothing, folklike melody ("Dalla città, all'occaso"—*To the west of the town*), Ulrica tells her to pick an herb at midnight under the gallows; Riccardo determines that he'll be there, too. Then, to a tune so glorious ("Consentimi, o Signore"—*Grant me, o Lord*) that it blazes its way into the mind at once, Amelia opens a brief concerted passage for herself, Riccardo, and Ulrica. The three express varied thoughts, but this short passage, is, like Amelia's opening melody, of great splendor, with the three voices rising falling, twining, swelling and, quite often, singing softly. Amelia exits, to her desperate theme. Her vocal part is exceptionally hard, benefiting by heavier voices of dramatic sopranos, such as Zinka Milanov and Maria Callas, Martina Arroyo and even Birgit Nilsson.

The remainder of the scene consists of Ulrica's prediction for the disguised Riccardo. Dressed as a sailor, he sings a convincing parody sea chanty, "Di' tu se fedele"—*Tell me if the sea*—in two sections, a lilting, slightly melancholy tune followed by a scrambling section and a rhythmically emphatic closing phrase. Ulrica looks at Riccardo's palm, detecting "Un grande, vissuto sotto gli aste di Marte"—*A great man who lives under the sign of Mars*—that is, a warrior. But disturbed by what she sees, she doesn't want to reveal his fortune. After coaxing, she tells him that he's to die soon, and at the hand of a friend; in fact, the next person to shake his hand. At this point Renato walks in, taking Riccardo's hand. Everyone in Riccardo's entourage, including the conspirators, is relieved, since Renato is Riccardo's best friend. Riccardo chuckles, then launches into the brilliant ensemble "È scherzo od è follia"—*What joke or folly is this prediction!*—which shows the amused and rational Riccardo mocking Ulrica's prediction. It's characterized by Riccardo's part, which hops elegantly along; against the composer's stated desire, many tenors insert laughter between the notes, as well.[2] With Amelia having left, Oscar takes the lyrical high part as Samuel and Tom mutter below. This witty, striking ensemble epitomizes the comic side of *Ballo*; it's wound down gracefully in preparation for the final chorus, a triumphant, marchlike hymn, "O figlio d'Inghilterra"—*Son of England* ("*the fatherland*" in the

Swedish version)—that juggles playfulness and pomp, perhaps to under-
score Riccardo's hubris.

Act 2 forms a remarkable dramatic unit, covering a wide range of
moods, from Amelia's terror to her ecstatic love duet with Riccardo to
the amusement of the conspirators, and more. Set at midnight at the gallows outside of town, the act opens with an orchestral introduction of
tremendous force. At its center rises Amelia's glorious melody from the
previous scene, given to the flute, then the strings, decorated by the flute
and clarinet. The grim mood of the opening returns, as the short but
telling orchestral essay in mood setting winds down. A terrified Amelia
enters looking for the herb Ulrica promised will end her suffering. A melancholy solo for the English horn sets the mood for the sorrow-laden, shifting melody of "Ma dall'arido stelo divulsa" (CD Track 9)—*But once I've
plucked that herb*—in which she mourns her love for Riccardo, but even
more, its approaching end ("Che ti resta, perduto l'amor . . . che ti resta,
mio povero cor?"—*What will remain when love is lost, poor heart?*), the
latter to a questioning, rising line. The bell chimes midnight, as Amelia
imagines ghosts rising from the ground, to music in the same mood as the
introduction. She calms down, ending this moving aria on a prayer—and
a delicate cadenza.

Riccardo enters, and the two begin their great love duet "Teco io
sto"—*Here I stand*—which, interestingly, is one of the few large-scale,
fully developed love duets in the master's output. Amelia tries to fend
Riccardo off, reminding him that her husband would give his life for him.
But the tides of Riccardo's openhearted melody ("Non sai tu che se l'anima
mia"—*Don't you know that even as my soul is torn by remorse*) soon wash her
defenses away, and she admits, over trembling strings with an articulate
melodic line for the cello, that she loves him, too. Beside himself, Riccardo
sings another big tune, "Oh, qual soave brivido"—*What a sweet emotion*—
in which Amelia joins, though her sentiments remain guilt-ridden. The
melodic line moves from its smooth, swift flow to athletic leaps in this
cabaletta-like passage that has none of a cabaletta's ordinariness or pre-
dictability. Note, when you listen, the excitement expressed in the shuddering figure for the violins. And again, the lovers join in a triumphant,
almost *Tristan*-esque vocal celebration of their love. This was composed
six years before Wagner's great work, but opera lovers can't help hearing
in the ecstasy of this passage one of Verdi's more Wagnerian moments.

An approaching figure breaks the tryst: it's Renato, who, aware that the conspirators hope to murder Riccardo that night, has followed to protect his boss. Of course, he has no idea who the veiled woman is. After much persuasion, Riccardo agrees to head for the safety of the town, as long as Renato agrees to escort the veiled woman back to the gates but never to ask her identity. A breathless and savage trio, "Odi tu come fremono cupi"—*Do you hear how the sounds of death carry*—for Amelia, Riccardo, and Renato follows, notable for its moaning affect and quick tempo, wipes away the love duet's ecstasy. As the conspirators approach, they are disappointed to find Renato rather than Riccardo, and as a scuffle breaks out, Amelia intervenes to protect her husband. Her veil falls off, and Renato is shocked, and the others amused, to find Renato in the peculiar position of having a tryst with his own wife ("Ve' se di notte qui colla sposa"—*See how the heroic lover comes with his wife*). Of course, this marvelous ensemble builds on Amelia's mortification and Renato's swelling rage ("Così mi paga se l'ho salvato!"—*This is my reward for saving him!*). But what really animates the structure is Verdi's urbane depiction of the conspirators' ironic amusement. For the only time in the opera they are on top of the situation, and they can't stop laughing and repeating, "Che commenti per la città"—*What gossip there will be in town!* Renato invites the leaders, Samuel and Tom (or Horn and Ribbing), to his home the next morning.

Some listeners find the third act, cast in three scenes, to be a half-step down from the brilliance of acts 1 and 2. And, although Verdi's inspiration is just as high if you look at the music section by section, it's true that act 3 can feel a bit long next to the crisp wit and energy of the first two. (Act 1, in two scenes, is actually a few minutes longer.) That's probably because it carries a heavier load of plot to be played out, as well as arias to comment on all the action.

Verdi opens it with another great, raging orchestral prelude, this one depicting the discord in Renato's household and heart. Betrayal has turned this reliable man into Amelia's persecutor and Riccardo's worst enemy. Dragging Amelia into his study, Renato tells her in a bitter dialogue that she must die for her guilt. Since he has determined to kill her, Amelia pleads for one favor, that he allow her to hold their young son one last time. Her cantabile "Morrò, ma prima in grazia"—*Then I shall die, but first, for pity's sake*—is one of the best known from the opera, and a great soprano showpiece, another affecting statement of Amelia's sorrow. Accompanied by a solo cello, the melodic line droops then rises in an intense phrase of supplication, first to a B-flat, then a C. Renato coldly grants her request and she leaves. Looking at a portrait of Riccardo hanging in the room, he addresses the image of his betrayer. It's not her frail heart that I should strike, he reflects, Riccardo's blood is what's really needed. "Eri tu"—*It was you*—Renato's aria, begins with alarming ferocity in a declaimed line over thudding strings punctuated by tremendous blasts for the brass. But he relents, in the second section ("O dolcezze perdute!"—*Oh, lost happiness*) on thoughts of the joy he had with Amelia, now gone forever. Flute and harp accompany this grandly expanding melody on which Verdi shrewdly ends, maintaining sympathy for a character who has, after all, been gravely wronged.

Samuel and Tom enter, to their trademark fugato theme in the low strings. Briskly, Renato informs them that he knows about their plot to kill Riccardo, and for reasons he won't disclose, that he's joining them. The three launch into an impressive oath trio, "Dunque l'onta di tutti sol una"—*The guilt of one is that of all*—a heroic melody set to an orchestral accompaniment in which a thrumming harp figures prominently. Its savagery is notable, as is its particular sound, which will bear late fruit in two powerful passages in act 2 of *Otello*. They decide to draw lots for the honor of killing Riccardo, and Renato cruelly forces Amelia to draw the lot, which he wins. Although she has no idea what she's drawing for, she senses that Renato and the others are up to no good. Verdi sets the drawing in an impressive brass-heavy passage showing the tension of the moment. Oscar enters, bearing invitations to the masked ball at Renato's; his bouncy music, filled with trills and staccato high notes as though from another world, contrasts as powerfully as it might with Amelia's anxiety and the excitement of the conspirators, now including Renato, eager for another chance to kill Riccardo.

The second and third scenes of the act, set at Riccardo's residence, are linked. In the first, Riccardo, alone in his study, has decided to send Renato and Amelia back to England (or to their unnamed home country, in the Swedish version). The great melody symbolizing Riccardo's love for Amelia dominates the scene. The heart of the scene is Riccardo's mournful *romanza* "Ma se m'è forza perderti"—*But if I have to lose you*—often cut in older performances and recordings. The cut makes the act a bit shorter at the cost of an exquisite moment for the tenor. A *banda* is heard from offstage, marking the start of the ball in a simple, lively dance, which Verdi transforms with a few explosive accents and finally by passing it to the full orchestra into an idea of startling force. Riccardo sings the love theme ("Sì, rivederti, Amelia"—*Yes, to see you again, Amelia*) in which Verdi characterizes the fierce grip of his love in one last convulsive iteration.

The scene changes to the ballroom, where the guests have arrived. Renato, Samuel, and Tom enter, looking for Riccardo, who seems not to be present. Renato spars with Oscar, who sings a delicious canzone, "Saper vorreste" (CD Track 10)—*You want to know*—in which he teases Renato about Riccardo's costume in as lighthearted a bit of fluff (with a spine of steel), replete with trills and swooping tra-la-las, as you might imagine. Verdi impressively captures Oscar's playfulness and Renato's anger amid the general excitement of the ball. But eventually Renato learns what costume Riccardo is wearing. Amelia finds Riccardo and begs him to leave. In the background, a string orchestra heard from another room, plays a mazurka, a Polish dance with a hopping rhythm. Creating the sense of distraction and dazzlement one feels at a big, noisy party, this masterstroke sets the stage for one last agonized duet for the lovers, she pleading, he again swearing his love and repeating that he must look at her one last time, as the mazurka flits away imperturbably in the background. At first, their murmured exchanges, set against the bland dance, make for some potent dramatic irony. But before long, more passionate outbursts dominate and Verdi melds the mazurka to the vocal lines. Renato attacks. After some thundering phrases from the orchestra and chorus indicting Renato, the mazurka resumes from the other room then finally falters, as the musicians inside learn that something has happened. The ending of Haydn's "Farewell" Symphony, where the musicians stop playing one by one, may be Verdi's precedent for this astonishing example of stagecraft. Over sighing violins, the fatally wounded Riccardo begins his farewell ("Ella è pura"—*She is pure*) in which he informs Renato that Amelia has not dishonored him, then pardons everyone. The other principals and even the conspirators in a grand, harp-borne crescendo for the company lament the loss of so generous a soul. Riccardo gasps a few more words and dies, and a quick chorus ("Notte d'orror!"—*Night of horror!*) brings down the curtain.

# The Late Middle Period
## La forza del destino and Simon Boccanegra

he compositional period for the two operas we'll examine in this chapter in this chapter is long, running from 1857, when Verdi wrote the first version of *Simon Boccanegra* to its 1881 revision. *La forza del destino* falls in between, with its original version dating from 1862; Verdi's 1869 revision for La Scala in Milan has taken its place. The stylistic range covered in here is correspondingly wide.

By this time Verdi was regularly claiming to be done with writing operas; he was, at any rate, highly selective about his projects. But well-paying, prestigious commissions like that of *Forza* drew him out. Well known and popular, *Forza* is an important example of the composer's mature style. Verdi mixes in this ambitious work the high drama of the standard operatic types that are the main characters, who have one story line, with the ordinary lives of numerous humble character roles that also populate the cast. *Forza* contains two huge hits (as well as many smaller ones): a wonderful overture that's Verdi's most popular, and the act 4 aria "Pace, pace, mio Dio" for the heroine, surely one of the greatest for soprano by this or any composer. *Boccanegra*, far less familiar and less approachable for most listeners, is an unusual political tale, done in an uncompromising style. Although weighed down by an overcomplicated plot, some of the characters emerge as credible and interesting. What makes *Simon Boccanegra* worth more than cursory auditing is the fact that it's a lesser-known specimen of Verdi's late style, showing the composer at his most sublime in many long passages.

## La forza del destino

Verdi composed *La forza del destino*, a tale of the entangled lives of Leonora, daughter of the Marquis of Calatrava, Don Alvaro, her lover, and her brother Don Carlo di Vargas, for a high fee on a commission from the St. Petersburg Opera, where it had a triumphant premiere in 1862. The opera performed today is, as noted, an 1869 revision Verdi made for La Scala. This, the last libretto for the composer by Francesco Maria Piave, is an old-fashioned Spanish triangle-cum-revenge tale of the *Trovatore* type. Tossing Aristotelian unities out the window, the story takes place over about ten years. Piave had a stroke in 1867 and was no longer able to work, so the composer retained Antonio Ghislanzoni to make changes to the text for the revised version; Verdi would later tap Ghislanzoni to write the libretto for *Aida*. The main plot line, concerning Leonora, Alvaro, and Carlo, is drawn from *Don Alvaro; o, La fuerza del sino*, a Spanish play of the 1830s by Angel de Saavedra. But the scene that ends act 3 is from Schiller's play *Wallensteins Lager*—Wallenstein's Camp, which Verdi's friend Andrea Maffei (the librettist for *I masnadieri*) had translated, portions of which Verdi borrowed with Maffei's permission. The composer, wanting to write on a broader scale, decided to incorporate panoramic views of life in a Spanish village and in a military camp into the somber drama of Alvaro and the Vargas of Calatrava family.

Having three librettists, or four, if one includes Verdi himself, didn't help matters. Even though the opera's music is of unquestionable splendor, *Forza* poses a problem for even devoted Verdians who think the camp scene and the other scenes showing normal life don't belong in the opera. To them, *Forza* seems like two operas shoehorned uncomfortably into one. The grand opera portions have a darkly magnificent unity; with the overture, three duets for Alvaro and Carlo, the duet in act 1 for Leonora and Alvaro, another for Leonora and Padre Guardiano, Alvaro's difficult "Oh, tu che in seno agli angeli" at the beginning of act 3, and topping it all, her stupendous aria "Pace, pace, mio Dio" in act 4, very much on the asset side for the main story line.

While the opening scene of act 2, the camp scene that ends act 3, and Fra Melitone's that opens the last act are great on their own terms, for many the mix of styles is too much to swallow. Not even *Forza*'s fans claim for it the deft blend of comedy, drama, and tragedy of *Un ballo in maschera.* The chief reasons for the superior aesthetic unity of *Ballo* comes from its characters, who are credible, whereas *Forza*'s are flat; and from its situations, where, again, *Ballo*'s are essentially believable, and *Forza*'s, ridiculous. Defenders of the opera point out that it's a typical mid-nineteenth century artistic conception, ambitious in scale, with generously proportioned digressions, like fiction by Tolstoy or Dickens. Without doubt, it's a noble experiment, and Verdi is an artist whose instincts one trusts. In the end, you'll have to make up your own mind as to how *Forza* works for you.

A headlong fantasia (called here a *sinfonia*) on themes from the opera opens *Forza*. Verdi's most popular overture, its brilliant orchestration and swift pacing blend in a satisfying dramatic arc, from anxiety and conflict to an exciting resolution. Three blasts from the brass, symbolizing the unyielding grip of fate, begin it; then the tormented heroine Leonora's theme is stated, an anxious pulsing for strings, trombones, and bassoons, repeated three times, ending in a troubled sighing figure. Strong and striking, the theme dominates the overture and should stay in your memory with one hearing. Verdi quickly works it into a frenzy; the "fate" theme returns, followed by a piercing melody sung by Alvaro in act 4, here by woodwinds, while underneath Leonora's theme builds ominously. After another pause, the strings sing a hovering melody from Leonora's aria "Madre, pietosa Vergine" in the second act, with her troubled theme repeating ever more insistently in the lower instruments, then furiously taking over. An abbreviated version of Alvaro's tune precedes a free-flowing, open melody, sung memorably here by the clarinet, that comes from Leonora's act 2 scene with Padre Guardiano, then a more solemn tune of Padre Guardiano's, stated as a brass chorale. Amid a wild orchestral battle, Leonora's theme returns in a brighter, major key, after which the "Madre, pietosa Vergine" tune receives a blazing climax—"*grandioso*" is the composer's expression mark. With Leonora's agitated idea never far off, the composer teases us with fragments of themes, as he races to a dazzling ending.

As noted, the "fate" theme consists of a single tone, repeated three times. Although the composer makes much of the laconic motif in the overture, he hardly uses it over the course of the opera: he opens the first and second acts with it, but then drops it. The first act is short, tight, and exciting, both musically and dramatically. The curtain rises on the

Marquis of Calatrava's talking affectionately to his daughter Leonora ("Buona notte, mia figlia"—*Good night, my daughter*), glad that she's finally over her infatuation with the low-born Alvaro; Leonora shows her anxiety in a murmured aside: "Oh angoscia!"—*What anguish!* You'll notice immediately a new maturity of style in the vocal parts and fluid, rich accompaniment, mostly set mostly for strings. As soon as the Marquis leaves, Leonora pours her heart out to Curra, to her servant and confidante. Her recitative, and the *romanza* "Me pellegrina ed orfana"—*Exiled and orphaned*—into which it leads are superb new specimens under the old-fashioned titles. A solo cello opens the cantabile pensively, as subtle shifts of tonality underline Leonora's uncertainty about which course to follow, that of loyal daughter or woman in love. Pulsing strings lead to the lyrical climax of the marvelously flexible vocal line on the words "Colmo di tristi immagini"—*Tormented by morbid fears.* Leonora reflects mournfully that she'll never see this, the home where she grew up, again. Weeping winds and trembling strings add orchestral intensity to the singer's part as it again rises climactically on the words "dolor"—*pain*—and "ahimè"—*alas*—as this potent but free example of Verdi's mature style winds gently down.

Unsure of what she wants, Leonora wonders whether Alvaro will really come. His arrival on horseback is unseen but depicted in the galloping figure for strings; he then climbs through her window, to an ardent melody, "Ah, per sempre, o mio bell'angiol"—*From this moment, my darling*—in which he speaks of his love. Listen particularly for the phrase "Ma d'amor si puro e santo"—*But of a love as pure as mine*—that's even more intense, rising to a climax on the words "nostro palpito in letizia"—*our apprehension to joy.* Alvaro's expressive vocal lines show the nobility of his character, even though he's a South American of mixed race, for which the Marquis despises him. His line rises to an even grander peak as he describes tomorrow's dawn, when they'll be married ("Pronti destrieri"—*Horses are ready*). Leonora remains unsure, however, and Alvaro is hurt: "Gonfio hai di gioia il core"—*Your heart is full of joy.* The lovers begin a duet that's rapturous on Alvaro's part and anxious on Leonora's until she gives in: "Son tua"—*I'm yours.* Yet her vocal line continues to waver through shifting tonalities in the strettalike passage that follows.

Leonora's hesitation has been fatal; her father enters in fury as the orchestra wildly thunders out Leonora's main theme. Proud and sensitive,

Alvaro is prepared to die on the spot to save Leonora's honor ("Pura siccome gli angeli"—*Pure as the angels*), but the haughty Calatrava refuses to sully his hands with the blood of one he sees as so far beneath him. Alvaro drops the pistol he's holding, which fires, the shot accidentally striking the Marquis ("Io muoio!"—*I'm dying!*). The last moments of the act consist of the Marquis's curse of Leonora, some standard operatic exclamations of horror, and a rushing orchestral postlude based on Leonora's main theme. The absurdities of plot and Piave's banal lyrics are all swept along—somehow made convincing—by the music's hurtling tide.

Three blasts by the brass signal the "fate" motif, but instead of the high affect and drama of the first act, we are in the town square of Hornachuelos, a village near Seville where the opening scene of the second act is set. There's an inn and a church, and a busy square in which mule drivers and other greet one another in a cheerful chorus ("Holà!"—*Hey, there!*) set to a brisk rhythm led by the violins. The mayor is talking to a supposed student, who is actually Carlo, Calatrava's vengeance-driven son and Leonora's brother. Leonora, who's also staying at the inn, but disguised as a man, peers timidly out of a door; she notices Carlo immediately: "Che vedo? Mio fratello!"—*What do I see? My brother!* Carlo questions Trabuco, a mule driver (one of the many character roles in *Forza*) who was riding with the unknown young man, actually Leonora, but he gets nothing out of the stubborn peasant.

Preziosilla, an attractive young gypsy (another character type) enters to the delight of all the men. Before long, she launches into her light aria with choral interjections, "Al suon del tamburo"—*The sound of the drum*. This is accompanied, naturally, by a rattling snare. Her message being that war is great, Preziosilla promises glory for all who fight bravely, as its clinching line, "È bella la guerra"—*War is fine*—demonstrates. Musically, this French-styled aria with chorus is, typically for Verdi, stronger than its text warrants. The tune is catchy to say the least, with a memorable vocal leap on a weak beat. Studying Carlo's palm halfway through, Preziosilla says he's no student. A second verse follows, but the sound of pilgrims chanting from offstage interrupts its climactic point, showing the diverse nature of the material that makes up *Forza*. The merriment ceases as the residents join the prayer. Leonora participates the ensemble too, praying that Carlo not find her ("Ah, dal fratello salvami"—*Protect me from my brother*). Melody and rhythm soon stretch out in long, arching lines as a clarinet plays a rippling arpeggio and Leonora's voice soars above the rest of a complex and sophisticated ensemble.

As soon as the pilgrims have passed through, Carlo resumes his interrogation of Trabuco, who remains uncommunicative. Carlo suggests to the mayor that they paint whiskers on the stranger whose identity he wants to discover, but the mayor forbids the prank. Musically the scene pursues a comic tone, replete with sparkling trills, scampering runs, a bright, piccolo-dominated sound for the orchestra, and laughter for the chorus, led by Preziosilla. The crowd's interest turns to the "student," Carlo, whose suave narrative aria ("Son Pereda"—*I'm Pereda*) makes up a tale of a life very similar to his own, except that in it he's helping a friend who's looking for his sister and her seducer. An explosive undertone, expressed musically by sharply accented comments from the orchestra, and a heavier, more intense accompaniment to the faster-moving middle section, "Là e dovunque narrâr"—*Everywhere they told us*. The chugging brass and strings describe Carlo's real feelings beneath his easy manner, much as they will characterize Ford's simmering rage in *Falstaff*. It's here, too, that he relates the inaccurate news, which Leonora overhears, that the seducer has fled to America. The scene ends comically, as Preziosilla demonstrates that she has seen through the student's disguise, calling him "Marchese"—*Marquis*—and laughing at him. Everyone says good night, and the bustling violin theme from the scene's opening comes back. In a fine proto-cinematic pullback, Verdi's complex music shows the village square returning to life: Preziosilla's laughter (so similar here to Oscar's in *Ballo*) seems to dominate, but Carlo continues to tell everyone that he's Pereda, the mule drivers again call out to each other, and others sing, "Andiam"—*Let's go!*

The second scene contains some of Leonora's greatest music. Set at a monastery outside Hornachuelos, it opens with her entering, terrified, to her main theme. She muses, in a sweeping accompanied recitative, of her brother's horrendous tale, and, in a phrase of piercing sorrow ("Ed or mi lascia"—*And so he left me*), expressing her emotions on learning, incorrectly as we'll see, that Alvaro abandoned her and fled for America. She then embarks on her great aria "Madre, pietosa Vergine"—*Virgin mother, full of pity*—in which she begs the Virgin Mary for mercy for her sins. The vocal line begins in the middle of the range, in convincing mimesis of a spontaneous but desperate prayer. The accompaniment consists of a nervous rustling for the strings and a moaning phrase for flutes and clarinets. More declaimed than sung, the vocal line rises steadily to a peak on the words "Pietà di me, Signor"—*Have mercy on me, Lord*. After a long pause, Leonora continues: "Deh! Non m'abbandonar"—*Don't forsake me*—to the shattering melody first presented in the overture, over the same trembling strings; unforgettable even in its first avatar, it's even more moving here, especially when sung by a great soprano voice. (It's also similar in profile and tessitura to Aida's "Numi, pietà.") Note the contrast between the rapid, partly declaimed opening phrases and the long notes, supported by a fully open voice in this lyrical climax. Leonora's musing is interrupted by chanting from inside the church giving her comfort and inspiration: "Ah, que'sublimi cantici"—*What a sublime song*. But she falters as she tries to rise and knock on the monastery door ("Oh, misera Leonora, tremi?"—*Poor Leonora, you tremble?*) as the original, nervous accompaniment returns. But she finds strength once more in prayer, twice repeating and ending her aria with the soaring tune, to ever-richer commentary from the orchestra.

Drama turns to comedy as Leonora rings the bell and Fra Melitone, the irritable monk with whom she must deal at her moment of crisis, asks what's so urgent; "Un infelice"—*A misfortune*—she replies. Leonora's sweeping tragic theme as well as the glorious melody of her last aria, return to accompany her worried reflections as Melitone goes off to fetch Padre Guardiano, the abbot and sage of the monastery. Padre Guardiano arrives, and after sending Melitone off, embarks on the enormous dialogue that ends with Leonora's taking up life as a hermit. Leonora reveals, to Padre Guardiano's surprise, that she's a woman. She then launches into a lament ("Infelice, delusa, rejetta"—*Unhappy, deluded, rejected*) in which she bewails her condition, her vocal line marked by big leaps and stabbing dissonance.

Padre Guardiano solemnly welcomes her to the way of the Cross; then, to a melodic line that twists then rises, Leonora replies that she already feels calmer. A very beautiful concerted passage for the two, begun by the abbot's line "Chi puo legger nel futuro"—*Who can read the future?*—follows, their lines twining; Leonora's then soars above a rich accompaniment as Padre Guardiano warns her that this is not a decision to rush into. Questions about her father, lover, and brother bring Leonora fresh pain, as she pleads passionately ("Se voi scacciate"—*If you drive me away*) that the abbot grant her request. Padre Guardiano praises God, to the melody heard as a chorale in the overture, here in a sturdier rhythm and to an accompaniment of plucked strings, but still easily recognizable. He calls Melitone, whom he instructs to summon the monks. Padre Guardiano then tells her that she'll dress as a monk, and that he'll bring her, at dawn, to a cave on the mountainside where she'll take up her new life of isolation and prayer ("Sull'alba il piede"—*At dawn you'll walk*). Leonora then thanks God, to the wonderful tune given by the clarinet in the overture ("Tua grazia, o Dio"—*Your mercy, o Lord*). Again their voices blend, now brightly in hope, to end the scene.

The final scene of the act, set in the church attached to Padre Guardiano's monastery, shows the ceremony of Leonora's transformation as a hermit. Deliberately static, the scene is notable for its slow tempos, which Verdi interrupts only with orchestral and vocal fire in the thunderous imprecations at its center. It opens with a prelude for organ, followed by a long orchestral passage that meditates on the great melody of "Deh! Non m'abbandonar." The monks enter, followed by Padre Guardiano and Leonora, dressed as a monk. The abbot enjoins the monks not to disturb this new occupant of the mountainside cave, to which they agree, in a powerful chorus, dominated by the orchestra's pounding triplets as well as flashing scales that anticipate the Requiem. Then, as the monks sing a hymn, "La Vergine degli angeli" over an accompaniment of arpeggiated triplets, Leonora joins in, first apart from, then above the chanting monks, in lovely descant. There's a big crescendo for all, followed by a somber falling figure for the strings as Padre Guardiano leads Leonora off. This, and a diminuendo—a lowering of volume—provide a fade-down that makes an effective ending to this solemn tableau.

Act 3, is set several years later in Velletri, Italy, during the War of the Austrian Succession. Although unknown to each other, Alvaro and Carlo are both fighting with the Spanish army. A brash orchestral introduction and a chorus of soldiers offstage opens the act, followed by a long solo for clarinet that floats nostalgically over a gentle orchestral background. With the mood set and some themes of his cantabile anticipated by the clarinet, Alvaro, enters, musing about his wretched life ("Invano morte desìo"—*In vain I wish for death*). Accompanied by the sad tones of an oboe and a bassoon, he reflects in majestic recitative about his royal Incan ancestry. He then sings his great cantabile "Oh, tu che in seno agli angeli"—*You, who in the bosom of the angels*—a prayer to Leonora, whom he believes to be dead, to forgive him and intercede for him in heaven. The clarinet finally joins Alvaro in his lament, another great Verdian tenor aria that's exceptional in its vocal demands as well as convincing in its spacious expression of the character's sorrow.

Carlo enters hurriedly, pursued by soldiers who have accused him of cheating at cards. Alvaro chases them off, and the two introduce themselves, both using false names; false Alvaro thanks false Carlo for saving his skin. Carlo has already heard of (false—you get the idea) Alvaro for his heroic deeds in the war. In a thunderous, very masculine concerted passage far too brief to be called a duet ("Amici in vita, in morte"—*Friends in life and death*), they swear brotherhood. After an orchestral depiction of battle that shows how far Verdi has come from the days of *I Lombardi*, Alvaro is brought in, badly wounded. Carlo offers him a knighthood in the Order of Calatrava for his courage, but Alvaro blanches at the mention of the name. The two principals then sing a fine, short duet, "Solenne in quest'ora"—*Swear to me in this solemn hour*. Carlo makes Alvaro swear to burn a packet of his letters should he die, as expected; overcome with grief over the loss of his brave new friend, Alvaro agrees ("Amico, fidate"—*Friend, have faith*). This somber passage is lightly scored until the cellos and winds comment sweetly in burbling triplets on Alvaro's relief that he can now die in peace. The vocal lines twine nobly as both characters show their best sides. It's a great moment for tenor and baritone, who share the limelight equally. As soon as Alvaro is carried off, though, Carlo begins to wonder, to stinging string commentary, why the Calatrava name made Alvaro shudder. He opens Alvaro's case, and after a brief struggle with his conscience, persuades himself that his family's honor outweighs his oath to destroy the letters. His cantabile "Urna fatale"—*Fatal lot, sent by destiny*—is another fine specimen of interior monologue for baritone, at first angry, then regretful over a situation that has the better of him; it's reminiscent of Renato's "Eri tu" from *Ballo*, though less fierce, as it opens with softly pulsing triplets, then rising intensely, to a quicker accompaniment, on the phrase "Un giuro è sacro per l'uom d'onore"—*An oath is sacred to a man of honor*. The singer has to hit a number of high F-sharps, and rounds the aria out with a suave cadenza. Biting strings again accompany him as he wrestles with his conscience, opens the letter, and seeing Leonora's name, has his suspicion confirmed that Alvaro is the man who killed his father and dishonored his family. Upon hearing that Alvaro will live, resumes his mission as vengeful son in the cabaletta-like "Egli è salvo"—*He is saved!*—rejoicing in the prospect of revenge, and spurning his oath to Alvaro. This climactic moment includes an unusual phrase for madly chattering winds.

An attractive chorus of a rustic tint for soldiers opens the second scene, still set in the Spanish camp at Velletri. Alvaro has had an unexpectedly swift recovery, and as Carlo enters greets his new friend to whom he's now grateful for saving his life. But the moment Carlo addresses him as "Don Alvaro, l'Indiano"—*The Indian*—he knows his trust has been betrayed, as he cries out in the first of many tremendous outbursts that makes this scene so exciting. Still Alvaro tries to conciliate, refusing to fight one with whom he has sworn brotherhood. But in their duet, Carlo, bent on revenge, mocks his overtures, repudiating their friendship and revealing, to Alvaro's shock, that Leonora is still alive. Alvaro still tries to dissuade Carlo from his vengeful course, even calling him "friend," but Carlo calls him "stolto"—*fool*—insulting him viciously and telling him to a violent orchestral uproar that first he then Leonora must die. To the wildest music in the opera, an enraged Alvaro tells Carlo that he's the one who should prepare to die. They draw swords and start to fight, but are separated by soldiers, who drag Carlo off. Appalled by his own behavior Alvaro throws down his sword, then resolves in a ringing phrase to sort out his torment in the peace of a monastery ("Al chiostro, all'eremo"—*To the cloister, to the retreat*). Alvaro's vocal part is challenging throughout this extraordinary duet, with two climactic Bs toward the end, the first leaped at with very little means of approach. With two duets so closely scored, this second one is occasionally cut from live performances.

It is the final scene of act 3 that above all gives *Forza* doubters pause. The composer intended a vivid slice of army camp life, but to many it seems more like a bizarre variety show, albeit with exceptional music. And as though the entire plot were not already overburdened with coincidence, somehow Preziosilla *and* Fra Melitone *and* Trabuco have come to Italy with the Spanish army, whom they are there to encourage and profit from. First, Preziosilla sings a *canzone* ("Venite all'indovina"—*Come and have your fortunes told*) accompanied by the chorus, charmingly decorated by a pair of piccolos. Then in a whining quasi-Slavic melodic idiom, Trabuco trades with the soldiers. On a more serious note, peasants whose farms have been destroyed by the war beg mournfully for bread ("Pane, pan, per carità"). This being southern Italy (though barely, as Velletri is just south of Rome), Preziosilla as mistress of ceremonies calls for a tarantella, which proves entertaining enough on its own terms. Although Melitone's presence is hard to explain, his "Predica"—sermon—("Toh, toh, poffare il mondo"—*Whew, what a world*) with chorus is a masterpiece of comic writing, again, clearly anticipating *Falstaff* with some of its passages sounding just like Falstaff's monologues. Crazy, witty, and filled with nasty puns and sarcasm, Melitone's castigation of the human race seems infused with more energy than Padre Guardiano's pieties. And finally, Preziosilla's well-known "Rataplan" (a nonsense word that imitates the sound of the drum), makes a brilliant if heartless end to the act. Without question, it's a virtuoso showpiece for the singer, the chorus, and the drummer. Verdi's compositional range and skill are on display in this glittering demonstration of his rhythmic drive. "Rataplan" may be the best-known number in this curious mélange, but Melitone's satiric sermon deserves more attention.

Melitone's comedy dominates the opening scene of act 4. More than five years have elapsed, and everyone, as it happens, is back in Spain. Under the eye of Padre Guardiano, Fra Melitone is ladling out soup to a shoving crowd of beggars. This well-drawn scene is satisfying musically and dramatically, as the composer captures the moods of the beggars, and Melitone's irritation in free and fresh sounding exchanges. The urgency of the beggars' hunger is underlined by rising waves of volume, while Meltione's sour affect is here rendered with an initially gentle touch, though Padre Guardiano needs to remind him several times to be patient. Melitone finally begins a buffo aria, "Il resto, a voi, prendetevi"—*Take the leftovers*—a bustling, quick-time complaint, with chattering winds imitating the vocal part, demonstrating that Rossini's comic style was still very much alive even in the 1860s. (He died in 1868.) But the thunderous unisons of the stretta ("Via di qua!"—*Get out!*) that ends it do, again, anticipate Verdi's treatment of character in *Falstaff*. Melitone and Padre Guardiano then chat about another monk, Father Raffaele, who's dark "like an Indian," and a bit touchy; he is, of course, Don Alvaro, who has found retreat in this very monastery. Padre Guardiano reassures Melitone about his tortured-looking friend and colleague. The bell rings and Don Carlo enters, seeking Father Raffaele. Padre Guardiano brings him and

Carlo informs him stiffly that the time has come for blood: "Col sangue sol cancellasi"—*Blood alone can expiate*—telling Alvaro that he has even brought him a sword with which to fight. Alvaro tries to stay calm in the face of Carlo's insults, though he nearly flies off when called "codardo"— *coward*. To the plangent melody first heard in then overture, Alvaro explains that he will not be provoked. "Le minacce, i fieri accenti"—*Your threats and fierce words*—develops into a duet set to that piercing tune. Its temperature rises as Carlo continues to insult Alvaro, as a nervous, repeated fluttering for the violas paints the growing strain on Alvaro. But, referring to Leonora to an angelic phrase ("Sulla terra l'ho adorata"—*I loved her in this world*), Alvaro gets control of himself once more. Carlo has not come to patch things up and continues with his insults. To a panting orchestral phrase that depicts his fraying temper, Alvaro even offers to kneel to ask Carlo's forgiveness, but this only provokes a new insult about his parentage, "Ah, la macchia del tuo stemma"—*The stain of your ancestry*. This proves too much for Alvaro, who grabs the sword offered by Carlo and dashes off to fight his persecutor.

The second scene, set at the cave where Leonora has lived in retreat, opens with her troubled theme. Then, emerging from her cave, the unhappy woman broods magnificently on her fate in her aria "Pace, pace, mio Dio" (CD Track 11)—*Peace, my God*—revealing in this meditation a depth of character not hinted at before. The opening line, built of two sighs for "Pace, pace" followed by the opulent phrase to which "Pace, mio Dio, pace, mio Dio" is sung only twice, and echoed by the woodwinds. Yet it dominates the aria, which is titled "Melodia" in the score. The words of the aria almost don't matter, so clear though subtle is the blend of affects from sorrow to bitter regret to resignation, carried on the vast sweep of its lyric structure. Leonora reflects, in a seamless fusion of *declamato* and cantabile, regal in the fall of its phrases, on the fatal tragedy that separates her and Alvaro ("Fatalità," with the trumpets adding two soft but steely notes), and that she still loves him. She implores God to let her die, finally singing that she still lacks the peace she hoped to find here ("Invan la pace qui sperò"). The orchestral accompaniment remains light, with the harp a constant, flowing companion to the voice, and the winds and strings providing delicate harmonic and metrical punctuation. Verdi brings back her anxious theme before the end, but Leonora seems to find a measure of tranquility in an exquisitely floated B-flat. The pace of the accompaniment accelerates as Leonora reflects that the bread she subsists on only prolongs her wretched life ("Misero pane"). Sounds of approaching men frighten her ("Maledizione!"—*The curse*), and she retreats to her cave.

Verdi wrote arias as great as "Pace, pace, mio Dio," but none to beat it. Leonora's plot-burdened torments may be improbable, yet her testament "Pace, pace, mio Dio" seems to summon and speak of pain, regret, and world-weariness for us all. More than a showpiece for dramatic sopranos of the top tier, it's one of the profoundly moving moments in opera, in music, in art.

We hear Carlo's voice from offstage, crying that he's wounded. Alvaro enters, in despair at having again shed Vargas blood. Leonora curses them for disturbing her but Alvaro recognizes her, telling her he has killed Carlo. When she runs offstage to see her brother, Carlo stabs her. Padre Guardiano enters, supporting the wounded Leonora and the three begin a noble trio, "Non imprecare"—*Do not curse*. Leonora tells Alvaro she'll await him in heaven. She dies as Padre Guardiano sings the opera's punch line: "Salita a Dio"—*She has ascended to God*. Of course, the plot has to be tied up, and the music of the final scene is genuinely great. But don't be surprised if you find it anticlimactic after the grandeur of Leonora's aria.

## Simon Boccanegra

If this opera's plot has left you confused, you can get in line. Surely the most frustrating aspect of this flawed masterpiece is the incoherent plot that shows how desperately Verdi lacked a librettist with skills that complemented his own. The important facts to remember are: that Amelia is Boccanegra's lost daughter and Fiesco's lost granddaughter; that Fiesco holds his grudge against Boccanegra until the very end, when it's too late; that Paolo is the villain; and that Gabriele hates Simone, too, but comes to be his ally and successor.

There are two *Simon Boccanegra*s: an 1857 original version, libretto by Piave, with additions by Giuseppe Montanelli, and an 1881 revision, with alterations and additions by Arrigo Boito, the great writer and musician who would create the librettos of *Otello* and *Falstaff* for Verdi. The 1881 version of *Boccanegra* is invariably the one performed today. The first version, which flopped at La Fenice in Venice, is an experimental work, singular in Verdi's output. An earnest political tale, it can be looked at as a precursor of *Don Carlo*. Working with the serious subject, complicated plot, and male-dominated cast, the composer created an intentionally lean style, uncushioned by prettiness, opportunities for vocal display, or juicy tunes, and reliant on the lower strings throughout. Verdi rightly saw the material as better matched to the "*declamato*" (declaimed, as opposed to cantabile) style of singing, and the first audiences did not like the austere score. While not particularly lovable, the first *Boccanegra*, falling between *Vespri* and *Aroldo* (and, more in the mainstream, *Ballo*) makes for interesting listening, fitting in comprehensibly as another link in the chain of the composer's development.

Over the decades that followed, Verdi's publisher, Giulio Ricordi, occasionally pushed the idea of a revised *Boccanegra*. By 1880, thanks again to Ricordi, the composer was starting to consider composing an *Otello*, with Boito as his librettist. Verdi himself came up with the idea of a council scene, for which Boito created the text. In the end, the most extensive changes were made to the prologue, and to act 1, including the great Council scene that ends it. Boito helped to bring several characters, including Paolo and Boccanegra himself, more to the forefront, much to the benefit of the drama, though the awful plot apparently had to stay. As is always pointed out, the greatest outcome of the revised *Boccanegra* surely is the successful, mature collaboration between Verdi and Boito. Without this, *Otello* and *Falstaff* as we know them would not exist.

By 1880, when Verdi revised the music of the old *Boccanegra* and added new material, he had composed *Don Carlos*, *Aida*, and the Requiem, and had grown into a composer not only of lyricism and power, but of immense sophistication, too. Only the Italian version of *Don Carlo*, *Otello*, *Falstaff*, and the *Quattro pezzi sacri* lay ahead. From the soft, subtle strings of the new opening to the fierce power of the Council scene, we're hearing the master at the height of his powers. *Boccanegra* is surely the least familiar opera written in Verdi's late style and what we hear of it in the revised work is as great at one would expect. Still, between its bewildering plot, predominance of low male voices, political subject, and declaimed vocal style, albeit deployed with deepened subtlety and skill, the opera remains tough going for many. Hard-core Verdians rightly admire the work. For others, *Boccanegra* may add up to a bit less than the sum of its parts. Its chief drawback may stem from the slightly uneasy mix of the composer's middle style in one of its more austere incarnations that forms a substratum to the plushness and freedom of his late manner.

The prologue, essentially a first act, that takes place twenty-five years before the main action of the opera, sets the stage for events to come. Confusing though the story may be, you'll have no difficulty recognizing a new level of sophistication and mastery in Verdi's music. The brief introduction for strings breathes a different air from anything you've heard before, revealing a cool freshness in the composer's instrumental writing and a new breadth to his harmonic thinking. Instead of a big chorus, the opera opens in medias res with a quiet dialogue between Paolo Albani and Pietro, Genoese plebeians on the make, who are plotting to make Simon Boccanegra, one of their own party, Doge. As soon as Pietro leaves, Paolo, a proto-Iago figure, snarls of his hatred for the patricians ("Aborriti patrizi!"—*Detested patricians!*). In a second dialogue, this with Simon himself, Paolo makes his suggestion, but the corsair thinks he's mad: "Vaneggi?"—*Are you joking?* But holding out the idea that election as Doge will make him a fit husband for his lover, the patrician Maria Fiesco, Paolo persuades Simon to become a candidate with relative ease as long as Simon agrees to share with Paolo the danger and power of the office. They swear an oath to a quick, unrhetorical passage, marked by one big brass chord that beautifully demonstrates the lack of fuss and fluidity of Verdi's late style. The remainder of the opening scene consists of an exchange between Paolo, Piero, and the chorus, acting as the plebeians whom they instruct to acclaim Boccanegra at a rally the next morning. Paolo sings the brief cantabile "L'altra magion vedete?"—*Do you see that building?*—in which he attacks the Fiesco family (the "Fieschi") in mysterious tones by telling the crowd how Maria, who loves Simon, is imprisoned there. Light and delicate, but effective, it's a narrative that's sufficiently hair-raising as to frighten the superstitious crowd. It's also lighter in tone than the somber scene that follows.

Jacopo Fiesco, who hates Boccanegra, emerges from his palace on the square. One of the finest basso roles in the repertory, Fiesco has an ironbound vocal line that is always one of the chief pleasures of listening to *Simon Boccanegra*. After a funereal orchestral introduction, Fiesco bids farewell to the place where that beloved daughter Maria has just died. In a majestic recitative, "A te, l'estremo addio" (CD Track 12)—*A last farewell to you*—he then bitterly curses Boccanegra as her seducer: "Oh, vile seduttore!" Before singing his great aria "Il lacerato spirito"—*The tormented spirit*—he even blasphemes, asking a statue of the Virgin Mary how she could have allowed this to happen, but then humbly recants. The aria itself, one of the greatest for the bass voice, is the agonized lament for a beloved child of a man who does not give his love easily. The second part, "Il serto a lei de'martiri"—*Heaven has given her a martyr's crown*—is more lyrical though still stern. An eloquent postlude for winds over trembling strings ends this profound passage.

Boccanegra, unaware of what has happened, returns, filled with hope for his and Maria's future. He and Fiesco enter into a long dialogue in which Fiesco attacks him for misdeeds against his family without, however, informing him of Maria's death. Boccanegra begs forgiveness, but Fiesco remains implacable. Simon offers to let Fiesco kill him then and there, but the proud and stubborn patrician refuses. To a shifting melody, Fiesco explains that he will forgive Simon if he gives up their daughter ("Se concedermi vorrai"—*If you will give up to me*). But Simon cannot, as he explains in a brief but poignant, nautically flavored passage, "Del mar sul lido"—*By the shore of a foreign land*. The woman who cared for her died, and the child has disappeared, a fact Verdi emphasizes with a mysterious harmonic shift. Without his grandchild there can be no peace, Fiesco says, turning his back on the now wretched Simon, while singing a sepulchral low F.

Simon rails against the Fieschi ("Oh de'Fieschi implacata, orrida razza"—*Stony-hearted, awful Fieschi!*) in a desperate phrase. He then decides to slip into the palace to visit Maria. With Fiesco watching, he enters, and to music that reflects the emptiness of the place, finds no living human, but Maria dead. His horror is jarringly interrupted by a busy choral movement, resembling the *Traviata* party music as the chorus acclaims him as Doge. Celebratory bells chime manically, contrasting ironically with Boccanegra's horror. But both he and Fiesco are disturbed as the prologue ends, both because Maria is dead, and Fiesco because the hated Simon is now Doge.

Act 1 opens with an orchestral introduction that again displays Verdi's command of the orchestra. A tone poem depicting dawn over the Mediterranean, this long-limbed, delicately orchestrated passage is based on trills for the violins and burbling decorative figures for woodwinds, with the piccolo lending its bright sound. The clarinet intones a long phrase over exotic harmonies in the strings, and the oboe and clarinet sing like birds, in sweetly clashing tones. The introduction also leads directly into Amelia's aria greeting the dawn, "Come in quest'ora bruna"—*How the stars and sea*. This pretty but substantial cantabile, which picks up as a continuation of the prelude's music, does little to advance the plot. But it does settle Amelia's identity for the audience as she recounts the identical personal history as what Boccanegra told Fiesco in the prologue. The sad part of her childhood ("Ma gli astri e la marina"—*But what do the stars and sea*) is set to muttering strings, but this passes, and the ecstatic opening music returns, made piquant by refined harmonic alterations. Verdi flatters the soprano voice here, with the line rising gracefully at the end to what should sound like a relaxed and comfortable B-flat.

Gabriele Adorno enters, and the two sing a long duet in which she expresses fear for his intrigues in Genoese politics. The heart of their impassioned exchange is a concerted passage begun by Amelia ("Vieni a mirar la cerula marina tremolante"—*Come and look at the shimmering blue sea*) in which trills for the winds depict the glistening sea she sings of; Gabriele joins in with an ecstatic reply ("Angiol che dall'empireo"—*Angel who from heaven*). The passage ends with the same kind of mincing figuration for violins and high winds the composer used for years, but here more boldly harmonized. The next portion is an anxious exchange between the lovers when Gabriele learns that the Doge, his enemy Boccanegra, will visit, coming to a huge climax on the phrase "Amanti oltre la morte, sempre vivrai con me"—*we shall be . . . lovers beyond death*. Another conversation follows, this one between Gabriele and Fiesco, Amelia's guardian who now confusingly calls himself Andrea. Fiesco tells Gabriele of her supposedly humble origins, but Gabriele says that "L'orfana adoro!"—*I love this orphan*—then asks Fiesco to bless their union. This the now old man does in a hymnlike "Vieni a me, ti benedico"—*Come to me, I give you my blessing*—a quasi-religious moment in which this darkly drawn character shows a benign side. Verdi sets his music to a choralelike setting, beautifully alternating, and then blending the string and wind sections.

A trumpet fanfare announces Boccanegra's arrival; Gabriele and Fiesco exit hastily. The Doge tells Paolo, who notices Amelia's beauty, that they must return to Genoa soon. He and Amelia then begin the long duet in which their relationship is revealed. First he shows her a document pardoning the Grimaldis (of which clan she is supposedly a member) for their various offenses. Simon also notes her beauty, asking why she lives outside of town, reading in her embarrassed manner that she's already in love. Amelia reveals that she isn't a Grimaldi, and in one more glorious link in the long chain of melancholy Verdian cantabiles for heroines, accompanied by eloquent woodwinds, tells him her story: "Orfanella il tetto umile"—*The lowly roof ... sheltered me, a poor orphan*. Again, the same kind of plangent oboe introduction and another sad, lilting melody and crushed harmonies, only here the style shows a new sophistication and polish. With growing excitement, Simon realizes that she might be his lost daughter: "Ah! Se la speme, o ciel clemente"—*Merciful heavens, if the hope*. This turns into another great father-daughter duet of melting warmth, deserving wider appreciation. A few quick questions reveal the truth, as to an ecstatic vocal and orchestral climax father and daughter are reunited. Another wonderful passage follows, begun by Simon ("Figlia, a tal nome io palpito"—*Daughter! At that name I tremble*). The duet has a long, rich postlude, based on the huge melody of Simon's phrase, played by the violins over arpeggios for the harp. This proto-Puccinian moment provides one of the few big tunes in a score in which as noted, the composer avoids them. The remainder of the scene briskly transforms Paolo's resentment of the Doge to full-blown hatred as Boccanegra tells him bluntly that Amelia is not for him. Paolo then tells his old henchman Pietro that he wants to kidnap her; Paolo agrees to help.

The mighty Council scene that rounds out act 1 belongs entirely to the 1881 version of the opera. Its stormy orchestral introduction is no mere flourish, but a controlled presentation of contrasting ideas. As the curtain rises, the Doge is conducting business of state with the council, composed of equal numbers of plebeians and patricians. The King of Tartary proposes peace; he reads a letter from the poet Francesco Petrarca, whom we know as Petrarch, begging for peace between Genoa and Venice, its commercial and military rival at the time. (Petrarca actually did write such letters to the Doge of Venice and the historical Simon Boccanegra.) The counselors want war, but the Risorgimento visionary in Boccanegra sees them as parts of a single Italian homeland: "Adria [Venice] e Liguria [Genoa] hanno patria commune"—*Venice and Genoa share a common fatherland*. Sounds of a mob from outside interrupt the proceedings; they are chasing Gabriele, but also calling for death to the Doge; there's an exciting and unusual high B for the women's chorus. Gabriele is somehow extracted from the mob and brought before the council; Pietro advises Paolo to flee, as it appears that their plot has failed, but the Doge, who mistrusts Paolo, forbids anyone to leave, saying that whoever does so is a traitor. As the mob continues to howl for blood and vengeance, the plebeian counselors begin to waver but the Doge faces them down with immense authority: "Morte al Doge? Sta ben"—*Death to the Doge? Very well!* The crowd bursts in, as to mocking squeals from the woodwinds Simon challenges them fearlessly, too ("Questa'è dunque del popolo la voce?"—*Is this then the voice of the people?*). Gabriele, who believes Simon was behind a failed abduction of Amelia that's about to be revealed, accuses him harshly. But as Gabriele tries to stab the Doge, Amelia enters and throws herself in his way.

To a sharp-edged string accompaniment, Amelia tells of how Lorenzino (whom Gabriele has killed, by the way) kidnapped her. Warning this weak player of the Doge's wrath, she bluffed her way out: "Confuso di tema, mi schiuse le porte"—*Shaken by fear, he unlocked the doors.* Patricians and plebeians in the chamber accuse each other of spawning the plot. After an orchestral flourish remarkable for its ferocity, Simon interrupts, laying forth in his aria "Plebe! Patrizi! Popolo dalla feroce storia"—*Plebeians! Patricians! Heirs to a fierce history*—at once an indictment, apologia, and plea for Genoese unity. One of Verdi's greatest baritone arias, this powerful passage falls into two parts, the first a raw recounting of the terrible feuds that have racked the city for generations. Then, switching to a major key but with no abatement of tension, the Doge's line takes on a more sorrowful tone ("Piango sulla mendace festa dei vostri fior"—*I weep for the deceptive gaiety of your flowers*). Boccanegra's heartfelt words soften the crowd and in a noble ensemble, the councilors except for Pietro, Paolo, and Fiesco, who, never one to let things go, still laments, his vocal line way down below the others ("Sta la città superba nel pugno d'un corsar"—*This city lies in the hands of a pirate*). There can also be no more clear-cut an example of "*declamato*" exposition, as opposed to cantabile singing, than Simon's tremendous appeal.

Relieved that Amelia is safe, Gabriele offers his sword to the Doge, who refuses it, but, as a pragmatist, insists that he remain a prisoner until the plot has been fully unraveled. The final passage is another titanic moment, as the Doge shows himself as a cunning politician, mass psychologist, and charismatic leader. Grasping somehow that Paolo was behind the failed kidnapping, he makes him repeat, "Sia maledetto"—*May he be cursed*—of the still-to-be-identified villain. With the chorus, whispering in awe, a quailing Paolo repeats it, then flees the chamber in terror, having cursed himself. This great passage is punctuated by a huge unison figure that stalks and snarls for the full orchestra. Its forerunners include Amneris's curse of the priests in act 4 scene 1 of *Aida*, and the "Tuba mirum" section of the Requiem. It's followed in this great chain by the "Credo" of Iago. A slow, sinister turn for the bass clarinet works in; but soon takes over, roared out by the bassoon, tuba, and low strings in a fearsome postlude.

Pizzicato strings suggesting Paolo's stealth introduce the second act, set in the Doge's room, to which Paolo and just about everyone else in Genoa seem to have free access. After telling Pietro to bring the prisoners up, Paolo broods bitterly ("Me stesso ho maledetto"—*I've cursed myself!*). In a compact but impressive monologue, "Vilipeso . . . reietto"—*Vilified and rejected*—he lays out his hatred for the community and tells of his plans to poison the Doge, which he sings while pouring the contents of a phial into his goblet. The dark and evil nature of this passage mean that it's also set in the *declamato* style, with dark-toned instruments, notably trombones and lower strings dominating the accompaniment. Gabriele and Fiesco, now prisoners, are brought in. In a briskly paced discussion between the two basses, Paolo proposes an alliance between them; but Fiesco, who mistrusts Paolo as much as he hates Simon, spurns the offer. When Paolo suggests poisoning the Doge, Fiesco reacts with disgust: "Osi a Fiesco proporre un misfatto?"—*You dare suggest a crime to Fiesco?* (The old man has standards for his intrigues.) This quick but impressive passage may remind you of the duet for Rigoletto and Sparafucile. Fiesco leaves, but Gabriele also dislikes Paolo's idea. But Paolo sends the hotheaded Gabriele over the edge by suggesting that Amelia is there to satisfy the Doge's "infami dilettanze"— *infamous pleasures*. To an orchestral accompaniment that surges like a wild ocean, Gabriele pours out his rage in another declaimed aria, "Sento avvampar nell'anima"—*I feel a fire of jealousy raging in my soul.* Gabriele's vocal line ranges restlessly up to a high A, and this stormy passage is any- thing but lyrical. To the accompaniment of weeping oboe, he realizes that he's crying ("Io piango!"). Then, unusually from a formal standpoint, he sings a genuine cantabile, "Cielo pietoso, rendila"—*Merciful heaven, restore her,* a more old-fashioned remnant from 1857, ending with a cadenza.

Amelia enters and the lovers embark on a tense duet based on Gabriele's misunderstanding of her position. Without letting him know that Simon is her father (although why she still can't is not really clear), she tells him that the love between her and the Doge is "santo"—*pure*. Agitated emotions are mirrored by syncopation in the orchestral accompaniment. Gabriele settles down a bit to beg her lyrically ("Parla, in tuo cor virgineo"—*Restore faith in your innocence of heart*), to which she replies in kind, over gently pulsing strings ("Sgombra dall'alma il dubbio"—*Banish doubt from your soul*). Gabriele, however, is not comforted. Trumpets herald the approach of the Doge, and to a fretful melodic idea and orchestral accompaniment Amelia begs Gabriele to leave. Boccanegra enters, to a somber figure for strings. When he asks Amelia to name her lover, he's appalled to learn that it's Gabriele: "Il mio nemico!"—*My enemy!* Gabriele's name is on the list of conspirators he's holding. She pleads with him to forgive Adorno, and after a poignant lament ("O crudele destino"—*Cruel fate*), he agrees to think about it, as long as Gabriele repents. He sends her off, then, in an impressively understated monologue, considers whether pity shows weakness or harshness, fear. Thirsty, he drinks from the poisoned goblet; somber chords for the trombones mark the moment. Exhausted, he begins to doze as a high-set figure for the violins depicts his slipping into sleep and then dream. To the ripe melody of his act 1 duet with Amelia, he sings as he dozes of his daughter's loving an enemy.

Gabriele enters, carrying a dagger to kill the sleeping Boccanegra, but it's harder to do than even this fiery young man expects, and Amelia enters before he summons the nerve. Simon wakes, defiantly telling Gabriele to strike. But now the truth comes out that he's Amelia's father. A shocked Gabriele drops his dagger and begins the trio that forms the lyrical climax of the act. To an interesting pizzicato accompaniment, Gabriele opens the passage ("Perdon, perdon, Amelia"—*Forgive me*), passionately declaimed rather than sung in cantabile style. Remorseful, Adorno tells her and the Doge that he's an assassin. Simon wonders how to act, and Amelia prays generically to her own mother, in heaven, for protection. This intense and noble passage is a high point of the act.

Sounds of another attack by enemies of the Doge are heard from off-stage. Simon tells Gabriele to go and join his people, but Adorno refuses. He says he will try to persuade them to change their view, but will fight for the Doge in case he cannot. Boccanegra tells him that in the event of victory he may marry Amelia afterward, and, to a wild fanfare, the act ends.

The last act picks up directly from the victory of the Doge and his partisans, with excited battle music and ironic cries of "Evviva il Doge"—*Long live the Doge*—from the offstage chorus, which knows nothing of his poisoning. Although defeated, Fiesco has been pardoned, but Paolo, crossing the stage under guard, has been condemned to death, as he informs Fiesco in a short but riveting narrative, "Il mio demonio mi cacciò fra l'armi del rivoltesi"—*My demon drove me to fight with the rebels*. Set to an agonized, winding melody, he still takes perverse satisfaction in having poisoned the Doge, as he tells a horrified Fiesco. The sound of an offstage bridal chorus for Gabriele and Amelia causes Paolo great pain, again expressed by the twisting of the accompaniment that backs his reflections. Fiesco finally figures out that Paolo was behind Amelia's abduction, and almost kills him on the spot, but thinks better of it: "Sei sacro alla bipenne"—*You are promised to the headsman's ax*.

A long sequence of fanfares for the horns surrounds a minor announcement from a captain that, to honor the dead, the Doge wants no unseemly celebrations. Verdi's dizzy three-note chromatic figures for strings paint the poisoned Doge's desperate condition as he enters. In another powerfully pictorial passage, Simon expresses his longing for a breath of fresh sea air, and for the freedom of youth and bold deeds ("Oh, refrigerio! La marina brezza!"—*What relief, the sea breeze!*). Verdi sets these lines to a long-limbed phrase for the strings, with the violas fluidly suggesting the movement of air and sea, and a cool sounding trill for the flute. Fiesco, who always seems the last to hear about everything, steps forward, looking forward to one last showdown with Simon. Fiesco's multipart aria begins somberly with a serious melody declaimed over pulsing strings ("Delle faci festanti"—*In the gleam of festive torches*). He tells Boccanegra, who at first does not recognize him, that "I morti ti salutano"—*The dead greet you*. Fiesco then sings, to a strange, whirling dance, that he's there like a phantom to right an old wrong: "Come un fantasima Fiesco t'appar." But Simon shocks Fiesco: He's filled with joy to see his old nemesis, who will become an angel of peace: "Di pace nunzio Fiesco sarà."

Simon then reveals the truth about Amelia, whom Fiesco will now watch over. Fiesco's initial shock melts into grief as he realizes the magnitude of the wrong he has done Simon: "Piango, perchè mi parla"—*I weep because the voice of heaven speaks through you*. The two old foes finally reconcile, as Simon embraces Fiesco as the father of his beloved Maria. Verdi uses the pulsing three-note rhythmic device of triplets to turn the duet into a sad waltz. And he gives prominence to the woodwinds, to which he assigns long, weeping phrases. Fiesco tells Simon about the poison, but Boccanegra already senses that he's dying. He asks Fiesco to allow him to bless Amelia once more.

The others enter; all are surprised to see the old foes together. Over an extraordinarily dark accompaniment, Simon tells Amelia, "Tutto finisce, o figlia"—*Everything is ended, my daughter.* Then, to the celestial and delicate accompaniment of high set, muted strings, Simon begins the big and exceptionally beautiful ensemble that ends the opera, "Gran Dio, li benedici"—*Almighty God, bless them.* Amelia and Gabriele sing high set descants of greater melodic intensity, as down below, Fiesco intones the moral of the story: "Ogni letizia in terra è menzognero incanto"— *Happiness on earth is a deluding spell.* Verdi lightens the orchestration as Boccanegra's death approaches; with his dying breath, Simon names Gabriele as his successor. Fiesco goes to the balcony to tell a shocked crowd that Boccanegra is dead and Gabriele Adorno is their new Doge. Solemn bells sound, and the opera ends on hushed chords.

# *Choral Works*

## The Manzoni Requiem and the
## *Quattro pezzi sacri*

A part from some stray juvenilia and the cantata *Inno delle nazioni*—Hymn of the Nations—of 1862, Verdi's important choral works consist of the Requiem in memory of Alessandro Manzoni of 1874, and the *Quattro pezzi sacri*, the four sacred pieces, his final works, written between 1889 and 1897. Rarely heard, the *Inno* is exactly the kind of occasional piece Verdi despised and turned down commissions for by the dozen. But he accepted this one only, for the 1862 London Exhibition. The Italian text, by a twenty-year-old Arrigo Boito, marks the first and least known of their collaborations.

## The Manzoni Requiem

Verdi's setting of the mass for the dead began as an idea to commemorate Rossini, who died in November 1868. Having composed the closing section, "Libera me," Verdi planned to invite other Italian composers to write the remaining movements. These forgotten names, including Carlo Coccia, Alessandro Nini, and Pietro Platania, demonstrate the extent of Verdi's dominance over Italian musical life. For reasons that aren't completely clear, the Rossini Requiem never came together. But when novelist and fellow Italian cultural icon Alessandro Manzoni, author of *I promessi sposi*—The Betrothed—died on May 22, 1873, Verdi revived the idea, this time to honor Manzoni. The work had its premiere in Milan on the first anniversary of Manzoni's death, making it likely that Verdi worked on the score in the years between Rossini's death and Manzoni's.

The form of the high Catholic requiem Mass—*high* meaning one set to music—as used by Verdi, consists of seven large parts:

1. Requiem aeternam and Kyrie
2. Dies irae, sometimes called the "sequentia," or sequence
3. Offertorio
4. Sanctus
5. Agnus Dei
6. Lux aeterna
7. Libera me

The Dies irae—day of wrath—the longest section by far, contains nine distinct parts to which Verdi gives individual settings, while linking them into a unit; the Requiem aeternam and Kyrie consists of two parts, which Verdi also unifies. He radically alters the standard sequential method of setting the litany by transplanting text and associated musical ideas from the opening Requiem aeternam and the Dies irae into the final section, the Libera me, creating a cyclical, intensely dramatic form. The Dies irae stands at the heart of Verdi's vision, the terror of death and divine judgment he evokes in this long movement (within the structure of which he also reprises words and music) acting as the motor that drives this mighty work. Another aspect of Verdi's dramatic conception of the Mass is that, like operatic characters, the four soloists, especially the soprano, sing their heads off. In addition to the soprano, mezzo, tenor, and bass soloists, there's a large chorus that's kept busy with unusually difficult material, and a big orchestra that gets to play one of the master's finest scores. The Requiem has been called his greatest opera; the trite joke is on the mark to the extent it recognizes his dramatic approach to the text, its violence and agitation surpassing the Requiems of Mozart, Cherubini, Berlioz, Brahms, or Britten, or the gentle specimen by Fauré.

It's fair to speculate as to why the atheist Verdi chose to set a Catholic service. Perhaps the dramatic qualities inherent in the subject of how man faces death seemed worthwhile to Verdi the musical dramatist, with the setting of the morbid Dies irae as an enjoyably spooky exercise. As a musical tragedian, all but two of Verdi's twenty-eight operas contain deaths of important characters, and the fatalist composer himself, marked by loss early on, is quoted as saying, "What is life but death?"[1] Verdi's setting of the Requiem text has countless moments of lyrical beauty. But its expression of terror and its crushing power are what will strike you initially. These come mostly in the Dies irae and the Libera me. If you don't know the work, be prepared: it's strong stuff, grand and awe-inspiring. And in a more than a few spots it's quite remarkably loud, as Verdi effectively uses volume to evoke awe. A good performance of the Requiem can and should overwhelm.

The Requiem opens very quietly, though, with a simple, falling seven-note phrase for the cellos, replied to quietly in full harmony by the other strings. The chorus softly sings, "Requiem aeternam dona eis, Domine"— *Grant them eternal rest, o Lord*—the falling melodic pattern giving the words the effect of sighing. The material in this passage sounds free, almost spontaneous, but it's memorable as well as musically dense. The line takes a more consolatory turn with a key shift to the major for the words "Et lux perpetua luceat eis"—*And may light perpetual shine on them*. Verdi changes the key again as the chorus sings a stern a cappella passage in a hymnlike polyphonic style, to the words beginning "Te decet hymnus, Deus, in Sion"—*A hymn, o God, becometh thee in Zion*. This powerfully expressive passage winds down, leading to a condensed reprise of the opening.

But afterward the music flowers, as the woodwinds and soloists join in a radiant phrase, led heroically by the tenor, joined in turn by the bass, soprano, and mezzo-soprano as they sing "Kyrie eleison," the Greek prayer for mercy that's part of the Catholic liturgy. Listeners familiar with choral music will recognize the words for "Lord, have mercy" as they normally open other musical settings of the Mass. A pulsing, long-short-short-long figure enters, driving the movement rhythmically until the end. Verdi moves the material around, adding the prayer for mercy to Christ, "Christe eleison," in a movingly expressive plea in which the composer changes harmony freely, passing themes from voice to orchestra then back. The long-short-short-long figure, set for the strings in a hopeful rising phrase, ends the movement but this is only to raise false hope and emphasize by contrast the ferocity of the Dies irae that follows.

The text of this long passage, dating to the thirteenth century, depicting the terrors of the Day of Judgment, is full of the morbid obsessions of a superstitious age. Verdi may not have believed a word of it, but he did an extraordinary job depicting it musically. The conductor who doesn't see that the four chords for the full orchestra that open it are sharply defined and not simply rapped out as one, two, three, and four, has done a poor job. The men's chorus sings the opening line "Dies irae, dies illa, solvet saeclum in favilla"—*Day of wrath, when the world dissolves in ashes*—in sharply accented notes, then in a dissonant incarnation that sounds like the buzzing of *very* angry bees. The opening chords are repeated, this time interspersed by fearsome thwacks on the bass drum. This goes on at high speed and volume, climaxing on an iteration of the words in a memorable long-short-short-long-long rhythm that will be the leitmotif for the idea of the Day of Judgment throughout the work. The music quiets a bit, but remains dark and agitated as trumpets and winds exchange muttering figures and the chorus softly whispers its part.

Trumpets on and offstage take over, as the "Tuba mirum"—*The trumpet, scattering a wondrous sound*—depicts the heavenly trumpets that will wake the dead. The on- and offstage fanfares build threateningly as the chorus joins in thunderously. Fanfares and chorus then join in one of the stupefying moments in the Requiem as trumpet fanfares and howling chorus are met by brass and strings that shudder and winds that shriek out a falling interval in one of the most enormous gestures in music. (Pay attention to this, even though it's hard to miss.) A sharp chord breaks the passage off, as the bass, to a stunned and broken march, sings the words "Mors stupebit," which describe the shock of the natural world, and of death itself, at the mighty summons that has just occurred. The mezzo-soprano then sings, "Liber scriptus proferetur"—*A book shall be brought forth*—beginning in a tightly bound declaimed phrase that opens into a broader melody on the words "Unde mundus judicetur"—*For which the world shall be judged*. But the chorus also begins to whisper the words "Dies irae," even as the mezzo's vocal line grows more eloquent. But her line tightens again as she sings, "Judex ergo cum sedebit"—*And so when the judge takes his seat*—to an ominous dragging rhythm, then a broken scansion of "Nil inultum"—*Nothing shall remain unavenged*—over a dry string accompaniment rendered in strange, shifting harmonies. She sings a final, majestic iteration of "Liber scriptus proferetur," as the muttering of the chorus and rushing of the strings heralds an outburst of the Dies irae motif for the full orchestra and chorus.

Verdi gradually quiets the uproar to prepare for one of the lyrical high points of the Dies irae, the "Quid sum miser"—*What shall I, a wretch, say?* This delicately orchestrated trio for the soprano, mezzo-soprano, and tenor expresses the grief and fear in a sinner's soul, so Verdi's interpretation, while providing a moment of repose amid the violence, still expresses an affect deeper than melancholy, as in Bach's passions and cantatas. Here, the composer depicts spiritual pain and remorse in music of aching beauty. Sighing winds and a winding figure for a solo bassoon open and unify the section, as the mezzo, followed by the tenor, and the soprano, sing their long, arching melody; the orchestra remains silent for a few bars, as the strings take up the sighing figure at the section's quiet high point. Toward the end, the soprano sings a high B, and the passage winds down as each sings, unaccompanied, the bleak questions that form the text.

As earlier, Verdi uses a quiet passage to set the audience up for a shock, in this case, the thundering of the bass chorus and orchestra in the next section, "Rex tremendae majestatis"—*King of dreadful majesty*—set in a stark downward figure in a sharply dotted (very short–very long) rhythm that has stood for majesty in music since the baroque era. The tenors repeat the phrase, in the same rhythm but softly, in repeated notes that suggest a humanity frozen in awe at the grandeur of God and Christ. The bass soloist enters, lyrically imploring, "Salva me, fons pietatis"—*Save me, fount of pity*—followed by the mezzo and the tenor. Then, climactically, the soprano urgently sings, "Salva me," joined by the full chorus, as the basses continue to roar out, "Rex tremendae majestatis." A bold change of key turn the passage lyrical for a moment, but the basses signal a crisis as everyone else pleads for pity, and the composer pits the two contrasted ideas together, working them into a climax that is stunning in its power and volume, and another of the Requiem's overwhelming moments. But then, from the shocked silence that follows, soloists and chorus beg, at first quietly, "Salva me, fons pietatis," in a fervent phrase that builds to another climax, this one not terrible in its force, as before, but moving in its humility.

Verdi uses a rhythmic figure played by the strings to bridge the next section, "Recordare, Jesu pie"—*Remember, merciful Jesus*. In this duet for soprano and mezzo, the vocal lines intertwine in a sweeter plea, as the flute and clarinet add rhythmic punctuation. Its three-part structure sets the middle part to a more flowing rhythm, with carefully indicated hesitations that anticipate the vocal passages of the Second and Third Symphonies of Mahler, who must have known these pages well. The third section, "Juste judex ultionis"—*Just Judge of vengeance*—is close in profile to the opening, except that the strings play tremolando.

The next section, "Ingemisco tanquam reus"—*I groan as one guilty*—is sung by the tenor. It opens in a sad, reflective tone that changes to wistful with the words "Qui Mariam absolvisti"—*You, who absolved Mary*—referring here to Mary Magdalene, whom Jesus forgave. These words, and the remainder of the section is set to this warmly expressive melody, rising to a peak on a B-flat, and decorated by the winds, with the bassoon given prominence. By citing examples of Christ's mercy, the tone of this part is more tranquil. The final section, "Inter oves lacum praesta"—*Give me a place among the sheep, separate me from the goats*—sets the "Qui Mariam" melody to a wider-ranging vocal line over a spinning accompaniment, as the tenor's plea rises to another exciting B-flat. Grinding strings set the tone of "Confutatis maledictis"—*When the damned are confounded*—for the bass, but this, too, is lyrical at its long central passage, in which the bass soloist prays to Christ. Beginning with the words "Oro supplex et acclinis"—*I pray, suppliant and kneeling*—over a pulsing string accompaniment, the singer delivers a calm, steady melody that reflects one soul's remorse. Two climaxes are reached on the lines "Gere curam mei finis"—*Take my ending into your care*, as another proto-Mahlerian trudging phrase for oboes over pulsing strings signals the coda of this section.

Instead it snaps unexpectedly over a sharp harmonic edge into a full and furious restatement of the Dies irae opening, complete with big chords and stinging choral lines. But Verdi condenses, building it into a climax that leads into the final section: "Lacrimosa, dies illa"—*That will be a day of weeping*—a huge quasi-cantata set to a grandly lamenting melody over a steady pulse given by the strings. The mezzo-soprano presents the melody first. It's then sung by the bass in a contrapuntal style, with the mezzo adding weeping figures seconded by the oboe and clarinet, which sound like a counter-subject. (This great, grief-stricken melody is one Verdi originally wrote for *Don Carlo*, for Philip and the ensemble after the murder of the Marquis of Posa. It has been restored in some recent productions of the opera.) The chorus joins in, then the other soloists; this is not a fugue, though it begins like one, and Verdi builds it into a big climax reminiscent of a fugal stretto. But then the soloists sing a long a cappella passage to the words "Pie Jesu, Domine"—*Merciful lord Jesus*—in a free, hymnlike format, and counterpoint is put aside. The harmony shifts through uncertain, twilit regions, as the chorus and soloists intone, "Dona eis requiem"—*Grant them rest*—then the key shifts massively into one that's distant and somber, ending this vast movement over trembling strings and muttering brass and winds. Although in a major key and quietly stated, the closing pages express only anxiety and fear.

The Offertorio—offertory—which follows is a more ceremonial prayer that pulls back from the personal points of view depicted in the Dies irae. At its heart lies the solemn "Hostias," an expression of hope that the prayers offered (from which the name of the section is drawn) will be acceptable to God. The Offertorio opens with an expressive rising figure for the cellos, answered gracefully by the flutes, oboes, and clarinets. Immediately you will hear that the tone has changed from the anxieties and terrors of the Dies irae to something more tranquil. The tenor and mezzo enter, singing in sweet harmony the words "Domine Jesu Christe, Rex gloriae"—*Lord Jesus Christ, King of glory*—imploring Christ to "libera animas omnium fidelium defunctorum"—*Deliver the souls of the faithful departed*—from the pains of hell. This long concerted passage, richly harmonized and orchestrated, provides relief from ears and nerves shaken in the Dies irae, though the rolling 6/8 beat here soon develops into a potent swaying motion. The soprano joins in on a long-held but softly sung note, as the harmony changes celestially around her words, and the other singers fall away for a moment. They soon rejoin her, though, as the music carries the words "In lucem sanctam"—*In holy light*—on an ecstatic, fluttering accompaniment led by the flutes, clarinets, and violins, in high pizzicato notes, a stunning effect.

In the next phrase, introduced by the bass soloist, Verdi uses counterpoint, to sketch with music the countless generations of faithful suggested by the phrase "Quam olim Abrahae promisisti et semini ejus"—*Which you promised of old to Abraham and his seed*. The bass opens this impressive passage, as the other soloists join in rapid entries of the busy theme, notable for its narrow range and battery of repeated notes, suggesting crowded years of sacred history, as chromatic accents seem to emphasize further the dizzying numbers implied in those generations. An emphatic iteration on long-held notes and rich orchestral backing prepares for the central "Hostias" that forms the heart of the Offertorio.

Over trembling strings, the tenor sings one of Verdi's great melodic inspirations, to the words "Hostias et preces tibi, Dominus, laudis offerimus"—*We offer unto you, Lord, sacrifices and prayers of praise*. The range of the tune is surprisingly narrow, but its turns eloquently express its text, including a trill that comes as from within and moving upward, hovering rather than moving forward. The accompaniment is light but telling, only the trembling violins and violas, with the cellos harmonizing and accenting with pizzicati its two melodic high points. The tenor's ten-bar phrase seems to last forever, but soon the bass and other soloists join in, as do horns and woodwinds. Verdi shifts this fervent melodic idea through a rainbow of harmonies, as the female singers decorate, then take over the gradually expanding line. This magical passage is brought gently to an end on murmurs of "Fac eas, Domine, de morte transire ad vitam"—*Do this, Lord, on behalf of the souls we commemorate.* "Quam olim Abrahae" returns, definitively breaking the spell as the full orchestra joins in powerfully. It all dies down as the soloists ask God again, this time in a more darkly hued phrase seconded by ominous strings to deliver the souls of the faithful. Trembling strings soar again with the melody of the opening section echoed by a solo clarinet and an arching phrase for the cellos, much like the one that began it brings a sense of symmetry to this big movement's closing page.

At three minutes' performing time, the "Sanctus"—*Holy*—is the shortest movement of the Requiem, as well as the most brilliant. This jubilant passage traditionally summons the image of heavenly choirs praising God, as Verdi does here. Opening with sharply rhythmical blasts from the trumpets, he begins this glittering fugue for chorus with a skipping subject, sung by the sopranos. Except for one more flowing and delicate episode lasting only for a few seconds, the composer keeps the textures thick and busy. Listen, too, for the chorus singing "Osanna"—*Hosanna*—to a skittering accompaniment by the violins and flutes. Finally, scales rise and fall in the orchestra. Verdi uses these passages to build power by shifting keys, and in the last one, back in the home key, he syncopates, breaking the steady rhythm. Although over quickly, these scalar passages form another tremendous display of power. It's hard to believe that the other composers Verdi nominated as collaborators for the Rossini Requiem had anything like this in their artillery!

The "Agnus Dei"—*Lamb of God*—is a prayer to Christ, as divine sacrifice and intercessor for humanity. Composers commonly put this simple text to music that's tender, reflecting Jesus's humanity, and somewhat melancholy, as Verdi does here. Set for the female soloists and full chorus, the prayer is made of one musical thought, a serpentine melody, sung at the beginning by the soprano and mezzo, which moves at one easy tempo. The chorus and orchestra join in, softly replaying the tune. It is then restated in the minor key by the soloists, decorated by the strings and high woodwinds, making it sound more fragile and pained. The chorus then sings it, back in the original major key, with a full orchestral backing. The soloists sing it once more, this time embroidered remarkably by three flutes. Verdi breaks up the text for the closing: the chorus and orchestra take it once more, and the movement ends on the soloists and chorus alternating, then sharing the phrases for "Dona eis"—*Grant them*—and "Requiem sempiternam"—*Eternal rest*—as the violins play a sweet, rising flourish.

Verdi sets up the penultimate part, "Lux aeterna"—*Everlasting light*—as a contest between analogies for light and darkness, alternating comforting and alarming ideas, major and minor keys, bright and dark orchestral sounds. The mezzo, tenor, and bass share this powerful passage; the composer holds the soprano for her appearance in the climactic Libera me, giving her seven minutes' needed rest. Over high-set, trembling strings, the mezzo declaims, "Lux aeterna luceat eis Domine, cum Sanctis tuis in aeternum"—*Let everlasting light shine on them, Lord, with your saints forever*—in a tone that's filled with hope, but that hope is immediately disputed by the bass who sings, "Requiem aeternam, dona eis" to a dirgelike tune accompanied by a funeral march for the timpani, low brass, and bassoons, leaving no doubt as to the more somber point of view he's arguing. The mezzo and tenor rejoin him, now mournfully. Then, the three sing a long a cappella passage, like a brave hymn. But the funeral march follows once more, with the bass singing the dirge and the others decorating his melodic line. But the bass's melody opens into a magnificently impassioned plea in which he's joined by the other singers. This leads to a brighter outlook in the orchestra and, again, more hope, if not exactly good cheer, for the singers. There's another a cappella phrase, closing out the hymn, as Verdi closely alternates bright and dark orchestral affects—primarily the funeral march against shimmering string tremolos and looping embroidery for high woodwinds. The singers repeat the same few words of the prayer over and over. The contest between dark and light ends in a draw as the orchestra plays a major-key chord, darkly voiced.

"Libera me"—*Deliver me*—is the prayer carried in the closing section of the Requiem that's built in sections, some of new material, others that revisit the Dies irae, and even the opening Requiem aeternam. The movement begins plainly with the soprano, who is the only member of the solo quartet to sing in this section, intoning the opening words of her prayer urgently in a quasi-spoken passage: "Libera me, Domine, de morte aeterna in die illa tremenda; quando coeli movendi sunt et terra"—*Deliver me, Lord, from eternal death on that awful day when heaven and earth will move.* But Verdi opens her line out enormously on the words *tremenda* and *movendi*, at which point dry strings shudder frighteningly below. Murmuring a cappella, the chorus echoes her prayer, dropping an urgent-sounding half-tone for the second phrase ("Quando coeli movendi sunt"). Strings playing tremolo then recall the Dies irae motto, as the soprano sings, "Dum veneris judicare saeculum per ignem"—*When you will come to judge the world by fire*—her line expressing her (and our) terror with a difficult leap.

The four bassoons gravely introduce her next lines, a cantabile passage set to a spinning figure for the violins, playing with mutes, which a chromatic falling figure for the other strings, also muted, transform into something that seems to move outside of normal time. "Tremens factus sum ego et timeo, dum discussio venerit atque ventura ira, quando coeli movendi sunt et terra"—*I am seized with trembling and fear for the trial and the wrath to come, when the heavens and earth will move*—are the words Verdi sets to this music that speaks of cosmic terror about as well as any; and though quiet, this is another tremendous moment. The music rises to a climax at the end, and is repeated, moving instead in another, seemingly milder tonal direction, in a quiet, open phrase. What follows, though, are the four massive chords of the Dies irae, followed, by a full exposition of that frightening chorus. This is where Verdi plays most freely with form. Composers all seem to set the liturgy differently, with many returning to the "Requiem aeternam" toward the end. But Verdi is alone in bringing back the "Dies irae." By reprising the terrors of the Day of Judgment and the enormous musical gestures associated with them, he disrupts the balance and growing sense of calm other composers evoke toward the end of the litany, denying the consolation typically offered in this final section of the Requiem. His strategy may not be particularly subtle, but it's bold and devastatingly effective.

As the music gradually quiets down, the soprano joins in, again with "Dum veneris." The bassoons, trombones, cellos and bass singers growl out the words "Dies irae" on a low F; far above, an oboe sings a high F; then everything stops. Suddenly, the soprano, accompanied only by the chorus, sing the "Requiem aeternam" from the very beginning, but here with its melodic span fully worked through. This remarkable passage is very difficult, especially for the soprano, who has to make a nasty octave jump from a middle to a high B-flat marked to be sung *pianissimo*, at the end. (This treacherous jump has skunked many, including some of the best, as can be heard in live performances under Toscanini by Zinka Milanov, one of the greatest twentieth-century Verdians, who wobbles in panic as the phrase approaches, then chokes. Another admirable Verdi singer, Leontyne Price, swoops up the octave in her otherwise glorious studio account under Fritz Reiner.) There's hardly a finer example of the primacy of the voice, or of the essential humanity of this composer's style and outlook, than this crucially placed meditation for voices alone.

The soprano sings the opening of the Libera me again, as the chorus and orchestra tear into the fierce fugue that again shows Verdi's technique put to an overwhelming expressive end. You won't miss the explosive chords for the full orchestra, shocking in their force, that seem to fling the vigorous subject forward. There's a slightly more delicate staccato episode followed by a thunderous one marked by heavy blasts from the brass. The entrance of the soprano provides a genuinely soothing moment amidst the choral and orchestral fury. The emphatic rhythm to which "Libera me" is set—*long*-short-short-short—gradually assumes a greater role as the fugue progresses. The soloist sings the phrase in a new rhythm (long-short-short-long-long), which the woodwinds echo. This Verdi now spreads out into a more quiet and dark-hued incarnation, with a spinning string accompaniment reminiscent of that from "Tremens factus." At first she sings her falling line, alone. But then, the chorus rejoins, with the springing rhythm of the opening subject. His contrapuntal mastery fueled by an immense rhythmic drive, Verdi builds the bounding thematic fragment into a climactic stretto of shattering force for the full orchestra and chorus. The soprano joins, her line soaring above it all to a high C; then, everything drops away, leaving only the falling melodic fragment and the spinning figure, low in the violins. Then, with the chorus singing "Libera me," the soprano intones her half-spoken prayer from the opening of the section, as, to a slight broadening of the tempo and over massive unquiet chords for the full orchestra, the chorus joins her to sing, "Libera me . . . libera me." There's no comfort or hope in this conclusion, only uncertainty and the terror that is the hallmark of this doubter's religious masterwork.

## Quattro pezzi sacri (Four Sacred Pieces)

Three of these four choral works are Verdi's last compositions; one, the Ave Maria, was written in 1889, after *Otello* and before *Falstaff*. All are great works, as one can expect from their dating, even if they are not entirely representative of the composer's attitude toward religion. If they're exercises they are glorious ones and considering their position and significance, don't get the currency they deserve. The four pieces were published together in 1897. But the composer never viewed them as a unit and did not expect them to be performed together.[2]

The first, an Ave Maria—Hail Mary—for unaccompanied mixed chorus, is a brief but complex study in vocal textures and harmony that looks back to the Renaissance choral masters. Next in the score is Stabat Mater, a setting of a mournful medieval Latin prayer to the Virgin at the foot of the cross. Another a cappella piece, the *Laudi alla Vergine Maria*, is next. Set to a text from Dante's *Paradiso*, this short work may be the most immediately appealing. Another old prayer, the Te Deum comes last in the score, and this masterpiece for double chorus and orchestra is the longest and most elaborate of the four. Verdi's final style, concise in the extreme, makes eloquent a text other composers sometimes turn into an exercise in pomposity.

These four works share a density of texture, high polish, and rarefied musical thought that only a great composer in full maturity can achieve. The lack of rhetoric we'll hear in the late operas is reduced even further here into a pure, telegraphic style purged of excess gesture and movement in a manner reminiscent of Mozart's final works. Everything is stripped down, with rhetorical and transitional material severely limited, as Verdi moves freely from one idea to the next. And the harmony is dense and sophisticated, much like that of other masters in their final styles.

# The Great Political Tragedy
## Don Carlo

D on Carlo, Verdi's study of love, politics, and intrigue at the court of Philip II of Spain is one of his greatest works. It is also the opera with the most complex history, its writing and rewriting occupying the composer on and off from 1866 to 1886. The history of the five versions of the opera is beyond the scope of this book, but explains why there are such major differences among performances. Verdi composed *Don Carlos* for the Paris Opéra. (Note the Spanish spelling, copied directly for the French versions of the opera; *Carlo* is Italian.) Based on a play by Friedrich Schiller, the opera's French libretto was begun by Joseph Méry and completed by Camille du Locle. Schiller's parable on liberty is very much a product of its time (the 1780s). The play's political message requires its characters, especially Rodrigo, Marquis of Posa, to express ideas that did not exist in sixteenth-century Spain. Another curiosity of the story, added by Verdi and his librettists, is the presence of a mysterious monk who also seems to be Charles V, the supposedly dead father of King Philip II. Acting as a deus ex machina, the monk rescues Carlo in the opera's final moments.

Leaving aside Carlo's rescue, what makes *Don Carlo* extraordinary are the six principal roles, all of which are interesting. Carlo himself, the Infante—crown prince of Spain—is a hypersensitive, credulous young man of unformed ideas and ideals, but wild ambition and mood swings; today he'd probably be diagnosed as bipolar. Carlo himself may be weak, but Verdi's portrayal is magnificently vivid, the master capturing the prince's hair-trigger upheavals with a rapidity that anticipates *Otello*. Elisabetta, the French princess to whom Carlo is momentarily engaged, is for once, a heroine with real backbone, willing to face down Philip, her intimidating older husband. Best of all is Verdi's portrayal of King Philip, the tough but lonely monarch, intrigued by the idea of change but checkmated into a reactionary mode by the ancient, symbolically blind Grand Inquisitor, arch-enemy of all liberal thought. These two dragons do battle in the first scene of act 4, where Verdi's portrayal of men of power reaches unparalleled heights. Rounding out the principals are the forward-thinking Rodrigo and Princess Eboli, an intrigue-loving courtier.

Verdi's study of public responsibility set against private desire and sorrow also reaches a new level; *Don Carlo* and *Aida*, his next opera, forming his two most thorough and profound examinations of this favorite topic: Everyone—except the Inquisitor—has to sacrifice. The atmosphere of the opera is noble and melancholy, and its *tinta*—its indefinable Verdian color—is dark but rich. New, too, is the feeling of spaciousness and an unhurried pacing no other opera by Verdi displays quite to this degree.

The character of the work depends as well on which version you see, but the five-act versions in vogue today seem preferable to the four-act ones operagoers of the last century invariably saw and heard. The five-act version shows the beginning of the romance between Carlo and Elisabetta, adding depth to that crucial plot line. Whether or not one likes the original opening scene, showing Elisabetta in all her goodness among her people, is perhaps more a matter of taste, but that, too, is worth hearing. Although the opera was composed in French, and some advocate for productions of the French versions, you're still far likelier to see or hear it in Italian; therefore, here quotations will be in the latter language.

The opening act of the long, full version of *Don Carlo* is set in France, in the forest of Fontainebleau. It's winter, and the music depicts with a grinding, repeated interval the harshness of the woodcutters' existence. Verdi sets the onstage action against a chorus of royal hunters, heard from offstage, their horn fanfare dominating the scene musically, but also contrasting the lives of the two classes, one of which is free to entertain itself. The woodsmen's chorus, "L'inverno è duro"—*Winter is hard*—expresses their desperation, as the music, with its stern character and tough orchestration, captures the brutal nature of their lives in winter. The chorus comments bitterly on the royal hunt, heard from all around ("Fortunata è la sorte d'un re"—*Lucky is the life of a king*). Their despair reaches an intense pitch, when Princess Elisabetta, popular for her generosity, appears with her retinue. The woodsmen and their wives approach, telling of their misery. She replies comfortingly that the war with Spain is ending, and gives a gold necklace to an old widow whose sons were lost in battle. Grateful for her kindness, the woodcutters and their wives thank her in a powerful chorus, which Verdi again contrasts with the hunters and their horns. Versions of the opera that omit this scene now begin, with hunting fanfares and offstage choruses of hunters, leading directly into Carlo's recitative and aria.

Don Carlo enters an empty stage. In a yearning monologue, "Fontainebleau, foresta immensa e solitaria"—*Fontainebleau, vast and lonely forest*—he compares the frozen wastes of France to the hot gardens of his native Spain. He has come disguised with the Spanish ambassadors negotiating peace with France, hoping for a look at Elisabetta, to whom he will be betrothed. He's had his look and liked what he's seen, as he sings in a warm *romanza*, "Io la vidi"—*I saw her*—introducing this principal as a sensitive and romantic young man. Verdi will bring the aria's gently swelling melody back ironically later in the scene, and at other points in the opera. Elisabetta and Tebaldo, her page, enter; the princess and her entourage have been separated and she is lost. Taking Carlo for an ordinary member of the Spanish embassy, Elisabetta remains with him while Tebaldo spots the castle and hurries off to secure her a proper escort. To music that describes his motions, Carlo chivalrously builds a fire for Elisabetta, and the two begin a dialogue, at first polite but quickly warming as she expresses her fear that her new husband will not love her ("Ah, terror arcano invade questo core"—*A mysterious terror besets my heart*) on a grand, rising phrase. Carlo ardently assures her that the prince "Vorrà viver al vostro piè, arde d'amore"—*Will want to live at your feet; he burns with love*. But his passionate answers make her wonder who he is, and as he presents her with a portrait of Don Carlo, the mystery is solved.

The two begin an impassioned duet, "Di qual amor, di quant' ardor"—*With what love, what passion*—to a broad, noble melody, as they exchange vows to a surging and complex melodic structure, rhythmically animated by triplets, and with a notable role for the clarinet. It may remind you of "Teco io sto" from *Ballo*, in its momentum, but there's a more mature expression of love here, even though the characters are younger than Riccardo and Amelia. Note the joy Verdi expresses in their sweetly harmonized phrase "Lo disse il labbro, il ciel l'udiva"—*Our lips spoke it, heaven heard it*—which seems to find an unearthly happiness.

In their ecstasy, the couple barely takes note of a cannon shots from the Château of Fontainebleau, marking the peace treaty and, they assume, their betrothal. But when Tebaldo returns with a full retinue, it's to honor Elisabetta as the wife of Philip, Don Carlo's father, the King of Spain. The triplet rhythm of the page's announcement carries over into the desolate strettalike passage for the lovers that follows, "L'ora fatale è suonata"—*The fatal hour has struck*. This dark passage claims as its ancestor *Ballo*'s act 2 trio for Riccardo, Amelia, and Renato ("Odi tu come fremono cupi") in its gloom and fierce rhythmic drive. A march of triumph is heard in the distance; the Count di Lerma, an elderly official of the Spanish court enters, transmitting Philip's formal proposal. The chorus of French women urges Elisabetta to accept, and with no alternative, she faintly agrees. The lovers bewail their fate as the chorus with unknowing irony blesses the Princess for her good fortune.

They resume their desperate duet ("Mi sento morir"—*I feel I'm dying*) over a triumphant chorus, much as Aida and Radamès will, as duty trumps their frail hopes. As Lerma and members of the two courts escort Elisabetta off, Carlo is left alone and despairing, in the wintry forest, at night. In Verdi's gripping fade-down, he must curse fate ("Ahimè"—*Alas*) for the first time, but not the last, against the voices of the chorus and the triumphant march as it fades off into the distance.

Act 2, which is broken into two enormous scenes, and the remainder of the opera, are set in Spain. A somber introduction for horns sets a mood of oppressive gloom. The setting is the tomb of the Emperor Charles V, father of Philip and grandfather of Don Carlo. The historical Charles, a Habsburg prince who inherited the Spanish throne, is the Don Carlo of *Ernani*. Charles abdicated in 1556 and retired to the monastery of San Yuste, where in 1558 he died and was buried. Verdi turns him—or his ghost, it's not clear which—into the deus ex machina you'll see here and in the final act. Monks are heard chanting a cautionary hymn in memory of the dead king, "Carlo, il sommo imperatore"—*Charles, the supreme emperor*. As they sing that Charles is now ashes, his haughty spirit trembling before God, alternating major and minor phrase endings summon disturbing intimations of eternity.

A basso "friar," who is either Charles V or his ghost, joins in, over the chanting, in a mighty warning that blends declaimed and cantabile delivery, that "L'orgoglio immenso fu, fu l'error suo profondo"—*His pride was immense, his error profound.* The monks repeat their chant, to eerie interjections by the brass and the winds, including the piccolo, echoing distantly above, again suggesting vast time and space. In one of the titanic moments in this opera, marked "*grandioso*" by the composer, the friar sings, "Grand' è Dio sol"—*Great is God alone*—to a surging, melodic line that's of passionate conviction and fearful intensity. The passage winds down majestically with an orchestral reflection on the friar's surging melody. Verdi turns what could have been an exercise in mood setting into a meditation on human suffering and its causes.

A sad Don Carlo enters, soliloquizing that his search for peace in the monastery has been in vain. Nor does the reappearance of the friar, who sings another solemn moral about earthly woes, put him any more at ease, as he nervously sings that the friar's voice sounded like his grandfather's, and "È voce che nel chiostro appaia ancor"—*They say he still appears in the cloister.* His close friend Rodrigo, the Marquis of Posa, enters and the two greet each other rapturously. Rodrigo tells Carlo that the people of Flanders, a Spanish possession, are suffering, and need his leadership. Carlo replies passionately that Rodrigo is his savior. Noticing Carlo's sorrowful manner, Rodrigo encourages the Prince to tell him its cause, but even Posa is appalled as Carlo admits to loving Elisabetta "d'un colpevol amor"—*with a guilty love.* (Carlo's guilt and Posa's horror seem odd, since Elisabetta is not Carlo's mother, but his stepmother, close to his age, and only recently his intended bride; but perhaps the plot twist worked for pre-Freudian audiences.) Carlo feels more alone than ever now that his friend is shocked, but Rodrigo immediately rallies: "Tu soffri? Già per me l'universo dispar"—*You're suffering? Then the whole universe is as nothing to me.* Rodrigo presses Carlo to get Philip's permission to govern Flanders. He also tells Carlo that Philip and Elisabetta are coming to visit Charles's tomb. Carlo is terrified at the prospect of seeing his beloved, but Rodrigo urges him to be strong.

They launch into their famous duet "Dio, che nell'alma infondere"—*God, to instill love and hope in our souls*—in which they swear an oath to liberty and to each other. Set to a rousing tune, and sung in harmony that's mostly old-fashioned and comfortable, too, the duet looks backward. It's catchy, though, as is the brassy but stirring orchestral punctuation. But the duet is interrupted as Philip and Elisabetta, now Queen, enter. As the monks resume their chant from the opening of the act, Carlo cries out in rising *declamato* interjections: "Ei la fe' sua ... Io l'ho perduta ..."— *He has made her his . . . I have lost her*—on seeing his beloved as his father's wife, his cries slicing desperately through the chanting. Here again, Verdi portrays the individual, symbolized by Carlo's voice, as it's hemmed in by circumstance, duty, and religion. Rodrigo comforts his friend, but the mysterious friar also chimes in again, and the effect of this complex, fast-moving ensemble is hair-raising. Carlo and Rodrigo resume their duet, ending on "Libertà" and a thunderous orchestral postlude hammers the melody of their duet home.

The enormous second scene is set in the garden of the San Yuste monastery, which Philip and Elisabetta are visiting. The ladies of the court, including the vain and colorful Princess of Eboli, are waiting at a fountain for the Queen. The scampering orchestral introduction tells us that the heavy mood of the opening scene has lifted. Tebaldo and the ladies of the court are chatting idly about the pleasant spot ("Sotto ai folti, immensi abeti"—*Beneath the huge, dense firs*). They decide to pass the time singing the "Saracen song," more familiar to opera fans as the "Veil Song" because the refrain begins with the words "Tessete i veli, vaghe donzelle"—*Weave veils, fair damsels*. The thundering orchestral introduction in a bolero rhythm sets an unmistakably Spanish tone. Eboli, with Tebaldo joining in for the refrain, sing a long duet that tells of a Moorish king who has tired of his queen, seeing a pretty girl behind a veil. He tries to seduce her, but she turns out to be the disguised queen he wanted to abandon, ironically prefiguring a situation of mistaken identity that occurs in the first scene of act 3. A great showpiece for mezzo-sopranos, it's notable for its trills and for two long cadenzas that take the mezzo up to an A and on passage of quick, low-lying notes marked by Verdi to be sung *"come un mormorio"*—like a murmur. Verdi added the "Veil Song" because Pauline Gueymard-Lauters, the first to sing Eboli, demanded a bigger entrance and had the clout in Paris to get her way.[1] But it's undoubtedly a great mood changer and act opener.

Elisabetta enters, her misery depicted by a sighing introduction for the strings and a solo oboe. Eboli comments on the Queen's mysterious sadness. Posa enters; he hands Elisabetta a letter from her mother in Paris, at the same time slipping her a note from Carlo. Rodrigo now shows his skills as a courtier, distracting the ladies, particularly Eboli, with chatter about fashions and goings-on at the French court so as to give the startled

Elisabetta a few moments to read the letter, in which Carlo begs a brief audience: "'Per la memoria che ci lega'"—*"For the memories that bind us."* Elisabetta is alarmed by his direct approach; and though Rodrigo flatters Eboli outrageously, this perfect narcissist somehow concludes that Carlo has fallen in love with her. Verdi's elegant music, reminiscent of the final scene of *Ballo*, depicts Rodrigo's ability to charm. Then, in a plea that captures his earnest side ("Carlo del Re suo genitore"—*Carlo has always found his father's heart closed*), he implores the Queen to grant Carlo an audience. Rodrigo takes Eboli's arm, and leads her to the back of the stage for more flattery while, to a somber phrase for woodwinds, Carlo enters for the meeting with his stepmother ("Io vengo a domandar"—*I come to ask a favor*). Although Carlo begins with deliberate calm, he is within moments growing excited as he tells Elisabetta that life at court is suffocating him ("Quest'aura m'è fatale") and though she displays only sympathy, he is soon singing, *"con disperazione,"* that he must be allowed to go to Flanders. With great control Elisabetta replies that she will ask the King. But Carlo's self-control, already shaky, has been shattered by seeing Elisabetta. To shuddering strings, weeping woodwinds, and bold changes of tonality, he drops all pretense of etiquette, asking how she can be so cool toward him ("Mi volsi a un gelido marmo d'avel"—*I have asked a cold, marble tombstone*). His agitated declaimed vocal line reaches to an excited B-flat. She replies that she's anything but indifferent, but that "Dover"—*Duty*—comes first.

Apparently demented, Carlo sings to her in one of the opera's most extraordinary melodies, and translucent orchestration, that he's ready to die of love at her feet; Verdi's bold harmonic shifts describe a love that is not of this world. Carlo swoons from passion; Elisabetta, wondering whether he has really died, prays that his suffering be ended, referring to him tellingly as "Colui che il ciel mi destinò"—*The man heaven destined for me.* But Carlo awakens, and, to a languid but lush melodic phrase, "Qual voce a me dal ciel," asks what voice has descended to him from heaven. She shares his emotion, but aware of their danger as he is not, displays a sensible alarm. Then, to a dark cabaletta-like passage ("Sotto al mio pie"—*Were the earth to open beneath my feet*), he tells her he loves her and embraces her. As she recoils, Elisabetta startles Carlo with a powerful phrase evoking the shade of Oedipus. Crying out that he's cursed ("Maledetto io son"), Carlo rushes wildly off.

To a dotted rhythm suggesting his innate authority, Philip enters. Seeing Elisabetta alone, he asks why she's unattended, against his specific order, and whose responsibility it was for the day. The Countess d'Aremberg, one of her French ladies-in-waiting, steps forward. He tells her roughly that she's to return to France in the morning. The chorus comments that he has insulted the Queen. Elisabetta then sings an exquisite, consoling cantabile to her attendant and friend, "Non pianger, mia compagna"—*Don't weep, my companion*. This three-part cantabile opens with a weeping melody English horn and limping strings, followed by a consoling major-key section as she recalls France fondly, and gives the Countess a ring as a keepsake. The deeply expressive vocal line touches on B-flat, and there's an A at the end, but the vocal line remains comfortable and easy, and should give no sense of strain or showiness.

The ladies and the court exit. Philip orders Rodrigo to stay behind; the dialogue that follows is another highlight of the score. The King asks Rodrigo why he, a brave warrior for Spain, has never asked for a favor. Posa replies that he has no need of royal favor; the law is his shield. Philip warns, "L'audacia perdono . . . non sempre"—*I pardon boldness . . . but not always*. Seizing his moment, Posa raises the dangerous issue of Spanish tyranny in Flanders. He reports in a lurid description that war has brought the province to ruin. The music accompanying his rapid *declamato* narrative paints the turbulence and horror of the words in lamenting accents and hollow harmonies. Philip replies that he could only achieve his goals "Col sangue sol"—*With blood alone*—and that all is peaceful here in Spain. Philip mentions "i novator"—*the innovators*—whose ideas of freedom seduce the people. This anachronistic reference comes from Schiller, who placed eighteenth-century ideas into Philip's world. To a raw, nearly atonal accompaniment, Rodrigo shouts that Philip's peace is "Orrenda pace! la pace è dei sepolcri"—*Horrid peace, the peace of the tomb*. He tries to persuade the King that by granting freedom his reputation will change and make him like a God to his subjects. Calling Rodrigo a strange dreamer, Philip warns him, to a memorable phrase backed by heavy chords for the full orchestra all the more threatening for their *pianissimo* delivery, that he has nothing to fear from the King, but to beware of the Grand Inquisitor. Our sympathy for Philip soars as we see him as intrigued by Posa's idealism; we wonder if he was an idealist when young. Won by Posa's independence, Philip pours out his heart as he has to no man, that he is wretched with suspicion over his son and the Queen. Before the King's words are out, Rodrigo defends Carlo: "Fiera ha l'alma insiem e pura"—*His soul is both proud and pure*. Philip tells Rodrigo that he needs one man to confide in, and that he is that man. We now see Philip the autocrat of the opening of the scene in an utterly different light, as isolated, unhappy, and of real depth. To himself, Rodrigo rejoices in a rising phrase that the inscrutable Philip has revealed himself: "S'aprì quel cor che niun potè scrutar"—*That heart which none could read has opened*. Hoping that access will allow him to influence the King politically, Rodrigo continues to rejoice, to his rising phrase. Philip warns Rodrigo once more of the Grand Inquisitor, to the same heavy chords. The King extends his hand as a mark of favor; Rodrigo kneels and kisses it as the curtain falls on this brilliant study of how power is gained and exercised.

Act 3 is big, like its predecessor, but also more fluid and better pro-portioned. The first scene is based on some of the most well used operatic conventions—that of mistaken identity and an assignation gone bad in the dark of night—but Verdi's passionate and propulsive music makes it fly. A tranquil prelude based on the melody of "Io la vidi," Carlo's *romanza* from the first act, for clarinets, bassoons, horns, and cellos, opens the scene set in the Queen's garden in Madrid. Carlo enters reading a letter he believes to be from Elisabetta, setting a midnight meeting. The unsigned letter is, however, from Eboli. Never on an even keel, the Prince declares he's drunk with love ("Ebbro d'amor"); and his excitement builds as Eboli enters, veiled. "Sei tu, bell'adorata"—*It's you, my beautiful love*—he sings to a wavering, agitated melody. For the moment, Eboli is just as happy; as Carlo sings a leaping melody of epic cut, rhythmically animated by trip-lets ("L'universo obliam"—*Let us forget the whole world*). But this glory is cut short as Eboli unveils herself and Carlo foolishly exclaims, "Ciel! Non è la Regina!"—*It's not the Queen!* To an intimate melody, marked by repeated notes ("V'è ignoto forse"—*Perhaps you don't know yet*), Eboli asks Carlo what is wrong, says she loves him, and suggests Posa and his father are allied against him. As courteously as he can, Carlo tries to extricate himself: "Il vostro inver celeste è un core"—*You have a divine heart*—but finally putting it all together, Eboli realizes that Carlo loves the Queen.

Rodrigo enters, telling Eboli that Carlo is demented. But Eboli is sure of what she has heard. Rodrigo threatens her, but she replies that she knows his strength as the King's confidant, but he does not understand hers, referring to the as yet unrevealed fact that she is Philip's mistress. This all passes very quickly, to a violent, Beethoven-esque accompaniment. The three principals open a concerted passage, opened by Eboli's stinging line "Al mio furor"—*From my fury*—in which each expresses a different affect. Eboli sings that she's a wounded tigress; Rodrigo tries unsuccessfully to intimidate her, and Carlo laments his folly. Rodrigo even draws his dagger and threatens to kill her. A horrified Carlo restrains him, and soon Posa throws down his weapon, saying, "No, una speme mi resta"—*One hope remains*. He has, as we'll see, decided to place himself in the path of the Inquisition. The three tear into a stretta of tremendous ferocity, opened again by Eboli ("Trema per te, falso figliuolo"—*Fear for yourself, false son*). Setting this to a melody of sharp profile and marked by biting triplets, Verdi develops the rhythm into a new pulse stuttering with rage, building the trio to a quick and exciting ending, as Eboli storms off. Rodrigo asks Carlo for any personal documents that might incriminate him. The Prince hesitates, asking ironically whether it's safe to give them "all'intimo del Re"—*to the King's confidant*—but Rodrigo's sad reproach returns him to his senses as the scene ends to a recapitulation of their oath theme.

The second scene, set in a square in Madrid, depicts an auto-da-fé, those blends of prayer and punishment for which the Spanish Inquisition is infamous. A fierce introduction in a "Spanish" rhythm and pealing bells set the scene. The chorus sings in praise of Philip ("Spuntato ecco il dì d'esultanza"—*The day of rejoicing has dawned*) then, to a funeral march dominated by ominous low winds, monks of the Inquisition escort heretics who are to be burned at the stake. The opening chorus is repeated to massive fanfares. The church doors are opened, revealing Philip, wearing the crown; an organlike fanfare for the full orchestra proclaims his majesty. He explains, in recitative, why it is his duty to "Dar morte ai rei col fuoco e con l'acciar"—*Put the wicked to death by fire and sword*. But Carlo enters, leading six Flemish deputies; with poor timing and exceptional tactlessness he approaches his father. These six bassos, in a smooth but sad melody punctuated by a weeping figure for the oboe, implore the King for mercy. Of course, Philip must obey stated policy in so public a setting. He accuses them harshly of rebellion, as do the monks, in a menacing unison. But the court, including Elisabetta, Carlo, and Rodrigo, begs him in lyrical phrases to show mercy. Carlo and Elisabetta's vocal lines rise above the huge ensemble but Philip angrily orders the Flemings away. Again, Carlo approaches Philip, asking him to be made governor of Flanders so he may learn to rule ("Se Dio vuol che il tuo serto questa mia fronte"—*If it be God's will that one day your crown will circle my brow.* Enraged, Philip says that Carlo will use his new power against himself; Elisabetta expresses terror; Rodrigo succinctly says, "Ei si perdè"—*He is lost!* Overexcited as usual, Carlo draws his sword, yelling that he will save the Flemish people. Philip calls for the guards to disarm him, but none are willing to touch the Crown Prince—except Posa, who steps up to his friend, saying, "A me il ferro"—*Give me your sword.* To a faint echo of their oath by the clarinets, Carlo hands over the weapon.

Philip promotes Posa to Duke; and orders that the ceremony continue, which it does to choral odes and brassy fanfares. The Flemish deputies comment in low voices on the barbarous injustice that Heaven is suffering, when an unseen high soprano voice, detached from the action, sings that the poor souls of the day's victims may now "Volate verso il ciel"—*Soar toward heaven.* Although only sixteen bars long, a voice of great purity is needed, as the Heavenly Voice touches B several times and trills conspicuously for one long measure. But a greater mystery than casting is just who or what she is. In spite of its sharply drawn characters, *Don Carlo* is not entirely realistic, but at times a dreamlike work in which primal conflicts and desires are played out. The Heavenly Voice, like the mysterious friar of acts 1 and 5, is a deus ex machina—a divine intervention—for the sake of the suffering heretics, dying for the edification and amusement of the faithful.

Verdi was proud of the scene, and critics and nineteenth-century audiences found it impressive and effective.[2] Modern audiences, unhappy with what it shows and the accompanying pomp of the marches and processions, find it less convincing than the opera's more personal moments. But to be fair, the scene is tightly constructed and effective in its representations of the conflict between father and son. Moreover, the Parisian audience wanted spectacle, and that's what Verdi gave them.

The fourth act is set in two brilliant scenes that overflow with great music. The opening scene shows a sleepless Philip, alone in his study, brooding on his unhappy marriage and existence. Verdi and his librettists grew a brief soliloquy from Schiller's play into an expansive, sorrow-laden moment that broadens and deepens our sympathy for this remarkable character. Sitting at his document-strewn desk, the King reflects of his young wife that "Ella giammai m'amò"—*She never loved me*. He recalls bitterly her sad look on first seeing his white head ("Contemplar triste in volto il mio crin bianco"). Shaking himself, Philip notes the late hour, his ennui, and his inability to sleep. I'll sleep, he reflects majestically, "Sol sotto la vôlta nera, là, nell'avello dell'Escurial"—*Only beneath the black vault of my tomb in the Escorial* [the Spanish royal tomb]. He wishes the crown gave him the power to read human hearts, then thinks bitterly on the dual betrayals he suspects of Carlo and Elisabetta.

Verdi's music for this soliloquy is all one could wish for, and more. The prelude, to which the aria is linked, begins with a grinding half-tone figure like the one that opened the opera, portraying before a word is sung the protagonist's grinding sorrow and the obsessive quality of his thoughts. (Verdi structures the aria so that its handful of musical themes and the words they carry are repeated, with the end mirroring the opening.) Then in the greatest of all his parings of a low male voice with the cello, here virtually a second voice, that instrument adds a nearly continuous commentary that speaks with all Philip's sorrow and dignity. Muted violins take up a rolling figure that obsessively covers the same notes over and over. Over trembling strings, Philip quietly declaims his opening line ("Ella giammai m'amò"). A long flute trill joins the eloquent cello commentary. Then in a more passionate phrase, rising to an E (difficult for Philip, a bass), he admits to himself once more that she has never loved him. As he pulls himself together, noting the late hour, the cellos play a rising figure. In a huge, falling phrase, he notes his sleeplessness. Following a "*lungo silenzio*"—long silence—written into the score, the grinding figure returns, now played by the oboe. The King's reflection on the sleep of death begins in a contained vocal line that opens out grandly at the end. The tempo of the piece never changes, but Verdi gives quicker notes to the accompaniment of his titanic setting of Philip's wish to read men's hearts, the aria's affective centerpiece and musical high point. Philip's line curls throughout, reaching a D, then an E-flat on a curving run: this omniscience is what he wishes for above all. Verdi brings the phrase to a climax on the word "leggere"—*read*—marked by a massive key change and a rising triplet figure for the bassoons and low strings. The cellos, moving swiftly now, but over a turning figure, accompany his bitter reflection on Carlo and Elisabetta. Verdi unhurriedly moves the aria toward its conclusion, repeating but condensing its ideas, then falling softly away, to a fluid figure for the cellos.

"Ella giammai m'amò" shows exactly what makes opera work. As singing adds time to the delivery of words, these must be kept brief, and the music has to let the ideas and feelings expand. Verdi finds a voice for those few thoughts running around Philip's mind late on another of his sleepless nights. If his character intrigues us, then this tremendous confession grows our sympathy for him geometrically.

The next scene, the King's confrontation with the Grand Inquisitor, displays still more sides to his character. To a dirgelike theme, reminiscent of the music that accompanied Rigoletto's conversation with Sparafucile, but made darker and more threatening by the sound of the brass, rumbling timpani, and the weird growling of the contrabassoon this fearsome personage enters. Ninety years old and blind, the Inquisitor proceeds to dominate the King, who has summoned him for advice on how to deal with Carlo. Philip, wondering whether he can take "Mezzo estrem"—*Extreme measures*—against his own son, receives shockingly easy approval from the old man, who draws on a bottomless reservoir of cant ("Per riscattarci, Iddio il suo sacrificò"—*To redeem us, God sacrificed his [son]*) to justify the horrific deed. When Philip asks if nature and love, of which he truly has little for Carlo, can be sacrificed, the Inquisitor replies readly, "Tutto tacer dovrà per esaltar la fè"—*Everything must be silenced to exalt the faith*. Verdi's music consistently portrays an extraordinarily dark orchestral palette, dominated by the trombones moving in a limping rhythm, the troubled King's questions and the certainty of the cagey old priest's replies, to chords on the beat, also darkly accompanied, of course. Verdi casts their relationship as a vocal contest, as each tends to answer the other at a slightly higher pitch. Much credit goes to Schiller, too, for the brilliance of his original dialogue, couched in an exciting stichomythia—those rapidly exchanged short lines.

Uneasy but satisfied for the moment, Philip has nothing else to discuss with the Inquisitor. But the old priest is not finished; listen for his remarkable low E on "Sire." Beginning blandly, the Inquisitor says that heresy has never flourished in Spain, but that a certain intimate friend of the King's represents a threat far more dangerous than Carlo. Again, the cello plays a crucial role, threading the orchestral accompaniment, this time with a more stern fixity in its line. As though accusing himself he notes, with the cellos rumbling authoritatively below, that he, the Inquisitor ("Io, L'Inquisitor"), has allowed this miscreant (Posa)—and the King—to go unchecked. Now on the spot, Philip replies, to a spare, bleak accompaniment, that he has found a loyal man to help him through his lonely days ("i dì dolente"). The Inquisitor replies that as King no man is his equal. Angrily Philip warns him to stop ("Non più, frate!"—*No more, priest!*). Assuming for a moment a blandly wheedling tone, echoed by mild woodwinds playing churchy, choralelike chords, the Inquisitor says the ideas of the innovators have tainted the King, and that he should return to obedience to the Church. He ends by asking the King to hand over Posa. Philip cries out "Giammai"—*Never!*—as the Inquisitor bares his fangs, arrogantly telling the King that he's ready to haul Philip himself "al tribunal supremo"—*before the supreme court*. Again, Philip protests, but in the final, and most chilling part of his exchange, the Inquisitor tells Philip that he has crowned two kings, and that he won't permit Philip to destroy his work of years ("L'opra di tanti dì"). The Inquisitor makes it clear that Spain is his creation, and that he's still in charge. Furious, the old man asks, to thumping chords for low brass, "Che vuol il Re da me?"—*What does the King want of me?* Philip buckles, begging for peace. He asks the Inquisitor to forget what has passed there, to which he gets the icy reply "Forse"—*Perhaps*—as the old man is led from the room, to the limping figure on which he came in. In a vast, despairing phrase containing a two-octave drop, Philip comments, "Dunque il trono piegar dovrà sempre all'altare!"—*The throne must always bow to the altar*, ending this power struggle masked as intellectual debate. You'll grasp its greatness on first hearing, and longer acquaintance will deepen your respect.

If the opening portions of act 4—Philip's monologue and his confrontation with the Grand Inquisitor—are transcendent, the three concluding sections of this huge scene merely show Verdi at his usual high standard. The King's bad day gets worse as Elisabetta storms in, demanding justice ("Giustizia, Sire!"—*Justice, my lord!*) and to know how her jewel casket, containing cherished items, has been stolen. Lifting the item from his desk, the King coolly asks whether that's what she's looking for. He opens it, finding Carlo's portrait. She warmly defends herself, replying ("Ben lo sapete"—*You know well*) that she has the memento from the time of her betrothal to Carlo. Philip, already angry, warns her not to provoke him further then to a furious orchestral accompaniment accuses her of adultery. She faints, and Philip calls for help. Eboli, guilty of having stolen the casket, enters as does Rodrigo, who chides Philip that he controls a vast empire, but not his own temper. The four sing a lyrical reflection, begun by the King, "Ah, sii maledetto"—*Cursed be the fatal suspicion*—in which he and Eboli sing of their separate reasons for remorse, Posa that the time for action has come, and Elisabetta that she feels hopelessly alone in this foreign land ("Io son straniera in questo suol"). The King's and Eboli's vocal lines are both mostly declaimed, but accompanied at first by a smooth cello line; Rodrigo's, too, as he sings resolutely that he's ready to die for Spain. Accompanied by celestial flutes, the Queen's long line rises above the others. Philip and Rodrigo leave, and Eboli throws herself at the Queen's feet. Dramatically she confesses to stealing the casket, to accusing Elisabetta of adultery, of loving Carlo herself, and finally she chokes out over a heavy figure for the strings that she has "seduced" the King. Elisabetta, shows her own regal bearing, telling Eboli coldly that she must leave the court in the morning for a nunnery or exile. No stranger to court politics, Elisabetta knows that she's striking back at Philip as well.

Alone onstage, Eboli sings her great solo "O don fatale"—*O fatal gift*—in which she laments the beauty that makes her vain and haughty. This well-known aria, one of the finest for mezzo-sopranos, begins with a declaimed pattern that rises and falls quickly, punctuated by a snapping figure for horns and strings. Unusually for a mezzo, the vocal line surges up to a B, with the next section, in contrasting cantabile in which Eboli laments her sacrificing the Queen for her own folly ("O mia Regina") to steadier, even notes, but her agitation and sorrow are still clear, only moving in a different affective direction, and rising to a B-flat. In the closing cabaletta-like section she resolves over thumping timpani to save the Prince in the one day she has remaining. A thrilling showpiece, "O don fatale" makes a powerful statement of contrition as well.

The heavy mood of the second scene of act 4 is set by a prelude for strings, to which the oboe adds a sad reminiscence of the love duet from the first act. Carlo is shown, imprisoned; Rodrigo enters and the two begin a dialogue in which the Prince says his energy is gone but that he's still tormented by love for Elisabetta. Carlo tells Rodrigo that he must carry on their struggle. Rodrigo replies, in his long aria "Per me giunto è il dì supremo"—*For me the final day has come*—that they will not see each other again. The first portion is a cantabile with an enormous, arching melody, immensely flattering to the baritone voice and a big audience favorite. The Prince is baffled; Rodrigo explains that he has Carlo's correspondence with Flemish rebels, and that he's now hunted as head of the liberation movement. As Rodrigo sings, an assassin shoots him, and, first telling Carlo to meet Elisabetta at San Yuste the next day, he launches into a long death aria that's a continuation of the thematic material from "Per me giunto." Verdi adds poignant touches, including a reminiscence of their oath duet, and the usual flutes and harps that speak of approaching death. Vocally the line reaches to a G-flat, and Rodrigo dies, rather bizarrely exhorting Carlo to "Salva la Fiandra"—*Save Flanders*. Rodrigo's long sequence works its suave baritonal magic better in the theater than on recordings.

At this point, two versions of the opera may be heard. Philip enters, accompanied by members of his court. The King offers his son back his sword as Carlo mourns Posa and accuses his father of murder, yelling that "Tu più figlio non hai"—*You no longer have a son.* Contemplating the dead Rodrigo, the King asks himself, "Chi rende a me quell'uom?"—*Who will restore this man to me?* Most performances have used the version that cuts directly to the riot that ends the act; but one early version has a long ensemble in which the King sings a lament to Posa, using the melody to which the composer eventually set the "Lacrimosa" section of the Requiem. Heard more frequently lately, this four-minute addition is quite interesting, but does slow down the action.

Bells ring, and the chorus offstage is heard crying for Carlo to be freed. Philip tells the guard to let the mob in; as together he and the Grand Inquisitor face the rioters down. "Vi prostrate innanzi al Re, che Dio protegge"—*Prostrate yourself before the King, whom God protects*—the Inquisitor roars. Since everyone is afraid of him, the mob falls to its knees. The music of this short scene races; dramatically everything happens so fast that some confusion about what the mob wanted might arise. What's admirably clear is that the King and the old priest work together, the King fronting for the church. Philip needs its support, and the Inquisitor holds the strings.

The relatively brief fifth act opens with a spacious orchestral prelude in which the trombones and tuba dominate a somber setting of the monks' chant from act 2 scene 1. But the violins, played high, join in a passionate and majestic expansion of that tight sequence. Then, as the full orchestra joins in, a new phrase presses ahead urgently, followed by a turning figure that will figure prominently in Elisabetta's aria. Waiting for Carlo at the tomb of Charles V, Elisabetta sings her great apostrophe to the dead king, "Tu, che le vanità" (CD Track 13)—*You, who knew the vanities of the world*. Verdi sets the grand opening phrase to wide-spanning melody with a *declamato* flavor, changing to the tonic major key and over pulsing triplets a sweeter setting for the words "S'ancor si piange in cielo"—*If they still weep in heaven*—with which she asks the dead monarch to carry her tears to God. The spinning figure enters in the violins, then the cantabile breaks off, as to a nervous staccato figure for the strings, she narrates in recitative that Carlo is coming; that she swore to Posa to protect the Prince, and that her life is now over. As the flute makes the act 1 love duet sound distant and fragile, Elisabetta, recalls her homeland nostalgically. The dreamy theme from Carlo's delirium in act 2 scene 1, she sings poignantly of the love that "Un giorno sol durò"—*Lasted only a day*. A more urgent short-long figure for the winds animates the next section, in which she bids farewell to "Bei sogni d'ôr, illusion perduta"—*Golden dreams and lost illusions*, ending on an emphatic statement that "Il cor ha un sol desir: la pace dell'avel!"—*My heart has one desire, the peace of the grave*. This thought brings the aria full circle, with a sense of terrible inevitability, to a restatement of the opening theme, only this time over a fiercely pulsing accompaniment. Verdi turns the second iteration of her request for Charles to lay her tears at God's feet into a richly scored climax, in which the singer touches A-sharp twice; but the feeling here is of deep sincerity.

Carlo enters, and the two begin their long duet of farewell. First they speak quietly, telling each other to be strong for Rodrigo's sake. But as the flutes utter a dreamy theme to pizzicato strings, Carlo sings not of love, but of his fantasized self-sacrifice for Flanders ("Vago sogno m'arrise"—*A lovely dream smiled at me*). He never seems crazier than here, when he describes himself as a savior. Nor does Elisabetta puncture his grandiosity as, to a march marked by chattering trumpets, she barks that his works make a god of a man ("Fa dell'uomo un Dio"), then for him to go to his Calvary ("Sali il Calvario"). This unpleasant passage moves by quickly, and musical matters improve as the two say goodbye, first to a weeping lament for Carlo ("Or che tutto finì"—*Now that all is over*), then to a piercing phrase ("Ma lassù ci vedremo"—*But above we shall meet*) first sung by Elisabetta but in which they both soon join, to the commentary of pulsing strings and a liquid clarinet. This beautiful passage forms the lyrical climax of the act. They even assume their formal roles as mother ("Mio figlio, addio!") and son ("Addio, mia madre!"). Philip and the Grand Inquisitor enter with armed officers of the Inquisition, interrupting their reverie.

Verdi conceived a few endings for the opera's various versions. All begin with the King repeating the last words of the interrupted duet, "Per sempre"—*Forever*—ironically agreeing with the would-be lovers. He says to the Inquisitor, "Io voglio un doppio sacrifizio"—*I demand a double sacrifice*—to which the Inquisitor replies that Holy Office will do its part. Carlo desperately tries to fight off the guards, to furiously busy strings. But to a crash from the orchestra, the Friar from act 2 appears, wearing the crown of Charles V, singing another moral about earthly strife and heavenly peace ("Il duolo della terra nel chiostro ancor ci segue"—*Earthly suffering still follows us into the cloister*). Over a thumping figure for the orchestra, the blind Inquisitor cries out, "È la voce di Carlo!"—*It's the voice of Charles!* A terrified Philip sings, "Mio padre!" Elisabetta sings, on a clinching high B, "Oh, ciel!"—*Oh, heaven!* To the monks' chant from the opening of act 2, here roared out by the brass, the Friar, whoever he may be, leads a bewildered Carlo into the cloister. One version of the final bars races furiously to a *fortissimo* closing that was for years the only one to be heard. The other, performed with more frequency lately, quiets down after the shocked exclamations and brassy reiteration of the chant, dropping away to a *pianissimo* final cadence. Both are great, but it may be that the quiet version is more in keeping with the spectral nature of the denouement.

Critics consider the deus ex machina ending unsatisfactory, a convention that was way out of date when Verdi used it. Schiller's tough ending has Carlo and Elisabetta surprised in her room by Philip and the Inquisitor, and the King handing both over. Although weaker, Verdi's ending still works, up to a point, surely because the Friar, or Charles V, is a real character in the opera who makes a huge impact with his appearance in act 2. Even though he and his action may not make sense, our skepticism over his identity is long abandoned.

# A Farewell to Grand Opera

## Aida

Verdi composed *Aida* on a commission for the opening of Cairo Opera House, where the opera had its premiere in December 1871, the Egyptian subject a tribute to the country where it was first performed. Antonio Ghislanzoni, a singer and writer who collaborated with Verdi on the Milan revision of *Forza* after Piave's incapacitating stroke wrote the libretto, with the composer's constant coaching. Verdi conceived *Aida* as a grand opera in the Parisian style but in a modified form. Instead of five acts, there are four; instead of one long ballet, there are three, all quite short. The well-known second scene of act 2, known as the triumphal scene, fits the Parisian model for grand spectacle. The 1840s and 1850s (when Verdi wrote *Les vêpres siciliennes* for Paris) were the glory days for grand opera. But it was still alive in the late 1860s when he composed his first versions of *Don Carlos* and began work on *Aida*. The public has always loved *Aida*, but as we'll see, critics have come to question aspects of the work.

Although among the most popular of all operas, the grand scale of *Aida* makes it difficult to produce, and one of the most misunderstood, too. Staging problems include the need for a large cast and chorus, all of whom (plus elephants and camels such as each company can muster) are needed for the act 2 triumphal scene. Verdi's conception of the opera's closing scene suffers without his two-level set, which is beyond the reach of many a smaller company. Singers with big voices capable of cutting through a large chorus and orchestra are needed for principal roles in the ensemble numbers of the first and second acts. All these factors and more add up to make *Aida* the turf of big opera companies. Yet while the opera is no intimate work à la *Traviata*, much of it is actually played out between two or three characters. Even the big scenes with chorus in acts 1 and 2 contain long solos as well as concerted passages among the four principal characters. And the opera's second half is more intimate, with even the choruses of priests typically adding color by singing from offstage.

*Aida* has a militarist flavor, as manifested in the marches of the first and second acts, which bothers some listeners. Verdi wrote music to glorify Egypt, the country that paid for the opera, which accounts for the national hymns; and since the scenario involves war, military music necessarily comes with the package. There's also a post-Risorgimento, nationalist aspect to *Aida*, with Egypt substituting for Italy, its marches and anthems taking the place of the patriotic choruses in *La battaglia di Legnano*. Although a patriot, Verdi was no imperialist, and in the high age of European imperialism he's on record as opposing Italian adventurism in Ethiopia.[1] Perhaps it's best to think of the military passages of *Aida* as another operatic affect.

The opera has also been accused of a cultural imperialism and of orientalism, adapting or inventing exotic, Middle- or Far-Eastern-sounding music to tickle the ears of Western audiences. Verdi went to a great deal of trouble to add what he hoped were authentic-sounding trumpets to the triumphal scene, and certainly in the second scene of act 1, set in the Temple of Vulcan, as well as in the ballet in act 2 scene 2, the composer creates an orientalist sound world. So, here the charge sticks. But Verdi composed *Aida* at the beginning of a fifty-year period in which orientalism was one of the most important trends in European music. If he is to be condemned, then so are Puccini for *Madama Butterfly* and *Turandot*, Mahler for *Das Lied von der Erde*, Richard Strauss for *Salome*, Rimsky-Korsakov for *Scheherazade* and Ravel for *Shéhérazade*, Debussy for *Pagodes* and other piano works, Sullivan for *The Mikado*, and innumerable others.

Perhaps the opera's most puzzling flaw is that only one character, Amneris, comes fully—and spectacularly—to life; thanks to the raw vigor of his role, Amonasro, Aida's father, is halfway there. But in spite of his vocal glories Radamès is flat, and even with some of the most beautiful and moving material in the soprano repertory to sing, Aida somehow remains pallid.

Short but substantial, the prelude plays off two of the opera's primary thematic ideas: the sighing, tender melody, stated softly at the outset by the violins, always associated with Aida; then the marchlike theme of the priests. This theme is begun very softly by the cellos, then joined by the other strings, and, finally, the full orchestra. Contrapuntal mastery is one of Verdi's hidden strengths, but in *Aida* he uses it more openly and with power as here where both themes are treated in a tight canonic pattern, then juxtaposed in more dramatic conflict. Dying away high in the violins, Aida's theme ends the prelude.

To a background of mellow strings, Radamès, the young captain of the guards, is in conversation with the high priest Ramfis, discussing a rumored invasion by the Ethiopians. With a meaningful look Ramfis tells Radamès that the goddess Isis has selected the warrior to lead the Egyptian troops into battle and that he must now inform the King who that is. To trumpet fanfares Radamès hopes aloud that he might be the chosen one ("Se quel guerrier io fossi"). But his martial ardor melts as he thinks of Aida, his beloved, for whose sake he hopes to win the war, telling us that love and military glory form Radamès's two chief interests. He then sings his famous, old-fashioned, beautiful, and very difficult cantabile "Celeste Aida"—*Heavenly Aida*. This *romanza* is in three parts, the opening rising sequence, and the middle ("Il tuo bel cielo"—*That I might bring you once more*) in a more mysterious minor key, with exquisite commentary by flute, oboe, and bassoon. The third section reprises the opening, but with an ecstatic accompaniment of detached, staccato strings. The tenor's line famously climaxes on two B-flats, the first loud, but the second a tricky *pianissimo* that's rarely observed in live performance. Low strings shift solemnly into remote keys to end the aria. Verdi does little new here, as you'll hear if you revisit Ernani's entrance aria "Come rugiada al cespite" (see page 29), but the master displays a freshness and sophistication of harmony and subtlety in the orchestral accompaniment. Listen to the discreet way the cellos echo Radamès's vocal line in the concluding section, or to the looping flute as it decorates his closing phrase ("Un trono vicino al sol"—*A throne for you, near the sun*). The aria's lilting 6/8 beat stands out refreshingly in this march-heavy score. And while the vocal line sounds graceful and almost easy when well sung, it's anything but: The tessitura is high and Verdi asks for a delicacy few tenors can muster, at least on stage. It's also difficult because the singer who's still tight and nervous has to deliver it within two minutes of the curtain.

Amneris, the Princess of Egypt, enters; she loves Radamès, who as we already know loves Aida and not her. To her theme, a warm, triplet-laden melody given here by the violins, she asks Radamès flirtatiously why he looks so happy ("Quale insolita gioia nel tuo sguardo"—*What joy shines from your face*). When he explains that he hopes to be named commander of the army, Amneris asks archly whether he has no hopes here in Memphis ("Non hai tu in Menfi desiderii, speranze?"). The impulsively jealous Amneris says to herself, "Guai se un altro amore ardesse a lui nel core!"—*Woe if love for another burns in his heart!* This is accompanied by a waspish theme that accompanies her often though not inevitably through the opera. Aida, who is one of Amneris's slaves, enters accompanied by her tender theme sung by the clarinet, and Amneris immediately observes Radamès's excitement.

Feigning warmth, Amneris calls Aida, hoping to tease information from her; the music betrays her calculations in the bassoon that anticipates her vocal line, just as thought anticipates speech. Aida replies that the rumors of war worry her. In a short, intense concerted passage, the three express their private thoughts, Amneris reiterating her jealousy ("Trema, o rea schiava"—*Tremble, guilty slave*). Radamès reads her expression ("Nel volto a lei balena lo sdegno ed il sospetto"—*Anger and suspicion burn in her face*). Poor Aida admits to herself that in addition to the rumor of war, she also sheds tears for an unhappy love ("Quello ch'io verso è pianto di sventurato amor").

Massive brass fanfares and weighty trills for the strings introduce the King of Egypt, who brings out a messenger bearing news that Egypt has been invaded by Ethiopia, and that "Un guerriero indomabile, feroce, li conduce: Amonasro"—*A fierce, relentless warrior leads them: Amonasro*. The Ethiopians' king also happens to be Aida's father, as she sings in an aside. Led by the King and Ramfis, the Egyptians take up an energetic war cry ("Guerra!"), and the King announces that Radamès will lead the army. The hero is thrilled, Amneris is excited for him, but Aida can only worry. The King directs Radamès to the Temple of Vulcan to be sanctified, and the Egyptians in chorus sing, "Su, del Nilo"—*Go to the Nile*—a heroic march in an aggressive affect. In case you've never heard it, listen for the rhythmic and harmonic irregularities Verdi introduces to make it interesting musically.

At the end of the march, Amneris calls out, "Ritorna vincitor!"—*Return victorious!*—in a splendid vocal gesture. The crowd, including Aida, echoes her thunderously as everyone but the heroine leaves the stage. To different, questioning harmony and a more hesitant rhythm Aida repeats the phrase. In a long, *declamato* passage, she reflects in dismay on exactly what Radamès's victory will mean: murdered brothers, and "E dietro il carro, un Re . . . mio padre . . . di catene avvinto"—*Behind his chariot, a king . . . my father . . . in chains.* To a weeping accompaniment of two clarinets, Aida considers her terrible conflict of loyalties ("I sacri nomi di padre . . . d'amante"—*The sacred words father . . . and lover*). This leads to the climax of this great cantabile on the unforgettable phrase "Numi, pietà"—*Gods, have pity*—a simple but shattering melody, calculated by the composer to make audiences weep. The accompaniment, too, is simple, only trembling strings echoing her desperate prayer. The vocal line rises only to an A-flat, but the poignancy of the melody is what counts, allowing the voice to express Aida's anguish. The line drops as the scene ends on a soft but eloquent postlude for the cellos.

The second scene shows Verdi's skills as an orientalist. But this relatively short scene set in the Temple of Vulcan is remarkable from an aural standpoint, as much of the singing is done from offstage, and its tempos range only from slow to moderate. Harps invoke a ritualistic atmosphere, as a priestess from offstage joined by a chorus, sings a prayer hovering mysteriously between major and minor tonalities, to the god Ptah ("Possente Fthà"—*Mighty Ptah*). Ramfis and a chorus of priests reply from far below in a hymn ("Tu che dal nulla hai tratto"—*You, who from nothingness drew the seas*), a call and response that seems motionless. A languid dance for the priestesses, led by the flutes, is purest hoochie-koo, but delicious, particularly in the beauty of the writing for woodwinds. Ramfis summons Radamès for his investiture. His stark invocation ("Mortal, diletto ai Numi"—*Mortal, beloved of the gods*) may remind you of the Grand Inquisitor, though here at least Ramfis is more benign. To an intense phrase ("Nume, custode e vindice"—*O god, guardian and avenger*), Ramfis asks Ptah to rain death on Egypt's enemy. This leads to a grandiose anthem, thundered out by all, with occasional quiet replies by the offstage chorus. Radamès takes up his sword, and the scene ends with a powerful hymn to Ptah.

As the second act opens, a chorus of slave girls discusses the victory of the Egyptian army under Radamès. Amneris, surrounded by slaves, is preparing for his triumphant return. Verdi portrays her love for him ("Ah, vieni, amor mio"—*Come, my love*) with such convincing warmth that we begin to like her, even though she will proceed to torment Aida. Her preparations are accompanied by a ballet, the "Dance of the Moorish Slaves," a brief (ninety seconds) but colorfully scored interlude. Amneris's mood changes as Aida enters. Jealousy takes over as she once again pretends to empathize with Aida over Ethiopia's loss. She tells Aida that love will soften her pain. Aida admits in an ecstatic aside set to her own wistful theme that "Ne' tuoi dolori la vita io sento"—*In your sorrow I find my life*—referring to love, as Amneris sharply observes her excitement. To a wheedling melody, echoed sharply by the woodwinds, Amneris tells Aida that Radamès "cadde trafitto a morte"—*has died on the battlefield.* Aida cannot contain her grief, but Amneris then tells her the truth that he lives, "Radamès vive!" Aida shouts her joy in a high A. Amneris warns her plainly and with a dignity that once again endears, that she herself, "Figlia de' Faraoni"—*Daughter of the pharaohs*—is her rival in love. Aida almost lets slip the fact of her own royal blood, but catches herself. Over a steady accompaniment led by one sad bassoon, she pleads, "Pietà ti prenda del mio dolor"—*Take pity on my sorrow.* Amneris warns, now with real venom, that she rules Aida's fate. In a concerted passage, the two continue, Aida to plead, and Amneris to threaten, as fanfares and a chorus singing "Su! del Nilo" mark the transition to the second scene. To a nervous melody, Aida finds another way to beg for Amneris's pity ("Che più mi resta?"—*What else is left me?*) as Amneris challenges her to a fiery *declamato* ("Apprenderai se lottar"—*See if you're worthy*). Amneris sweeps off, and Aida is left alone to pray again for pity in a shorter iteration of her glorious "Numi, pietà."

The grand triumphal scene that ends act 2 is famous and popular. Its celebration of Egypt's victory brings the plot to its point of crisis, the public side of the opera ending here; what follows is more intimate, a pattern Verdi will follow in *Otello*, where the big concerted number that ends act 3 is followed by the tragedy played out privately in the last act.

Brassy trumpet fanfares mark the final appearance in Verdi's oeuvre of the brass *banda*, and plenty of marches populate the scene, but the composer varies the music brilliantly. The scene opens with a rattling fanfare for the *banda*, followed by strings in a sharp march rhythm that captures the excitement of spectators flocking to the parade. And the huge choral hymn "Gloria all'Egitto, ad Iside"—*Glory to Egypt and to Isis*—displays tremendous power and sincerity of patriotic affect. To the falling march tune first heard in the prelude rendered contrapuntally the priests add their more somber contribution ("Della vittoria agl'arbitri"—*To the victory given by those arbiters*). The brassy "Triumphal March," the most famous tune in the opera and one of the composer's greatest hits, follows. (You've heard it.) Although a cliché, it's powerful and impressive when performed with sincerity and energy, and Verdi brings its hammering note pattern back to great effect at the end of the scene. Listen, too, for the jolting key change that dispels monotony. This leads directly into a four-minute-long ballet that's written into the score and cannot be cut, another reason that this opera is only for major opera companies to stage. Undeniably orientalist, this passage is wonderful for its melodic opulence, rhythmic fury, and colorful orchestration. A grandiose reiteration of "Gloria all'Egitto" follows.

The King salutes Radamès as the savior of his country; a blushing Amneris crowns him with the victor's laurel as the orchestra paints her joy and love for him with the string melody that introduced her in act 1. The King asks Radamès to name his reward; the hero requests that the prisoners be brought out, which they are, to a sullen march and the priests' ominous chanting in the background. Aida spots her father, Amonasro, among the prisoners, and cries out; the ensemble is shocked. "Non mi tradir"—*Don't betray me*—meaning as King, he mutters to her as they embrace. The King of Egypt asks Amonasro, who's dressed only as an officer, to tell his tale. To an explosive accompaniment Amonasro replies fiercely that "Fu la sorte a nostr'armi nemica"—*Fate was our enemy*—then falsely that the King was killed. He then throws out a fierce challenge set over throbbing strings and barking orchestral interjections that "Se l'amor della patria è delitto, siam rei tutti, siam pronti a morir"—*If love of country is a crime, then we're all guilty, and ready to die*. Abruptly changing his manner, Amonasro suavely implores the Egyptian King for pity: "Ma tu, Re, tu signore possente"—*But you, King, are a mighty lord.* So persuasive is his melody that Aida and the other slaves and prisoners take it up in chorus. The priests protest vehemently, "Struggi, o Re, queste ciurme feroci"—*Destroy, King, this ferocious lot*. Watching Aida, Radamès sings that her sorrow makes him love her more than ever. And watching Radamès, Amneris can't mistake his love for Aida. All these threads are woven into an enormous concerted passage that's one of the master's most potent and beautiful. After the ensemble reaches an urgent climax,

Radamès asks the King to free all the prisoners. The priests object, but Ramfis suggests holding Aida's father as a pledge of peace. The King agrees, then gives Radamès the hand of Amneris, who gloats in a powerful *declamato* phrase, "Venga la schiava, venga a rapirmi l'amor mio . . . se l'osa!"—*Let the slave try to steal my love . . . if she dares!*

The Egyptian anthem is repeated, now punctuated by orchestral lightning and thunder in the form of slashing chords and rolls for the timpani, again forestalling monotony. Aside, Amonasro tells Aida to be patient and brave ("Fa cor"). Radamès sings that "D'Egitto il trono non val d'Aida il cor"—*The throne of Egypt is not worth Aida's heart*—and once more all the divergent emotions and musical lines are woven into a immense climax for the ensemble. Then the "Triumphal March" returns with steamroller force, its hammered brassy notes depicting the tide of events that has swamped the love of Aida and Radamès.

Many listeners start liking *Aida* (or liking it more) with the third act, where, as noted, the drama and the music become more personal. The orchestral introduction to the act, surely one of the most boldly imaginative passages in nineteenth-century European music, is universally admired. With the scene set by the bank of the Nile, Verdi, by means of magical tone painting, captures the feeling of a hot night with insects buzzing. It starts with hypnotic broken figure for the violins, followed by the rest of the strings' contributing different elements to the atmosphere like the whistling, long-held high notes, known as harmonics, for half of the cellos. The flute enters with a strange, trill-laden melody that seems never to settle into a tonality, giving it an open, birdsonglike feel. The chorus is heard from offstage, chanting a hymn to the goddess Isis ("O, tu che sei d'Osiride"—*You, bride and mother of Osiris*), which continues the tonal uncertainty. Ramfis and Amneris enter; the high priest gently advises her to pray for the goddess's favor on the eve of her wedding. Amneris replies, "Si: io pregherò che Radamès mi doni tutto il suo cor, come il mio cor a lui sacro è per sempre"—*Yes, I'll pray that Radamès gives me his whole heart, as mine is given to him forever in sacred love*—singing with a warmth and sincerity that are more than merely touching, the orchestra emphasizing her emotions with trembling violas and carefully placed pizzicati for the cellos and basses to punctuate her line. This moment turns us again toward this fully drawn character, passionate in love as in jealousy, praying that the man she loves will come to love her, which she knows full well he does not. The two enter the temple, and the proto-Bartókian outdoor night music and chant pick up once more.

Aida enters, her theme played low by a flute, the violas playing a running figure that suggests the motion of the river. This broadens quietly into a phrase of somber gravity, depicting her despairing mood. She sings that she wishes Radamès would come, fantasizing that should he abandon her she'll find in the river "E pace forse . . . e oblio"—*Perhaps peace . . . but at least oblivion*. Aida's thoughts drift to the homeland she'll never see again. Her cantabile "O patria mia" (CD Track 14)—*O fatherland*—is one of the lyrical high points of the role and of the opera; its intimate pain and ecstasy contrast with the public pomp of act 2 scene 2. The lyric is straightforward: she misses her homeland, and now that her love is hopeless, she's especially melancholy. Verdi's music depicting Aida's words and mood is anything but simple, though, opening with the clarinet and oboe sharing a lilting, plangent folklike melody. To these Aida adds the opening line, not cantabile, but not declaimed, either: "O patria mia, mai più ti rivedrò"—*Fatherland, I'll never see you again*. But the music takes on an excitement and ecstasy as she begins to picture it in her mind ("O cieli azzuri . . . o dolce aure native"—*Blue skies and soft native breezes*) as the flute trembles, and Aida's line slides up from minor to major, giving a sense of breaking through subtly but unmistakably to joy. The oboe and bassoon sigh along with her, but again her imagination swells as she thinks of home, her ecstasy returning as she sings of the "Fresche valli . . . o questo asil beato"—*Cool valleys . . . blessed peaceful haven*. Verdi carefully pares the string section down to a chamber-size ensemble to provides a quiet animation to the accompaniment, never overstating, as she breaks through again on "Mai più"—*Never again*—her line rising to a C sung softly, very difficult. A brief postlude (and an A, yet softer) seems to wind the reverie down as Amonasro enters, surprising her. There's no need to hold back tears if they come as you listen to this extraordinary aria: that's what Verdi intended. Keep in mind, too, how far the composer has come from his rough early days as you take in his exquisitely crafted late style. And finally, remember that "O patria mia" isn't entirely about Aida and Ethiopia, but about a great soprano singing of Verdi's own love for Italy, as well.

Amonasro, shrewd and tough, has taken in Aida's plight and in an idyllic phrase ("Rivedrai le foreste imbalsamante"—*Again you'll see our fragrant forests*), which she echoes, as he proposes that she can have everything she wants, homeland and love. More somberly, he reminds her of Egypt's brutality in war. Aida replies with a soaring phrase ("Deh! fate, o Numi, che per noi ritorni"—*Grant, oh gods, that we may return*) in which she sings with touching naïveté of her wish for peace. Amonasro, always a few steps ahead, tells her insinuatingly ("Radamès so che qui attendi"—*I know you are waiting for Radamès*) that she can help the cause by making him reveal the route the Egyptian army will take. Horrified, she refuses. Amonasro attacks ferociously, summoning gruesome images of Egypt conquering Ethiopia. When she begs for pity, he redoubles the intensity of his attack, describing Aida's mother as cursing her. He ends his cruel manipulation by telling her, "Non sei mia figlia, dei Faraone tu sei la schiava!"—*You are not my daughter, you're the slave of the Pharaohs!* Crushed, Aida begs Amonasro for pity in an unusual long-spun *declamato*, ending on a despairing phrase that ironically echoes "O patria mia": "O patria . . . quanto mi costi!"—*Fatherland, what a price I must pay for you.*

As Amonasro hides, Radamès enters to a skipping rhythm suggesting his boyish energy and directness. In a brilliant phrase, he declares his love again. With pulsing triplets accompanying their dialogue, Aida asks how he can hope to overcome the circumstances arrayed against them. His plan, which he relates as a pair of trumpets rattle out a dashing, rather elegant tattoo, is to defeat the Ethiopians once more, then declare his love for Aida to the King of Egypt, who will be unable to deny him. Aida offers another plan, which is that they flee together to Ethiopia. To a suggestive phrase preceded by an insinuating introduction for oboe and marked by triplets in the vocal line and the dreamy, flute-dominated accompaniment, Aida shows some depth as she tries to manipulate her lover. The hero is shocked by her suggestion ("Sovra una terra estrania"—*You've asked me to flee*) but she continues with her seduction, hitting two more of the *pianissimo* B-flats that make this role so difficult. Finally summoning an image of Amneris waiting for him at the altar, Aida overcomes Radamès's resistance and the pair sing heroically of their flight and their future together in Aida's homeland: "Sì, fuggiam da queste mura"—*Yes, let us flee, far from these walls.* This thrilling cabaletta-like passage gives the leads—and the audience—an exciting release as their driving melody provides the opportunity to sing a few B-flats in full voice.

Supposedly in the interest of learning the safe route for their escape, Aida worms from Radamès what Amonasro wanted to hear: the name of the pass still unguarded by the Egyptians. Now a shocked Radamès finds out who Aida's father is. Amonasro then tries to persuade the appalled hero that what he did was not his fault, and that Radamès and Aida will someday rule in Ethiopia. But Amneris and Ramfis, leaving the temple, stumble into the conspiracy. With a propulsive orchestra taking the lead, Amonasro attempts to stab Amneris but Radamès blocks him, yelling for Aida and Amonasro to flee. As Amonasro drags his daughter off, Radamès hands himself stoically over to Ramfis on a sustained high A: "Sacerdote, io resto a te"—*Priest, I surrender myself to you.*

Amneris dominates the first scene of the last act, set in the palace of the King. Falling melodic phrases like the striking one for woodwinds that begins the act dominate this scene. The winds lead into a new, lighter but more urgent version of Amneris's waspish theme. Sad and worried, Amneris sings first with fury of Aida that "L'aborrita rivale a me sfuggia"—*My hated rival has escaped.* Then reflecting on Radamès, she grows enraged, denouncing him as a traitor and crying that he and Aida should die. But unable to deny her true feelings, she recants immediately and passionately, to the flowing melody of her love first heard in the opera's opening scene. Still hoping that he might love her, she desperately considers how to save him ("Oh, s'ei potesse amarmi! Vorrei salvarlo"—*If only he might love me! I want to save him*). She orders a guard to bring him, and the two begin a powerful duet also preceded by a falling figure for the orchestra, then a solo clarinet, the most important instrument in its accompaniment, along with the trumpets, which repeatedly tap out two softly ominous notes.

In majestic tones, she warns Radamès that the priests are now considering his fate ("Già i sacerdoti adunansi"—*The priests are now in council*). But her passion rises as she tries to persuade him to let her plead his case to her father ("Ti scolpa, e la tua grazia io pregherò dal trono"—*Clear yourself and I shall plead your case to the King*), her line rising then falling grandly. Radamès replies in a similarly impressive tone that although he revealed the secret incautiously, his act was unintentional. He will not defend himself: "Di mie discolpe i giudici mai"—*The judges shall never hear me.* Radamès's line also rises to a passionate A-flat, betraying the high emotion behind his soldierly bearing. Amneris warns that he'll die, but he replies that he despises life—"La vita aborro"—now that Aida, the source of his joy is gone. Now things really heat up. To a rising orchestral figure, with a stroke on the timpani emphasizing her urgency, Amneris pleads that he must live and be her love ("Ah, tu dêi vivere!"—*You must live!*). In reply to Amneris's sweeping phrase, again in kind, he accuses himself of betraying his country for Aida ("Per essa anch'io la patria e l'onor mio tradia"), then, his line climaxing on a furious B-flat, he charges Amneris with responsibility for Aida's death. But Amneris denies it, saying that Amonasro is dead, but Aida fled with the other Ethiopians. Happy to know she's alive, Radamès wishes Aida well. Once again, Amneris begs him to live and love her, but he refuses to a tense tremolando accompaniment. A furious orchestra marked by snarling trumpets portrays her rage. To a driving melody climaxing on a long B-flat she sings that she now hates him ("Chi ti salva, sciagurato"—*Who will save you, wretch*). Radamès replies in an enormous phrase of his own that death is now his greatest good ("È la morte un ben supremo") and with a stinging statement rare for him that Amneris's pity is all he fears ("Temo sol la tua pietà"). An orchestral postlude of high energy and fury marks the end of the duet as Radamès is led off to trial.

This concluding part of the scene is unusual because only Amneris is left onstage, listening in terror to the proceedings, which we hear from offstage and on which she comments in despair. Since Radamès remains silent, only Ramfis and the priests, who reappear briefly at the scene's end, are heard. To the descending march heard in the prelude and the triumphal scene the priests pass, entering the underground chamber where Radamès is imprisoned. Amneris laments the jealousy that has brought her beloved to this, and calling the priests "Bianche larve"—*White-robed ghosts*. The trial begins with a hovering a cappella hymn, not unlike a Gregorian chant: "Spirto del Nume"—*Spirit of the gods*. The trial commences, as Ramfis, calling Radamès's name three times, recites the three charges against him: revealing his country's secrets, deserting on the eve of battle, and betraying king and country, each charge stated more intensely than the last. When asked to defend himself Radamès remains silent, and the priests cry out, "Traditor!"—*Traitor*. Each time, too, Amneris cries out in anguish, "Ah, pietà! Ah, lo salvate!"—*Have pity, save him*—or a variant thereof. To an orchestral cataclysm, and led by Ramfis, the priests condemn Radamès to a traitor's death, "A te vivo fia schiuso l'avel"—that he be entombed alive in the crypt beneath the Temple of Vulcan. Watching the priests as they file out as the orchestra renders their march in its most ugly and inflected incarnation, Amneris shrieks at them, "Compiste un delitto . . . Tigri infami di sangue assetate"—*Bloodthirsty beasts . . . you have committed a crime.* (No question about Verdi's anticlericalism now.) They reply brutally, "È traditor, morrà!"—*The traitor must die.* Then, in one of the greatest moments in *Aida*, Amneris, accompanied by the full orchestra, shrieks out again a titanic, writhing melody expressing despair and rage more potently than any other, anywhere, "Voi la terra, ed i Numi oltraggiate!"—*You offend heaven and earth!* Then she flings one final curse at the priests: "Empia razza! Anatéma su voi! La vendetta del ciel scenderà!"—*Impious race, I curse you! May heaven's vengeance strike!* Then, to coiled trills for the trumpet, stalking figures for the strings, and sharply broken-off chords for the full orchestra, the magnificent Amneris storms off.

The final scene of *Aida* is famous for its staging, Verdi's own idea, requiring two levels, one showing the Temple of Vulcan above, and below, its vault where Radamès—and Aida, as we'll soon find—are entombed. As the curtain rises, Radamès is shown seated on the steps, as priests secure the stone that seals the vault from above. To a simple, somber accompaniment he reflects that he'll never see the sun or Aida again, the music starting in a tight recitative, but swelling as he mentions Aida. But he hears a sigh, as Aida steps out of the gloom. A falling phrase for the strings introduces Radamès's unforgettable cry, "Tu, in questa tomba!"—*You, in this tomb!* To heavy, repeated chords for low winds and strings, she relates that sensing his fate she slipped into the crypt to die with him. Radamès reflects to the first of several celestial melodies in the brief scene, set very high, that she's too young and full of love to die for him ("Morir, si pura e bella"). The tenor rises to A-flat several times in this short but touching passage, punctuated by light strings and woodwinds. Already delirious, Aida raves to another divine melody ("Vedi? Di morte l'angelo") that the Angel of Death is approaching to carry them to eternity. Her line, too, has a high tessitura with several B-flats, but the melody is simple and the overall effect of Aida's voice and the orchestral ensemble is one of growing lightness, both in pitch and the ever-diminishing size of the orchestral ensemble. Verdi reduces the strings, with the highest violins playing muted, others normally, and the lower strings pizzicato. Over quietly thrumming harps, priests and priestesses are heard chanting "Immenso Fthà," as in the second scene of act 1, as life outside the crypt resumes its normal patterns. Aida comments that it's "Il nostro inno di morte"—*Our funeral hymn.* In time to the strokes of the harp, Radamès bravely tries to move the stone, but in vain. In a powerful phrase Aida comments, "Tutto è finito sulla terra per noi"—*All is finished on earth for us.*

To an ethereal accompaniment of woodwinds, a few soft notes for the horns, two harps and strings, Aida sings the first line of their great farewell to earth, "O terra, addio." The melody is one of the master's most penetrating, partly because it begins on an unusual and memorable interval. Grand but simple, the tune is in three phrases, one ("A noi si schiude il ciel"—*Heaven opens to us*) being different, though not radically so; the melody is repeated twelve times as Radamès and Aida share it to the end. To describe the tune technically captures none of its piercing, penetrating, heartbreaking beauty, which you're sure to hear, so prepare for tears to flow. The chanting of the priests breaks in, sounding remote. Amneris enters the Temple—the upper part of the set—dressed in mourning. She throws herself on the stone, praying in broken phrases for peace for her beloved Radamès, breaking our hearts for her as well. The flutes play a languid melody in triplets from the priestesses' dance in act 1 scene 2, here more remote and dreamy. Aida's and Radamès's voices, sounding almost as one, interrupt each other gently in the soft rise and fall of their sweet melody as they share it. The priests are heard again; the three principals reach a musical climax as the lovers, below, sing a high B-flat, and Amneris, above, sings a low C, as though reaching through the stone floor toward each other. Verdi continually lightens the accompaniment, but the flutes return with their languid triplets, sounding as though time itself is closing the sad tale. Aida dies in Radamès's arms; Amneris murmurs her prayer to the very quiet end, one of the most touching, beautiful, and imaginative to any opera.

# Shakespearean Tragedy
## Otello

The birth of Verdi's great Shakespearean tragedy was prolonged and difficult. It seemed likely to the composer that *Aida* was his final opera, even though he was only in his vigorous early sixties with revisions and new productions of older works always there to occupy him. He managed his Busseto estate and business affairs with energy and occasionally conducted the Requiem. Verdi's publisher Giulio Ricordi gets credit for seeing that the supposedly retired master had much to give. And crucially, Ricordi saw Arrigo Boito (1842–1918), the musician and man of letters, as Verdi's ideal collaborator. The brilliant Boito had already written and translated librettos, including two for himself. Over decades Boito also wrestled nearly two operas of his own into existence: *Mefistofele*, a retelling of the Faust legend, and the unfinished *Nerone*, based on the life of the Roman emperor Nero. The former, a work of high ambition, has survived, demonstrating its creator's skill as a librettist first; as a composer he's good, not great. Ricordi's bigger problem was in getting Verdi to trust Boito. Although the two had collaborated on the *Inno delle nazioni* in 1862, their work entailed little interaction. After that, Boito had written articles that seemed critical of Verdi, and the composer, never one to take criticism well, held a grudge against his younger colleague. By the time the *Otello* project was under consideration, Boito had come to revere Verdi's work. At Ricordi's instigation Boito drew up an *Otello* scenario that Verdi liked. Next, Boito assisted Verdi with the 1881 revision of *Simon Boccanegra*. Verdi quickly came to appreciate Boito's skills, which were far superior to those of any of his previous librettists. He asked Boito to proceed with the *Otello* libretto. Verdi took his time with the composition, which he did not begin in earnest in 1884, the premiere taking place on February 5, 1887, at La Scala. The work was received rapturously and is considered one of the greatest and most revered operas in the repertory. Boito's contribution is enormous, his tight libretto inspiring the composer to a manner in which the music doesn't just reflect words and action but impels them forward. Boito made the inspired decision to cut the stringy first act of *Othello* in which much is narrated but little happens, starting the opera instead with the storm in Cyprus that opens Shakespeare's act 2, then transferring the story of Othello's courtship of Desdemona to the love duet that ends act 1 of the opera. This allowed Verdi to conceive one of the greatest opening passages in the operatic repertory, immediately establishing a stormy and tragic mood for the opera.

Perfection is a slippery concept, but with *Otello* Verdi seems to come as close to it as any major operatic work. *Otello* has little fat, frequently displaying a concentration that shifts into frightening intensity. Verdi's enhanced musical armory, manifested by a new flexibility, fluidity, and freedom are what make the difference. Set pieces, such as Iago's *brindisi*— drinking song—in the first act, or his "Credo" and the quartet in the second, or Desdemona's two consecutive arias in the last act, all fall within the Italian operatic traditions. Verdi treats them with such freedom and integrates them so artfully into their respective acts that while recognizable in form, they fall smoothly into the flow of the drama. The master makes more extensive use of arioso—short, intense melodic passages— than ever before, and to greater effect. Only *Falstaff* exceeds *Otello* is this respect. His harmonic vocabulary shows the sophistication and boldness found only in the top rank of composers, and his instrumentation too is at a new level of power and polish. Much has been made of Verdi's use in *Otello* of the recurring theme, à la Wagner. In fact, it's limited but effective, with the "kiss" motif from the act 1 love duet brought back in the last act to powerful effect being the chief instance.

Much more important is the musical vocabulary Verdi uses to characterize the principals. What's known as diatonic—meaning conventional— harmony and a prevailing cantabile manner typically depict Desdemona and her direct, trusting nature. Iago's part is notable for its almost exclusively *declamato* style of singing, with chromatic lines, trills, triplets, and abrupt stops and starts revealing the workings of his web-spinning mind. Torn between the two, Otello's line is pulled toward the one he's with, as in his disastrous act 3 meeting with Desdemona, in which he tries to act politely at first, following her sunny melodic line, growing more tormented, distorted, and declaimed as he loses control. Otello also has a proclamatory, trumpetlike vocal style to characterize him in every act.

There have been many fine Iagos in the performance history of *Otello*, but the other two leads are more difficult to cast. Desdemona needs a good singing actress who can rise to pity and fear in the fourth act. Otello himself is one of the most famously challenging roles in the repertory, with a wide tessitura: it requires a heroic voice with a bright, metallic edge (the trumpetlike quality known as *squillo*); a rich, dark middle octave; and stamina. Harder to find is one who can maintain dramatic intensity from first to last, without yelling, barking, and laying on other hammy mannerisms as too many, including some famous names, have done. The mighty score needs a strong hand at the helm, with Arturo Toscanini's famous 1947 recording setting the conducting standard for most, the maestro driving it on with even more than his customary fury, bringing to the work the sense of almost constant danger that makes a great performance of *Otello* nerve-racking and ultimately shattering.

And so it begins with the storm that opens the play's second act, and quite a storm it is, making the wildest operatic opening of all. A shriek and roar to an enormous dissonance engages the full orchestra, then the volume drops abruptly. Horns moan, and skittering high woodwinds depict lightning. "Una vela"—*A sail*—a few members of the male chorus hesitantly sing. The observations by Montano, the Venetian governor of Cyprus; Cassio, a captain and Otello's lieutenant; and others on shore, continue. But when you listen, pay attention to the rhythmic impetus that drives this extraordinary musical depiction forward: these come from the cries of those on land, as well as from the furious orchestral textures. A cry ("Fende l'etra un torvo e cieco spirto di vertigine"—*A blind and hideous vertigo splits the sky*) finally emerges in a full phrase. Snarling trumpets suggest the wind as described by the chorus ("I titanici oricalchi squillano nel ciel"—*Titanic trumpets peal in the sky*). The chorus breaks into a hymn ("Dio, fulgor della bufera!"—*God, the splendor of the storm*) that's at once anxious and majestic, forming the first full melody in the opera, through which the trumpets of the storm continue to hammer, the orchestral accompaniment capturing both the grandeur of the hymn and the wildness of the storm.

Iago calls out "È infranto l'artimon!"—*Her mainsail's burst!*—then, as others call for help, he comments to himself and his puppet Roderigo, "L'alvo frenetico del mar sia la sua tomba"—*May the heaving sea be his tomb.* Now he is singing of Otello, his general, and we know from his second line how he feels. But the ship is saved, as the chorus cries, and in a moment, Otello makes one of the grandest operatic entrances: "Esultate!" (CD Track 15)—*Rejoice!*—as he relates to a line of nearly intolerable splendor, punctuated richly by horns, timpani, and strings, that the Turkish fleet has sunk—glory to themselves, heaven, and the storm. Thus we meet the hero at his pinnacle, seeing him in the godlike state from which he falls. Otello's radiant vocal line, though brief, is very difficult, leaping on his fifth note to a G-sharp, then up to A and a B that's a grace note; and as for more than one Verdi hero there's no time to warm up onstage.

The music for the storm and Otello's entrance has shaken us to our core; now Verdi needs to dissipate the tension so the story may proceed. He does by means of a quick, rhythmically driving chorus ("Evviva! Vittoria!"—*Hurrah! Victory!*) over a chattering accompaniment led by the trumpets. As the storm's last shudders are heard we may notice that a sound present from the opening suddenly ceases: it's an organ, in an unusual effect playing three pedal notes in a tone cluster, something we've felt rather than heard, and when it stops the last bit of the storm's tension ends.

Iago and Roderigo discuss the latter's desperate love for Desdemona. Rather incredibly, Iago suggests he can help the weak-minded gentleman, revealing his contempt for Cassio and hatred for Otello. In this fast-moving monologue we hear Iago's complaints as well as a complete lexicon of the trills, abrupt gestures, chromatic inflections, and snaking triplets ("Ed io rimango di sua Moresca Signoria . . . l'alfiere"—*And I remain the Lord Moor's . . . ensign*) that mark his part throughout the opera. As they exit beyond hearing, Verdi introduces a chorus around the bonfire that simultaneously seals our contentment and sets the mood for a very different moment in the drama, where Iago lures Cassio to drink, causing the lieutenant to lose his job: The chorus itself, "Fuoco di gioia"—*Joyous fire*—moves on a lively rhythmic figure. The chorus is a pleasing interlude, amplified by beautiful woodwind writing. Although it begins like a set piece, Verdi moves directly from the chorus into the action that follows, picking up intensity as Iago offers wine to Cassio ("Roderigo, beviam!

Qua la tazza, capitano"—*Roderigo, let's drink! Your cup, captain!*). Cassio refuses repeatedly, but cannot once Iago proposes a toast to Desdemona, whose beauty and kindness Cassio praises and, indeed, drinks to. Aside, Iago warns Roderigo that Cassio is a crafty seducer who can't hold his liquor ("S'ei inebria è perduto. Fallo ber"—*If he gets drunk, he's lost. Make him drink*). Thus Iago improvises his plot around the opportunity. He launches into his *brindisi*, a simple lyric ("Inaffia l'ugola"—*Wet your whistles*) set to music that starts jolly but soon grows menacing. The accompaniment is a rolling figure for bassoons and low strings, and Iago's line is marked by chromatic descents and an abrupt drop on the word "tracanna"—*drink deeply*. Cassio replies at first coherently but soon less so. Verdi's accompaniment grows thicker yet somehow more nimble as Iago works his mischief, as snarling trills for the winds, a skittering figure for the strings, and jumping chords for the trombones join in what turns into a frighteningly quick pattern. Soon Cassio is quite drunk as Iago coaches Roderigo to provoke the captain, who draws his sword just as Montano enters, telling Cassio that the guard he's supposed to command is waiting for him. He's shocked by Cassio's condition; losing no opportunity for villainy, Iago softly tells Montano that "Ogni notte in tal guisa Cassio preludia al sonno"—*Every night this is the prelude to Cassio's sleep*. Cassio attacks Montano, who is wounded; singing to a falling chromatic line, Iago sends Roderigo off to cry riot, then hypocritically pleads for the combatants to stop. Flying madly forward, the music builds to a savage, trill-laden climax.

Otello enters, again displaying his innate authority: "Abbasso le spade!"—*Put down your swords!*—instantly halting the fight. To an imperious rising figure for the strings he chides the combatants. Wanting to get to the bottom of the trouble, he asks "Onesto Iago"—*Honest Iago*—what has happened. With carefully considered pauses, a seemingly stunned Iago says he has no idea: "Non so . . . qui tutti eran cortesi amici"—*I don't know . . . all were friends here*—again adding a hypocritical comment that he wishes he'd lost the feet that brought him there. Furious, Otello asks Cassio how he let himself go; the captain can only stammer apologies; Montano's injury enrages Otello further, and to the imperious string figure and in a thrilling *declamato*, he strips Cassio of his rank: "Cassio, non sei più capitano!" Iago gloats, then receives Otello's order to lead the guard and restore peace. Desdemona, who was awakened by the racket, joins Otello.

Then in another commanding phrase ("Io da qui non mi parto"—*I shall not leave*), he says he will watch over the square until all have left.

We have twice watched Otello as a natural leader, now we see him in the role of lover. The love duet opens with a quartet of cellos in a tenderly beautiful introduction. Otello's line "Già nella notte densa"—*Now in the depth of night*—opens this huge duet written in several sections. First, Desdemona joins him in the introductory part, calling him her "superbo guerrier"—*proud warrior*—as she invites him to look back over their love. Then to a swaying accompaniment in which woodwinds and harp dominate, Desdemona opens a new section, "Quando narravi"—*When you told me*—in which she recalls the adventures he related, and he recites, to muttering trumpets and rushing strings the dangers of battle he faced. To pulsing violins, she talks of his torments as a slave. The woodwinds wind warmly through his reply, as he describes her reactions to his story, which made him love her. Then to a molten phrase ("E tu m'amavi"—*And you loved me*) first Otello then Desdemona talk of their growing love. In growing rapture, Otello sings to a new harmony, "Venga la morte"—*Let death come*—of his untoppable joy. Desdemona prays that their love never diminish; Otello agrees. Overcome with joy, Otello loses his breath ("Ah, la gioia m'innonda"—*My joy overwhelms me*). He steals a kiss ("Un bacio") and then another and another as the yearning, richly harmonized "kiss" motif representing their passion sounds in the orchestra; Verdi will reprise it to devastating effect in act 4. A gently rising arpeggio for the harp begins the closing passage of the duet, then the whole orchestra seems to quiver in ecstasy as the couple heads slowly off. Note when you listen to its wandering harmonic scheme with which Verdi, a shrewd old craftsman, suggests successively higher levels of joy and, paradoxically in spite of the ever-shifting harmonic backcloth, a relationship that seems the essence of stability.

Iago dominates the action of act 2 from start to finish. The brief orchestral prelude paints a brilliant portrait of the character from the inside out. It opens with cellos and bassoons repeating a bare, grinding figure that shows his malignity in its unadulterated form, then opens out in to a more relaxed phrase summoning up his false candor and charm, then moves to a more thoughtful mode containing tied string lines that suggest web spinning. Iago is spinning his web around Cassio as the curtain rises, telling him not to worry, that he can help him regain his post. As the spinning music continues, he suavely advises Cassio to plead his case with Desdemona, "Il Duce del nostro Duce"—*Our leader's leader.* As he sends Cassio off, the grinding figure returns forcefully, leading into Iago's famous "Credo" (CD Track 16), announced by a seething, angular unison theme roared out by the full orchestra that's the distillation of all such themes over Verdi's career. Over cackling trills and in purest *declamato*, Iago proclaims his allegiance to "un Dio crudel, che m'ha creato, simile a sè"—*a cruel God who has created me in his image.* A freely bounding string figure, marked to be played "*aspramente*"—harshly—accompanies his declaration "Vile son nato. Son scellerato"—*I was born base. I am evil.* Then to a melodramatic and Spanish-sounding figure for trumpets, he declares ironically that his belief is as firm as that of a young widow in church, that evil is his destiny ("per mio destino adempio"), as the spinning string theme is brought to a climax for the full orchestra. Iago then mocks, "Il giusto è un istrion beffardo"—*The just man is a foolish actor*—whose tears and honor are false. He calls man the sport of fate "Dal germe della culla al verme dell'avel"—*From the germ of the cradle to the worm of the grave.* And finally, to eerie harmonies and an accompaniment that dwindles nearly to nothing, he considers death: "La Morte è il Nulla. È vecchia fola il Ciel!"—*Death is nothingness, and heaven an old wives' tale!* The orchestra backs his thoughts with a mighty shout on the bounding figure and chattering brass, but to a shocking change of key.

Cassio is seen approaching Desdemona, who appears in a garden in the background. They converse, then Cassio leaves. Iago urges Cassio on to a nervously excited string accompaniment. He tells himself, "Al posto ... all'opra"—*To my post ... to work*—as he observes Otello approaching. Feigning not to have noticed him, Iago pretends to say to himself, "Ciò m'accora"—*That concerns me.*

In the scene that follows, Iago uses subtle tricks of speech to create suspicion about Desdemona and Cassio where none existed in Otello's mind as Verdi's music shadows the text subtly and with astonishing fidelity. Iago and the accompaniment echo Otello's tone, first insinuatingly, then exasperatingly, as in the exchange when Iago asks whether Cassio knew of Otello's love for Desdemona. First, a single stabbing note by the cellos shows Iago's hook sinking in as the first doubt enters Otello's mind. Verdi puts Iago's questions into a falling five-note curling phrase that passes quietly from strings to wind and back. This reaches a climax as Otello, who has taken in all of Iago's hints, finally loses patience ("Pel cielo, tu sei l'eco dei detti miei"—*By God, you're repeating my words!*). In urgent *declamato* Otello orders Iago to speak his mind, but instead the villain warns him, to a menacing phrase, here stated in a slippery chromatic setting, to beware of jealousy, describing it in an ominous melody, "È un' idra fosca, livida, cieca"—*It is a grim, pale, blind hydra*—his line ending on a big trill in the orchestra. Although agitated, Otello is still rational, laying out his own direct approach in determining loyalty. Now that his web is working, Iago tells Otello that generous natures like his may be taken advantage of, and he croons suggestively that he should "Vigilate"—*Be watchful.*

A group of Cypriot sailors, women, and children now enter, serenading Desdemona. This interlude's dramatic purpose is to show her purity, but musically it also cools things down for a few minutes; with everything that follows in act 2 set at the highest dramatic pitch. The serenade ("Dove guardi splendono"—*Wherever you look*), set to the orchestra and a guitar, mandolin, and a bagpipe, is purely diatonic, unshadowed by chromaticism or ambiguity. The girls offer Desdemona flowers; the sailors, pearls and coral. As it ends, Desdemona sings of the beauty of the day; Iago comments ironically and Otello, won back over, sings, "S'ella m'inganna, il ciel sè stesso irride"—*If she deceives me, Heaven mocks itself.*

As in the play, Desdemona, who is attended by Iago's wife, Emilia, greets Otello by raising the worst possible issue, that of Cassio. "Tu gli perdona"—*You must forgive him*—she urges in her open-hearted way. "Non ora"—*Not now*—he replies, calmly enough; but when she persists he becomes agitated. Unwilling to say the real cause of his disturbance he complains of a headache; when she tries to tie her handkerchief around his head to relieve him, he throws it roughly to the ground. The four characters (Emilia is not quite a principal) sing a long quartet known by Desdemona's line "Dammi la dolce e lieta parola del perdono"—*Give me your sweet word of pardon.* The quartet, during which Iago wrestles the handkerchief from Emilia, precipitating the tragedy, also places the personalities under delicate scrutiny. Desdemona's long-spun cantabile shows her sweetness and genuine concern. We see another side of Otello now, insecure and credulous ("Forse perchè gl'inganni d'arguto amor non tendo"—*Perhaps because I do not understand the deceptions of love*), having absorbed Iago's deceptions. Iago demands the handkerchief from Emilia, who refuses him ("Io tuo nefando livor m'è noto"—*I know too well your wicked ways*). But Iago, who calls her his "Schiava impura"—*Impure slave*—manages to snatch the handkerchief. Otello's line is half cantabile, half declaimed; Iago's and Emilia's parts of their argument are fully declaimed. The quartet is not a showpiece but a character study, and the better one knows *Otello*, the more sense and weight this slightly undervalued ensemble takes on.

Now Otello can only torture himself, muttering, "Desdemona rea"—*guilty*—as Iago watches his misery with pleasure ("Soffri e ruggi!"—*Suffer and rage!*). Otello attacks Iago as he blandly greets him, raging that no torment is worse than this suspicion. In a titanic farewell to his life and work set to a thrumming march beat marked by the harp, Otello sings, "Ora e per sempre addio"—*Now and forever farewell*—as trumpets echo his military imagery. Too short to be an aria and far too elaborate to be considered an arioso, this tremendous passage shows Otello irrevocably deciding to play out his jealousy. Trumpets have a big part in this remarkable passage; and Otello himself in trumpet voice, has a B-flat on the climactic line "Della gloria d'Otello è questo il fin"—*Otello's glory's gone*. To violent orchestral backing he attacks Iago, demanding proof. The villain pretends to be offended and to quit, but for all the magnificence of his rage, Otello must beg him weakly to stay: "No, rimani. Forse onesto tu sei"—*No, stay. Perhaps you are honest*. Again, the clever Iago makes Otello come to him, asking in reply to the latter's furious demand for proof, "Avvinti vederli forse?"—*Perhaps to see them together?* Instead Iago proposes conjecture, then fabricating his tale of Cassio's dream, in which to a rocking, dreamlike accompaniment he tells of how he recently heard Cassio moaning for Desdemona in his sleep, and in a particularly nasty stroke, quoting Cassio as saying, "'Il rio destino impreco che al Moro ti donò'"—*"I curse the cruel destiny that gave you to the Moor."* The setting of Iago's narration begins plainly enough, but Verdi continually increases its chromaticism, giving the final lines an almost dizzy sound. Otello is nearly convinced already, but Iago offers as one more item of proof the handkerchief he has stolen. Otello's tenderness is touching as he recalls, "È il fazzoletto ch'io le diedi, pegno primo d'amor"—*It's a handkerchief I gave her, a token of first love*. Iago tells him he thinks he saw it in Cassio's hand.

Beside himself, Otello rages memorably for Cassio's blood ("Ah, sangue!"), though in notes (ending on G-sharp), not shouts, as it's too often performed. Kneeling, he sings, in a trumpetlike repeated E that finally rises to an A over a twisting theme deep in the orchestra, that he will have vengeance: "Si, pel ciel marmoreo giuro"—*By the marble heaven I swear*—Verdi's greatest oath duet by a long way. Iago kneels with him, and to a more chromatic accompaniment, sings the tune as rumbled out before by the low instruments, to which Otello's voice adds its rigid harmony; we now see that, as one commentator puts it, "Iago calls the tune."[1] Woodwinds and slashing strings add the lightning and thunder they swear to. The orchestra roars in a way only Verdi can achieve as he introduces shattering syncopations and savage jolts of harmony to the closing. Some conductors slow down here, though the score indicates no ritardando, because what Verdi paints in those crashing chords is the sound of Otello's life coming down around his ears.

Act 3, the longest in *Otello*, opens with a brief prelude based on the dark melody sung by Iago on jealousy ("È un' idra fosca, livida, cieca") showing jealousy doing its poisonous work. Otello and Iago are in discussion as a herald enters, announcing the arrival of a ship carrying officials from Venice. Iago tells Otello in recitative how he will get Cassio to reveal his true attitude. Seeing Desdemona approaching, he suggests to Otello, "Finger conviene"—*Better pretend*. But then when Iago mentions the handkerchief, Otello in a leonine gesture backed by a sharp chord warns him off ("Va! Volentieri obliato l'avrei"—*Go! I would gladly forget it*). Although only seconds long, this restores Otello to some of his heroic stature.

The great scene that follows displays Verdi's late style in all its freedom and power, moving as swiftly as musical drama can. Trying at first to pretend, Otello speaks with elaborate courtesy to Desdemona, although the acrid clarinet that doubles his vocal line reveals his anger. Desdemona, who still has no idea of the change in her husband, addresses Otello with good cheer ("Dio ti giocondi, o sposo"—*God keep you merry, husband*). But, of course, when she raises the issue of Cassio again, he cannot keep his composure. As in act 1, his head begins to hurt, and when Desdemona cannot produce the handkerchief he gave her, he warns her in a mysteriously threatening passage that she must not lose it: "Una possente maga"—*A powerful sorceress*—wove magic into it, and its loss will bring catastrophe. Amplifying Otello's words with astounding fidelity, the swift movement of the violas and cellos suggests the spinning of the fabric, while strange shifts of harmony emphasize its dark magic. Thinking Otello must be joking, Desdemona tries to resume their polite dialogue. Otello keeps interrupting her pleas on Cassio's behalf, his agitation expressed in a rising vocal line ("Il fazzoletto!"—*The handkerchief!*). Treating Desdemona as never before, Otello grabs her face, demanding that she state who she is. "La sposa fedel d'Otello"—*Otello's faithful wife*—she replies, as, to a whirling pattern for strings and bassoons that builds to a savage climax, he tells her to swear, and damn herself ("Giura e ti danna!"). Bewildered and now frightened, Desdemona sings that she feels his fury ("In te parla una Furia"), her *declamato* leaping expressively, but she doesn't understand it. To a more pleading line, she asks him to witness her first tears of sorrow ("Mi guarda! Il volto e l'anima"—*Look at me! I reveal my face, my soul*). This exchange builds as Otello finally calls her a whore ("Una vil cortigiana"); to a B-flat, she denies it spiritedly. After a pause, Otello surprisingly resumes the supposedly courteous tone in which he opened. Again, edgy winds underline his words. But at the end, as his voice rises wildly, he cries out that he mistook her for "Quella vil cortigiana che è la sposa d'Otello"—*That vile whore who is Otello's wife*. Here his vocal line rises to a shriek on the word "cortigiana," and then falls, Verdi carefully marking that the line be sung *"cupo e terribile"*—hollow and terrifying— then with *"voce soffocata"*—suffocating voice. As he pushes Desdemona away, the orchestra thunders in pity and terror.

The thunder quiets, moving into a dotted (short-long) motif for the strings that slides desolately downward in a strange and distant key; Otello, still with *"voce soffocata,"* sings the great declaimed monologue ("Dio! Mi potevi scagliar tutti i mali"—*God! You could have thrown at me all the evils*) in which he sings that he could have weathered any trial better than this one. The blackness of the music depicts the terrible conditions Otello mentions. But his tone shifts ("Ma, o pianto, o duol"—*But, o tears, o sorrow*) as he sings that this has hurt where his soul lay content, extinguishing the sun of his happiness. In the extraordinary third verse, Otello sings with a last bit of warmth that clemency must now put on the mask of hell ("Tu alfin, Clemenza"), as the strings warmly second the idea. But as his thoughts move to what's ahead, his tone changes, the music not just moving with his words and ideas but impelling them forward. As he loses control of himself, demanding proof as Iago enters, Verdi tightens the rhythmic pattern that backs him. When told that Cassio is coming, he shrieks, "Là? Cielo, oh gioia!"—*There? Heaven, what joy!* But as he imagines their illicit deeds his tone shifts instantly, and the accompaniment with it. It's a wild ride, paradoxically created by Verdi's iron grip on the text and the music.

To fierce blasts from the brass, Otello hides behind a column, as Iago has instructed him. Knowing that neither singers nor audience can continue at such intensity, Verdi sets the concerted passage, opened elegantly by prancing woodwind figures, among Cassio, Iago, and the hidden Otello as a playful scherzo with a dark undertone. Keeping an eye on Otello, Iago controls the dialogue so that Otello can only hear part of what Cassio says, as when Cassio mentions Desdemona's name, but not that of Bianca, Cassio's own mistress. The central panel of this three-part passage is begun by Iago ("Essa t'avvince coi vaghi rai"—*She captivates you with sparkling glances*) and set to another elegant but more slippery theme in the orchestra. When Iago provokes Cassio to laugh, Otello assumes it's at his expense. Shocked for a moment at the extent of his own fall, Otello asks himself when he strains to hear Cassio, "Dove son giunto?"—*What have I come to?* Finally, Cassio produces the beautiful handkerchief that has mysteriously appeared in his room. Iago maneuvers Otello closer to see the item, and the hero is devastated ("Ruina e Morte!"—*Destruction and death!*) as the orchestra thunders and trills. The final part of this great passage is a strettalike trio at a very quick tempo in which Iago ironically describes the handkerchief, "Questa è una ragna dove il tuo cuor casca"—*This is a spider's web where your heart is caught.* Cassio agrees, but Otello can only rage at his betrayal: "Tradimento!" his fury darkening the ensemble's otherwise brilliant close.

Trumpet fanfare and cannon signal the arrival of the Venetian ship. Iago sends Cassio off. To a background of fanfares and choruses welcoming the Venetians, Otello enters, horrifyingly asking Iago, "Come la ucciderò?"—*How shall I kill her?*—and stating that "È condannata"—*She is condemned.* Otello asks Iago to procure poison, but so as not to implicate himself, Iago obscenely advises Otello to suffocate her "Là, nel suo letto"—*There in the bed where she has sinned*—and coolly that he himself will see to Cassio. Otello promotes Iago to captain. As Iago goes to fetch Desdemona, Lodovico, the Venetian ambassador and his party enter, to a fanfare of great splendor and the chorus welcoming "Il Leon di San Marco"—*The Lion of St. Mark*—the emblem of Venice. Lodovico presents a letter from the Doge to Otello, whom he addresses with unknowing irony as "L'eroe trionfatore di Cipro"—*The triumphant hero of Cyprus.* Emilia asks

Desdemona why she looks so sad; her reply is that a shadow has fallen over Otello's mind and her destiny. Iago greets the officials; Lodovico asks for Cassio. Iago replies, "Con lui crucciato è Otello"—*Otello is annoyed with him.* When Desdemona says that he'll soon return to favor, Otello, over trembling strings, and still pretending to read, asks, "Ne siete certa?"—*Are you sure?* Iago provokes her into yet another statement of her concern for Cassio, and Otello, enraged, makes as though to strike her: "Demonio, taci!"—*Silence, demon!* Now everyone sees that something is terribly wrong. Lodovico is shocked, but when he asks Iago what's going on, the villain answers noncommittally. Otello orders Cassio be brought. In an undertone Iago asks why; Otello tells him to observe Cassio closely. He then reads the Doge's instructions: he is to return to Venice, leaving as governor "Mio vessillo, Cassio"—*He who carried my banner.* Iago is furious. Otello proclaims that they will sail tomorrow, then grabs Desdemona and forces her to the ground, singing furiously and high in his range, "A terra! E piangi!"—*On your knees! And weep!* The orchestra sounds a chord sequence of enormous power, into which Verdi injects a note of sadness, four times, opening the ensemble that ends the act.

Built on three phrases sung by Desdemona, the passage begins with apparent simplicity. Her first, "A terra! Sì ... nel livido fango"—*On the earth, yes, in the pale mud*—is marked "*declamato*," struggling, like Desdemona herself to rise. The next, "E un dì sul mio sorriso"—*Once, hope lived in my smile*—over pulsing woodwinds, soars, however, then falls again. The third and most glorious phrase, "Quel Sol, sereno e vivido"—*The sun, serene and vivid*—moves radiantly, like the sun itself over an accompaniment that shimmers quietly. In the next section, sung a cappella, the chorus comments on the shock of what has just happened, as Emilia, Cassio, Roderigo, and Lodovico express similar emotions, each slanted by the character's place in the drama. (Roderigo, for example, mopes that Desdemona will be leaving.) As the orchestra reenters, Iago begins to advance his plot, urging Otello to strike tonight and saying again that he will take care of Cassio. A weeping figure appears in the orchestra, complementing the lament of the chorus. Iago then goads Roderigo into action, telling him that Desdemona won't be able to leave if Cassio is killed. The weeping figure assumes more prominence in the orchestra. As Iago eggs Rodrigo on, Verdi pulls the musical forces, until now deployed lyrically, into place for a stretta and climax of power and beauty.

First the trumpets hammer out Desdemona's first phrase, which climaxes majestically; then the second, which leads to an accelerating passage in biting triplets for everyone except Otello, who stands silent for the moment. This leads to an extraordinary climax on Desdemona's third phrase over a thundering orchestra, for which Verdi broadens the tempo. But in high agitation, Otello interrupts, cutting the final note of the climactic phrase off. "Tutti fuggite Otello!"—*All, away from Otello!* Lodovico attempts to lead Desdemona away, but out of concern she approaches Otello: "Mio sposo!"—*My husband!* With a huge snarl for the trumpets and a ringing A-sharp for the singer, he curses her: "Anima mia, ti maledico!"—*Upon my soul, I curse you!* To another colossal Verdian orchestral uproar, the stage empties, except for Otello and Iago. Dizzy with rage and grief, Otello mutters disjointed phrases from Iago's brainwashing, ending with, "Il fazzoletto"—*The handkerchief!*—and then swoons. To a still, single tone from low winds, strings, and brass, Iago calmly comments, "Il mio velen lavora"—*My poison is working.* As the chorus praising Otello is heard from outside, hammered notes introduce his penultimate line: "Chi può vietar che questa fronte prema col mio tallone?"—*Who can stop me from crushing my heel into his forehead?* As the chorus praises Otello again ("Gloria al Leon di Venezia"—*Glory to the Lion of Venice*), Iago contemptuously replies, a trill in his final note, "Ecco il Leone!"—*Behold the Lion!* Another violent and jolting orchestral postlude ends the act.

The fourth act is Desdemona's for more than half of its thirty-minute length. There can hardly be a better example than this act of the power of anticipation in narrative art, as our dread only adds force to Verdi's uncompromising rendering of Desdemona's murder. But with the public humiliation of the third act done, act 4 opens in a mood of lyrical intimacy and desolation as Desdemona waits for the catastrophe she senses is coming but still can't fathom. A very beautiful prelude for woodwinds and horn opens the act, playing the melody of the "Willow Song," the first of Desdemona's two linked cantabiles. Sung by a melancholy English horn, the melody is punctuated by a comment from the flute, then three hollow chords for the clarinets, followed by a short quasi-contrapuntal fantasy for the woodwinds and horn, all ending on a bare falling phrase for strings, as Verdi sets a mood from which hope has gone.

Desdemona and her confidante Emilia are in Desdemona's bedroom as Desdemona prepares for bed. Desdemona tells Emilia that Otello seemed calmer. She asks Emilia to lay out her white bridal gown, and then in a passionate arioso sings that she wants to be buried in it should she die before Emilia, who tries to dismiss her morbid mood. "Son mesta, tanto, tanto"—*I am sad, so sad*—Desdemona replies in a phrase that rises then falls sharply, expressing her overwhelming sorrow. In a particularly affecting recitative Desdemona introduces the "Willow Song" (CD Track 17) as having been sung by Barbara, a beautiful young maid in her mother's service who was abandoned by her lover. As in the prelude to the act, the woodwinds introduce the song and play a crucial role in its accompaniment. After they play a fragment with a folklike tinge, ending strangely but solemnly on a note shared by the English horn and piccolo, Desdemona sings the opening line, "Piangea cantando nell'erma landa"—*Singing, she wept on the lonely hearth*—to the tune that introduced the act. Falling woodwinds, again in starkly simple harmony mark the next line, "Piangea la mesta"—*The sad one wept.* Unaccompanied and *"come una voce lontana"*—like a faraway voice, in Verdi's instruction—she sings the desolate refrain, "O salce, salce, salce"—*Willow.* The English horn twines with Desdemona's voice for the next line, "Sedea chinando sul sen la testa"—*She sat with her head bent on her breast.* The word "cantiamo"—*let us sing*—is set to a sigh, followed by the stark falling figure "Il salce funebre sarà la mia ghirlanda"—*The weeping willow shall be my funeral garland*—is followed by a longer version of the fragment for winds heard at the start of the aria. The second verse, which describes Barbara's flowing tears, mixes strings and weeping winds for a fuller but still delicate accompaniment; the third, in which the birds that flock to hear Barbara's "dolce canto"—*sweet song*—are depicted in chirps for the flutes and piccolo. Most poignant of all are the sighing winds and trembling strings matching Desdemona's piercing vocal line as she describes how the stones themselves were moved to pity by Barbara's weeping. Desdemona thinks of poor Barbara—"Povera Barbara"—singing to a gently rocking line colored by a pathos-laden shift to the major key, the simple end of the tale: "Egli era nato per la sua gloria, io per amar"—*He was born for glory, and I to love.*

Desdemona's rendition is interrupted three times: the first, a quiet request to Emilia to hurry, and the second, asking her to hold a ring she gives her. But in the third, set to music of pictorial terror, Desdemona is alarmed by a sound, "Odo un lamento"—*I hear a wailing*—as she's overwhelmed by dread of her own approaching doom; Emilia reassures her that it's only the wind. But although brief (only ten bars long), and over in seconds, Verdi's wailing winds and shuddering strings render it potent and unforgettable. (Unfortunately, this passage is omitted from the recording on the CD.) Desdemona resumes and concludes the "Willow Song," then heavy-heartedly bids Emilia good night. As her friend leaves she cries out in desperation for a loving touch; to a passionate phrase Desdemona says not good night but farewell ("Emilia, addio!"). The women embrace as a bitter seven-note phrase over a sinking chromatic passage for the orchestra captures Desdemona's fear and grief in a few concentrated measures.

Alone, Desdemona prays in the second part of this unusual double aria. Her lovely, soft appeal to the Virgin ("Ave Maria") begins in a murmured version of the standard prayer, but blossoms into something more personal. It has to be admitted that sometimes (although never in the Requiem) Verdi's rendering of prayers and religious rites have a perfunctory air about them, understandable given the composer's atheism. But not this "Ave Maria," which is more to depict Desdemona's goodness than her faith, anyway. Very slow in tempo, the prayer rises on a tender melody, with few high notes but a leap of a sixth that stands out expressively. Verdi adds a catch in the form of a soblike grace note for the violas that depicts the character's underlying grief. Desdemona prays earnestly, "Nel peccator . . . per l'innocente, . . . e pel possente, misero anch'esso"—*For the sinner . . . the innocent . . . the powerful, and for the grieving, too.* The final verse is the clincher, as she prays aloud, "Nell'ora della morte"—*At the hour of our death*—as the accompaniment, only strings here, sinks. She prays to herself, as the orchestra carries on with the accompaniment as if she were singing, moving gently behind her pantomime. Desdemona picks up, meaningfully, again at "Nell'ora della morte." In the closest approach to vocal display in this cantabile, she completes her prayer on a long, soft A-flat ("Ave"), then an "Amen" murmured low.

Celestial strings end Desdemona's prayer; she lies down and sleeps. Otello slips in through a secret door, his final entrance as remarkable musically as his first. Verdi deploys the eerie and rarely heard timbre of the muted double bass in a long, hair-raising passage to depict Otello's stealthy entrance. An instrument almost never heard on its own, the double bass is the bedrock of orchestral sound, but which unlike its sibling the cello, few find pleasing. Verdi's goal is not to create a pleasing sound; rather, an alarming one, and he succeeds. The rising contrabass melody takes on genuine eloquence, though, before it's met by a nine-note staccato figure played first by the violas, which assumes an enormous role in the terrible events that follow. A single thud on the bass drum concludes this unnerving sequence, which Verdi builds to a big climax for the full orchestra to accompany Otello's pantomime of fury, as he advances on the bed, then stops himself. An impassioned rising phrase for English horn and bassoon backed by tremolando strings, and similar in profile to the double-bass melody seems to express all Otello's passion, as he watches the sleeping Desdemona; then to the yearning "kiss" motif from the act 1 love duet, he kisses her three times. "Chi e là? Otello?"—*Who's there?*—she asks, awakening to a cadence of the deepest gravity.

The nine-note tiptoe figure, strengthened by the brass at the end returns as Otello begins his ritualistic interrogation prior to what he sees as justifiable murder, which Verdi treats with urgency. First he asks Desdemona whether she has prayed; as we know, she has. In his trumpet-voiced mode Otello then says that if she has any other sins she needs to confess, to do it. When she asks why, he tells her that he would not kill her soul. Verdi expands the staccato string figure into longer sequences that ratchet up the tension, already high, unbearably. On a high A, showing his loss of control, Otello accuses her of loving Cassio, which of course she denies. He asks about the handkerchief, but again Desdemona can only profess her innocence. Frantic, she cries for help ("Aita!") with Verdi's trembling orchestra shrilly capturing her terror. She asks for Cassio to be brought in, but Otello tells her coldly that he's dead. Her despair ("Son perduto! Ei tradito!"—*I'm lost! And he's betrayed!*) enrages Otello as the staccato motif rushes ahead with unstoppable energy, taken up by more and more of the orchestra. The terrifying dialogue also tightens as Desdemona begs with increasing desperation and he loses all control: "È tardi!"—*It's too late!* Finally, to the most terrible of all Verdi's orchestral outbursts, Otello smothers Desdemona with her pillow.

As the instrumental turmoil subsides Emilia is heard knocking. "Calma come la tomba," Otello comments, to a simple, somber harmony, then faltering as he notices the knocking. Verdi renders the exchanges between him and Emilia in very quick recitative, with as little orchestral punctuations as is needed. Emilia brings news that Cassio has killed Roderigo; a massive chord for the orchestra underlines Otello's shock. As only happens in even the greatest operas, Desdemona, not quite dead as it turns out, gets to sing a few touching words before she dies: "Muoio innocente"—*I die innocent*—she sings weakly. To another big chord for the full orchestra, Emilia asks who did this; "Nessuno . . . io stessa . . . al mio signor mi raccomanda . . ."—*No one . . . I did it . . . Commend me to my lord . . .* Desdemona adds, nobly trying to absolve Otello. In rapid exchange, Otello admits killing her because "Fu di Cassio la druda"—*She was Cassio's whore.* Emilia shrieks for help, and instantly Cassio, Iago, Montano, and Lodovico enter, uttering cries of horror. Iago's plotting is quickly exposed, and the villain flees the room. To a powerful scale played in a shockingly remote tonality Otello cries, "E il ciel non ha più fulmini?"—*Have the heavens no more thunderbolts?*

To heavy chords played softly by the full orchestra, Otello begins his final monologue. "Niun mi tema"—*None need fear me*—he sings, "Ecco la fine del mio cammin"—*This is my journey's end.* A big chord accompanies his rueful "Oh Gloria! Otello fu"—*Oh glory! Otello's done.* An eloquent phrase for sighing woodwinds precedes his apostrophe to Desdemona, "E tu, come sei pallida!"—*And you, how pale you are!*—sung at first unaccompanied, in an arioso of Monteverdian gravity and freedom, this phrase the peak of this opera and perhaps of Italian lyric tragedy. Strings and timpani take up a dirge as Otello notes that Desdemona's "Fredda come la casta tua vita"—*Cold as your life was chaste.* When in his next line he sings of her rising to heaven, the flutes accomplish in under two measures and with a poignantly melancholy shading what formerly took the master minutes to accomplish. He looks at her again, and sings despairingly, "Ah, morta, morta, morta!"

Otello stabs himself with a hidden dagger; the others cry out in horror. As the impassioned English horn theme from before the kisses that awakened Desdemona, now sounding in infinite pain, he sings his matchless farewell: "Pria d'ucciderti . . . sposa . . . ti baciai . . ."—*Before I killed you, wife, I kissed you.* The English horn sounds again, as Otello's line breaks, in his agony. "Or mordeno . . . nell'ombra . . . in cui mi giacio"—*Now dying in the shadow where I lie.* The kiss theme sounds again for each of the three times he struggles to kiss Desdemona, as he sings, "Un bacio . . . un bacio ancora . . . un altro bacio," dying on the last attempt. Above the quiet shuddering of the double basses and timpani, the full orchestra sounds six terrible soft chords, ending *Otello* in a pure and trembling passion.

# Shakespearean Comedy
## Falstaff

Photographs of Verdi from the 1880s and 1890s show a change in the man. In candids taken with Boito or the Ricordis he leans backward, hands planted firmly against his lower back in a characteristically self-reliant gesture, but smiles and is unmistakably relaxed. Another, less well known, shows him chatting with a resident of the Casa di Riposo, the Milanese rest home he built for old and poor professional musicians. Verdi is standing and talking, the nameless beneficiary sitting; both are smiling. So, time seems to have softened this tough man, at least to some degree. Depressed he may have been at times, as when Giuseppina and old friends died, but somehow he found enjoyment and amusement in his last two decades; and somehow he found a pathway back to comedy.

The idea for *Falstaff* was Boito's, but Verdi, after a few protests about his age—seventy-six when he began work in the summer of 1889—was excited by the project, completing it toward the end of 1892. *Falstaff* premiered on February 9, 1893, to respectful reviews as might be expected but the rapidity of the music and action made the opera rather a puzzle for early audiences. Those with sharper ears, including the composer Richard Strauss who in 1895 wrote Verdi gushingly about *Falstaff*,[1] and the conductor Arturo Toscanini who championed the opera from the beginning until his own retirement in 1954, knew its greatness. As director of La Scala, Toscanini programmed *Falstaff* repeatedly, even though audiences remained cool to the work. Although the score's brilliance will be obvious even to first-time listeners, its speed and subtlety demand repeated hearings and long acquaintance. It's no coincidence that the opera's reputation and popularity grew once recordings allowed audiences to get to know it at leisure.

Much credit goes to Boito, who merged three Shakespearean plays into one triumphant libretto—a masterpiece on its own—that follows the plot of *The Merry Wives of Windsor* with interpolations that deepen the characters from the history plays *Henry IV Parts I and II*, as well as material from Boccaccio's *Decameron* for color. It's a battle of the sexes that the women are always winning, if not always by much. Throughout the opera Verdi treats the female characters with deep love, as for example in their lyrical ensemble in act 1 scene 2, where the lilting beauty of their parts contrasts conspicuously with the men's foursquare ranting.

The ultimate triumph is Verdi's for an opera that for many has the highest trajectory of all. In addition to the fleet-footed music, which moves from one idea to the next without ceremony, displaying an uncanny sensitivity to action and words, the orchestration shows all the master's force but also a new delicacy and refinement. Harmonic movement has a new freedom. The hair-trigger ensembles achieve a new level of sophistication and intricacy. There's a Haydn-esque freshness to *Falstaff* that's one of its most appealing qualities. Complaints that the work is Wagnerian in structure and that it lacks the melodic richness of Verdi's earlier work are wrong: the opera represents a purely Verdian renaissance, and overflows with melody. The nature of comedy as the mature Verdi sees it places forward motion as the chief priority, and the composer adds, then drops, melodies as the action demands. And, although *Falstaff* is genuinely funny, you will sooner or later perceive the vein of seriousness that places it among the elite operatic comedies. Sometimes *Falstaff* seems like the last burst of classical style, Mozartean in its elegance and purity, and its raging orchestral climaxes that sting with a Beethovenian power.

The opera opens with a characteristic Verdian gesture of two explosive chords from the full orchestra into which a falling figure for chugging winds and strings is built. Dr. Cajus, whose blustery theme this is, enters the Garter Inn, yelling for Falstaff, who ignores him. In a swift dialogue, Cajus accuses Falstaff, who meanwhile calls for another bottle of sherry, of beating his servants, breaking his horse's back, and "Sforzata la mia casa"— *Violating my house.* "Ma non la tua massaia"—*But not your housekeeper*— Falstaff replies. To a tranquil, rising scale in an unexpected key, Falstaff calmly confesses; when Cajus threatens to appeal to the Royal Council, Falstaff ironically wishes him luck. Infuriated, Cajus turns on Bardolfo, one of Falstaff's two henchmen, whom he accuses to a whining figure for the oboes and clarinets of getting him drunk the night before. Bardolfo agrees that they were indeed drunk, but when Cajus accuses him of having picked his pocket, Bardolfo disagrees. To the calm, rising theme Falstaff summons his other hanger-on, Pistola, whom Cajus then accuses. Less patient than Bardolfo, Pistola chases Cajus around with a broom, the two exchanging tasty insults ("Gonzo"—*Fool*—"Spauracchio"—*Scarecrow*—"Gnomo"—*Gnome*). In the end, Bardolfo sums up Cajus's weak case over the rising scale and giggles from the woodwinds and strings: "Costui beve"—*He drinks* . . . "Poi ti narra una favola ch'egli ha sognato mentre dormì sotto la tavola"—*Then he spins you a tale he dreamed while sleeping under the table.* Falstaff advises Cajus to go in peace ("Vattene in pace"), and on a thumping five-note gesture for the trombones, Cajus swears that if he ever gets drunk again, it will be with "Gente onesta, sobria, civile e pia"—*Honest, sober, civil, and pious company.* Bardolfo and Pistola accompany him out, singing "Amen" in bad counterpoint. The entire opening scene, packed with dialogue and music, runs just over four flying minutes that feel even shorter.

Falstaff advises his assistants, "Rubar con garbo e a tempo"—*Steal with grace and at the right moment*—to which they reply with another creaky "Amen." Falstaff reads the bill from the Garter Inn, the last item "Un' acciuga"—*One anchovy*—to a whine from the flutes and piccolo. But his purse is nearly empty. Falstaff pays a surprisingly touching, lyrical tribute to Bardolfo's red nose ("Tuo naso ardentissimo") that lights his way home every night. But both he and Pistola cost too much, he concludes, and are wasting his flesh: "Mi struggete le carni." To a keening melody, backed by the unusual combination of piccolo and cello, he sings that if he grows thin no one will love him; to a genuinely majestic accompaniment he praises his paunch, as do Pistola and Bardolfo ("Falstaff immenso!" "Enorme Falstaff!"). A mighty orchestral explosion punctuates his imperial proclamation "Quest' è il mio regno. Lo ingranderò"—*This is my kingdom. I will extend it.* As in *Otello*, Verdi establishes early on that the title character is the opera's dominant personality, its figurative "king." Both fall, albeit differently.

Changing tone, Falstaff tells Bardolfo and Pistola that it's time to sharpen their wits. He asks whether they know the burgher Ford, richer than Croesus . . . whose beautiful wife, Alice, holds the purse strings, Pistola adds. To an exquisite, gently rocking accompaniment, Falstaff sings the praises of the fair Alice Ford, "Un fior chi ride"—*That laughing flower*. Pay attention to the springlike freshness of this moment, as Verdi captures youthful impulses and follies that still come to old men. The music moves with the speed of thought as he describes how she smiled at him one day when he was in the street: "Sul fianco baldo, sul gran torace, sul maschio piè, sul fusto saldo, erto, capace"—*On my gallant flank, my broad chest, my manly foot, my sturdy, upright frame*—his grotesque vanity caricatured by a waddling accompaniment dominated by the bassoons, and his line fantasizing her thought, "'Io son di Sir John Falstaff'"—*"I am Sir John Falstaff's"*—sung in falsetto. He then mentions a second affluent married woman, Margaret Page ("La chiaman Meg"—*They call her Meg*) who likewise holds the key to her family coffers. Falstaff hands two "lettere infuocate"—*fiery letters*—to Bardolfo and Pistola, asking them to give one to Alice and Meg, respectively. With dignity, Pistola replies that he's a soldier, not a pimp, then Bardolfo also demurs. Why? Falstaff asks, to which Bardolfo replies, "L'onore"—*Honor*.

Dispatching the letters with a page, Falstaff in a great monologue, "L'onore! Ladri!" (CD Track 18)—*Honor! You thieves!*—first takes apart Bardolfo and Pistola and then deconstructs the idea of honor itself. First calling them "Cloache d'ignominia"—*Sewers of baseness*—he says that when even the great Falstaff has to resort to "Stratagemmi ed equivoci"—*Stratagems and deceptions*—then who are they, with their ragged clothes and shifty looks, to mention honor? "Che ciancia! Che baia!"—*What rubbish! What a joke!* A huge orchestral trill describes his contempt. He then asks rhetorically what honor really is: Can it fill an empty stomach or mend a broken leg? To each question he answers, "No," accompanied by a note burped out by the clarinets, bassoons, and double-bass. Finally, he concludes to an airy phrase from the flutes that honor is merely a word, made of air: It does nothing for the dead, and "gonfian le lusinghe"—*falsely puffs up*—the living. To sum up, he wants none of it, and to a scurrying accelerating accompaniment, he declares grandly that he's had enough of his unsavory companions, as well. Picking up a broom, he discharges them: "Vi discaccio"—*I'm throwing you out*. To a thrilling and swift orchestral postlude marked by some powerful trills for the woodwinds and brass, Falstaff chases them out.

Often thought of as a companion piece to Iago's "Credo," Falstaff's great aria is also paired more immediately by Ford's on jealously in act 2 scene 2, as well as Falstaff's own in act 3 scene 1. Verdi sets this extraordinary *declamato* monologue with dazzling, sometimes minimalist brilliance, as in the litany about the efficacy of honor, where the instruments grunt their agreement. Falstaff's vocal part is very difficult, from the batteries of Es, Fs, and even a detached G, unusual for a bass (less for bass-baritones, who often sing the role) to the need for the utmost subtlety in delivering the words, no job for amateurs. *Falstaff* may be a comedy, but as "L'onore" demonstrates, it's a profound one, a comedy of ideas as well as actions.

The second scene of act 1 introduces the women who drive the plot ahead. A short prelude of a lovely, symmetrical melody showcases Verdi's extraordinary writing for the woodwinds, the tune taken by the flutes and piccolo with the other winds and horns below. Set in the garden next to Ford's house, the four women—Alice Ford, her daughter Nannetta, Meg Page, and the older Mistress Quickly—enter and greet one another airily, their music telling us without fuss that they are intimate friends. Verdi portrays the relationships among the women throughout with touching tenderness; Quickly's greeting as she strokes Nannetta's cheek is "Botton di rosa"—*Rosebud*. Both Alice and Meg have received letters, identical it turns out, as they read them together ("Qua 'Meg,' là 'Alice'"—*Here "Meg," there "Alice"*) accompanied by the English horn, they note the duplicate texts and to a satirically swelling accompaniment, the four sing the letter's closing line, "E il viso tuo su me risplenderà come una stella sull'immensità"—*And your face will shine upon me like a star on the vast deep.* The four burst into two fleet bars of shimmering laughter. Calling Falstaff a monster, they agree that he must be punished, as Verdi launches boldly into a new rhythm, a flowing 6/8, for their short but exquisite quartet "Quell'otre! Quel tino!"—*That wineskin! That barrel!*—in which they make fun of Falstaff's weight, vanity, and pretensions and agree that he must pay for his folly. Boito's image-heavy mock Elizabethan text is astonishingly clever, but even in Verdi's delicate setting it's impossible to make out, only a word here and there emerging. The tone of the passage is cheerful, containing no menace. That is left for the men—Bardolfo, Pistola, Dr. Cajus, Fenton, and Ford—as they enter in a squarish two-beat rhythm and much heavier orchestral accompaniments, including timpani and threatening trumpets. As with the women, they are singing elaborate, deliberately wordy texts from which Verdi allows crucial and colorful words to escape. Bardolfo (reformed, he says, for reasons of health) and

Pistola have come to warn Ford about Falstaff; Cajus agrees, warning him against Bardolfo and Pistola, too; young Fenton, Nannetta's lover of whom Ford disapproves, offers to puncture Falstaff. In a passage miraculously combining lightness and complexity, Verdi joins the men and women's ensembles without changing their nature or, perhaps more important, their clashing rhythms, which the composer juggles with dizzying ease.

As Pistola sums the matter up to Ford ("L'enorme Falstaff vuole"—*Enormous Falstaff wishes*), the ex-hangers-on warn Ford emphatically to beware of Falstaff, who ogles all women, and who in Bardolfo's words would crown Ford with a cuckold's horns. Here, hammering trumpets second Ford's response ("Sorveglierò la moglie"—*I'll watch over my wife*). But as the men notice Alice, Fenton and Nannetta spot each other, too. As the women except for Nannetta go offstage, and the men move to the side to continue their conference, the lovers sing a short (about one minute and forty seconds long) duet unlike any from Verdi before, and in its own class for delicacy. They kiss quickly, beginning the call and response duet as Nannetta sings, "Labbra di foco"—*Lips of fire*—and Fenton responds, "Labbra di fiore"—*Lips like flowers*. Fenton declares his love, as Nannetta warns him, "Vien gente"—*Someone's coming!*—then darts off to lighter-than-air arpeggios for woodwinds and strings. Fenton sings the melancholy closing line of the madrigal that he and Nannetta share, "'Bocca baciata non perde ventura'"—*"Lips that are kissed lose none of their allure"*—as Nannetta replies to a long, lovely A-flat on the last word, "'Anzi rinnova come fa la luna'"—*"They renew it, like the moon"*—which the strings tenderly underline.

The strings turn heavy as the senior women return to the stage in a strongly rhythmic phrase suggesting their anger at Falstaff has taken on more of an edge. They agree that Falstaff ("Monte di lardo"—*That mountain of lard*, as Alice calls him) deserves punishment. As they contemplate how to pay him back, Verdi depicts their joy and love of fun in a spirited and in fact moving—though swift—concerted climax for the four based on the rhythmic phrase that opened the passage ("Che gioia"—*What joy*).

Verdi needs little new musical material to complete the scene, but reuses what he already has with concentration and brilliance. The lovers continue their duet with new verbal conceits (He: "Torno all' assalto"—*I return to the assault*; She: "Torno alla gara"—*And I to the defense*); the men bluster angrily, as Bardolfo and Pistola swear allegiance to Ford, and the women pursue their own plot in a quick recapitulation of the rhythmically conflicted ensemble. But as the men leave the stage the women's irresistible rhythm wins out in a driving, dancelike passage. Alice, their leader, sums it up: "Vedrai che quell'epa terribile e tronfia si gonfia"—*You'll see that awesome and boastful belly puff up*—then, to a collapsing scale for bassoons and trombones, "E poi crepa"—*And then burst*—as all the women join her. Sarcastically Alice repeats the flattering phrase from Falstaff's letter ("Ma il viso") in which all join, then burst into musical laughter.

A burly, thumping phrase for the orchestra brings us back to the masculine Garter Inn, where Bardolfo and Pistola beat their chests in pretended penance to Falstaff as act 2 opens. Bardolfo introduces Mrs. Quickly, on the women's mission to sting Falstaff. Quickly enters to a curtsey in flawlessly depicted music that is one of her trademark phrases for much of the opera. "Reverenza," the word she repeats with her six-note phrase, meaning "I bow to you," which she does literally at her entrance. Quickly offers her services while feigning obeisance to Falstaff, who is all too ready to swallow everything she says. As they go through an elaborately courteous ritual, she begins to get her story out, mentioning Alice's name, then another trademark phrase, "Povera donna"—*The poor woman*—and aside that Falstaff is a "Gran seddutore"—*A great seducer*—to which he blithely replies that he knows. Quickly says that Alice is in turmoil over Falstaff's letter, and that her husband always goes out "Dalle due alle tre"—*Between two and three*—a third motto set to a more lively rhythm. (Verdi reuses these pithy motifs effectively later in the opera.) Falstaff excitedly repeats the phrase, as Quickly goes on to warn him that poor Alice "ha un marito geloso"—*has a jealous husband.* Falstaff tells Quickly to promise Alice that he will be there. Bearing a response from Meg as well, Quickly reports that she, too, finds him bewitching, but that her husband seldom goes out. "Povera donna," Quickly repeats, now about Meg. Falstaff admits to having "un certo qual mio fascino personal"—*a certain personal magnetism.* Falstaff thanks, then tips Quickly, as one sharp chord shows her astonishment at how cheap he is. To her musical curtsey, Quickly exits.

Falstaff exults ("Alice è mia!"—*Alice is mine!*) to a strutting tune of repeated notes decorated by grace notes over one of Verdi's trademark moving bass lines giving it great momentum. Then, to a grunting march of lower-pitched instruments, he congratulates himself on his own excellence in the marvelous arioso, "Va, vecchio John, va, va per la tua via"—*Go, old*

*John, go your way*—basking in the satisfaction that women "Si dannano per me!"—*Risk damnation for me!* Subtle harmonic shifts undercut his preening, as the orchestra then repeats the strutting tune. Bardolfo announces "Una certo Mastro Fontana"—*A certain Master Brook*—who wishes to meet Falstaff, offering by way of introduction a gift of wine. Falstaff struts a bit more as Bardolfo goes for Mr. Brook, actually Ford. Ford apologizes for visiting without ceremony; Falstaff welcomes him. Ford gets to business (and to Falstaff's entrapment) by stating that he has money to squander. Overly cordial and to a memorable falling phrase ("Caro Signor Fontana"—*My dear Master Brook*) that will be repeated ironically later, Falstaff says, his thoughts already on his new acquaintance's money, that he wishes to know him better. Bardolfo and Pistola chatter as they watch the action; regally Falstaff shushes them. Holding out a bag of money, Ford says that since gold opens every door, he's hoping he can give his to Falstaff for one deed: to seduce the beautiful Alice Ford, who has spurned his advances ("C'è a Windsor una dama"—*There is in Windsor a lady*). A jingling figure accented by the clang of the triangle portrays the gold in Ford's bag. Ford's arioso goes on to describe the efforts and money he's lavished on Alice for naught, leaving him singing a madrigal about the pain of love, which opens with the only vocal cadenza in *Falstaff*. He and Falstaff sing the madrigal together, alternating lines, to a gurgling accompaniment in which the bassoons and piccolo take the lead.

Naturally enough, Falstaff wonders what he can do to help. Flattering the knight, Ford describes him as military trumpets sound as "Un uom di guerra . . . un uom di mondo"—*A man of war . . . and of the world*—to whom he will gladly give his money to win Alice. Saying that Falstaff has a better chance of seducing her, and that "Da fallo nasce fallo"—*One slip leads to another*—he asks Falstaff to give it a try. Taking the sack of money, Falstaff guarantees "La moglie di Ford possederete"—*You will possess Ford's wife*. In fact, he has already been invited to visit her today, "Dalle due alle tre," at which time Alice will be in his arms. To a single dry chord, the shocked Ford bellows "Chi?"—*Who?*—as Falstaff calmly replies that she has already informed him through a messenger that "Quel tanghero di suo marito"—*That blockhead of a husband*—is out every day at that time. Pulling himself together, "Mr. Brook" asks Falstaff whether he knows Ford, in response to which the knight cruelly mocks Ford and his kind: "Vedrai, te lo cornifico, netto, netto"—*You'll see, I'll cuckold him neatly!* The orchestral accompaniment to this stunning *declamato* passage is brilliant with bright piccolo sounds, then deeper as trilling strings echo Falstaff calling Ford "Un bue"—*An ox*—four times, the trills suggesting the animal's lowing. Telling Ford to wait while "Farmi bello"—*I make myself handsome*—he leaves the stage to a stinging, quasi-Beethovenian incarnation of a leaping phrase from his short aria.

Falstaff's swift aria acts as a prelude to Ford's, where many of its themes are repeated, albeit to completely different effect. The most frankly serious passage in the opera, Ford's aria opens in a hovering, open harmony as he asks himself, "È sogno? O realtà?"—*Is this a dream or reality?* His thoughts coming without clear order, he proclaims in horror, "Due rami enormi crescon sulla mia testa"—*Two enormous horns are sprouting on my head*—his vocal line rising monstrously in pitch (ending on a G-flat) and volume. Over an animating accompaniment Ford rouses himself as he reflects, the orchestra mirroring his agitation, that his wife is abusing "L'onor tuo, la tua casa, ed il tuo letto"—*Your honor, your house, and your bed.* A bleak phrase by the horns, their use carrying a double meaning, Ford considers that "L'ora è fissata . . . sei gabbato e truffato"—*The hour is fixed . . . you are duped and cheated.* A powerful phrase is given to his ironic reflection that people say a jealous husband is crazy. The orchestra rages powerfully behind his twin analogies, "O matrimonio: inferno! Donna: demonio!"—*Marriage is hell. Woman: a fiend.* Stabbing figures for the violins punctuate his harsh analogies of women's faithlessness with a German's love of beer or a gluttonous Dutchman in a kitchen, as Verdi works echoes of Falstaff's diatribe quietly into the background. Again nearly losing control, Ford thinks on the symbols of cuckoldry, also thinking of Falstaff, about whom he mutters, "Capron"—*Goat.* He nearly chokes again on the words "Le corna"—*the horns.* His part marked to be sung *"con violenza,"* Ford swears, "Vendicherò l'affronto"—*I'll avenge this outrage.* To a line that rises and falls and a powerful orchestral backing, he thanks "La gelosia" from the bottom of his heart. Ford plays the villain in *Falstaff* by default. But we can only sympathize with him here as he lays out his horror at Alice's perceived betrayal, so clearly does Verdi delineate his mental process and pain.

The raging orchestra dies down, as a ridiculously dandified Falstaff enters to a mincing tune. He politely asks Ford, who has regained his composure, to walk part of the way with him. An "after you" routine ensues, in which each tries to outdo the other in courtesy. Finally Falstaff takes

Ford's arm and the two leave together, to Falstaff's triumphant strutting theme from earlier in the scene.

The climactic second scene of act 2, set inside Ford's house, opens as to chuckling strings Alice busies herself in preparation for Falstaff's visit. Meg enters, then Quickly, who describes her successful entrapment of the knight in a narrative passage, "Giunta all'albergo della Giarrettiera"— *When I arrived at the Garter.* She describes his lordly manner, imitating his pompous greeting ("Buon giorno, buona donna") and bovine voice. Then playing herself, Quickly curtsies and sings her trademark "Reverenza." To a stinging phrase, she says he swallowed her story, believing both women are madly in love with him, and, to the now familiar motif, he'll be there between two and three. (Verdi added this narrative after auditioning Giuseppina Pasqua, who would sing the first Quickly, in appreciation of her acting and vocal abilities.) In addition to bringing back thematic material from the previous scene, it also puts the brakes on the pacing of the opera, slowing its pace a bit in preparation for the more static third act.[2] Alice calls two servants in to move furniture, and most important, to bring the laundry basket, in which Falstaff will be hidden before being dumped into the Thames. Nannetta, who entered with Quickly is crying; "*singhiozzando*"—sniffling—is Verdi's instruction. Through her tears she says that her father has told her that she must marry Dr. Cajus. Instantly the other women, calling Cajus a pedant, fool, dolt, and dimwit, agree that this will not happen, making clear once again who runs the show in Windsor. To a single, delicate iteration of Cajus's theme from the opera's opening, a relieved Nannetta rejoices, then joins in the others' gleeful mood. Alice moves a chair and a screen and places her lute on the table to the same string figures that opened the scene, broken into phrases that match her movements. In a broad, freely declaimed phrase, Alice declares, "Fra poco s'incomincia la commedia!"—*The comedy will soon begin!* Her arioso "Gaie comari di Windsor! è l'ora"—*Merry wives of Windsor, it's time*—set to a lilting, lighter-than-air melody may be the sublime core and most sacred moment in *Falstaff.* In this ninety-second passage, Alice declares the joyous intent of their escapade ("Splenda del riso l'acuto fulgor!"—*Let the bright gleam of laughter shine!*), her line rising sharply to a high C; then, tenderly underlined by the strings, she sings, "A noi"—*It's up to us.* The three chief conspirators—Alice, Meg, and Quickly—agree on a few final signals as Nannetta will watch from the door; in an unforgettable phrase, Alice says that they'll show the men that honest gaiety is proper, as in a ponderous voice that contrasts strikingly with the gravity-free passage in which it sits and echoed by the violins, she sings that "Fra le femine quella è la più ria che fa la gattamorta"—*Among women the worst is the one who acts the prude.* Then, to chattering woodwinds, the four repeat Alice's ecstatic melody. Quickly spots Falstaff approaching, as to graceful scampering arpeggios for the winds and hair-trigger ensemble singing, the women take their places ("Al posto"—*To our posts*).

Posing prettily with her lute, Alice strokes a few chords, played by a guitar in the orchestra. Falstaff, enters, singing a lyric ("'Alfin t'ho colto, raggiante fior'"—*"At last I pluck you, radiant flower"*), then stating that he can die happily after this hour of love. His words trailed by a mocking bassoon, he confesses a sinful thought, which is that Master Ford might pass on to a better life so that Alice could be his lady and Falstaff her lord. Again, gargling bassoons echo his fantasy ("T'immagino fregiata del mio stemma"—*I can picture you adorned with my crest*), his phrase expanding with satiric comments by the piccolo and oboe then expanding into a climax for the full orchestra. Alice seductively replies that she spurns gold, and is more comfortable in simple dress and a flower in her hair ("E in testa un fior"). She dodges Falstaff as he tries to embrace her, but he ardently declares his love to a more chromatically inflected, longing accompaniment, saying that it's no sin to obey the needs of the flesh. "Se tanta avete vulnerabil polpa"—*And you have so much flesh*—she answers. Falstaff replies in his sublime, moments-long aria "Quand'ero paggio del Duca di Norfolk, ero sottile" (CD Track 19)—*When I was page to the Duke of Norfolk, I was slender*—set by Verdi with infinite mellowness over the easy chug of strings, expanded and commented on by the woodwinds and horns. Falstaff sweetly recalls his "Verde aprile"—*Verdant April*—and his "Lieto maggio"—*Merry May.* Dazzling for the fullness of expression Verdi packs into the aria's tiny dimensions, its effect is to make us love the life force that is Falstaff again—in case we ever stopped. Alice accuses Falstaff of deceiving her, and of really loving Meg. "M'è in uggia la sua faccia"—*I can't stand her face*—he replies, advancing more aggressively on Alice.

The theme of demonic energy that carries the rest of this scene and the opening of the next begins quietly with staccato lower strings. Quickly enters, panting that Meg is advancing on the house and carrying on. Alice tells a nervous Falstaff to hide behind the screen. Now Meg enters, crying that Ford is on his way home, cursing all women and shouting that he'll cut someone's throat. Under her breath Alice reminds her not to laugh. But Quickly reenters, genuinely alarmed, yelling that Ford really is coming, as the violins take up a busy, fiddly theme that also plays a major role in the big ensemble that ends the act. Ford enters, bellowing ("Malandrino!"— *Scoundrel!*), with Cajus and Fenton in tow. In quick, declaimed patter he tells them to bar the doors and search everywhere. Bardolfo and Pistola enter, ready for action ("A caccia!"—*To the hunt!*). Ford asks his wife what's in the basket. "Il bucato"—*Dirty linen*—she answers, as he snarls that she's wicked ("Rea moglie!"). Searching the basket and finally overturning it, Ford makes a mess but still can't find Falstaff. Barking irrational orders to the other men, Ford runs upstairs to search, giving the women a moment to hide Falstaff inside the laundry basket. After a moment's concern that he's too fat to fit, Falstaff squeezes in, is covered with the dirty linen, and hidden under the closed lid.

Fenton reenters, and he and Nannetta hide behind the screen, where they comment on what's taking place ("Casa di pazzi!"—*It's a madhouse!*), as they bless the screen that's hiding them. Cajus enters, yelling, "Al ladro!"—*Stop, thief!*—shattering the musical reverie of the young lovers. To the fiddly theme the men (without Fenton) carry on noisily in their search, but at the climax of their shouting, a kiss is heard from behind the screen, as Cajus and Ford freeze like hounds: "C'è"—*There!* Now begins the wonderful ensemble that ends the act as the men on one side plan their assault on the screen, behind which they believe Alice and Falstaff are hiding, as the women try to keep the really hidden Falstaff in check, and Fenton and Nannetta croon lovingly behind the screen. For complexity and brilliance this ensemble seems to outdo them all—and it's funny, too. There's a lot going on, but Verdi captures all in vivid detail. Even though it takes a while to get to know, you'll enjoy its sweep and wit immediately; also note the Mozartean symmetry of its phrases. Along the way, Falstaff wails that that he's stifling ("Affogo!"), later begging for a tiny airhole ("Un breve spiraglio, non chiedo di più") as Quickly firmly pushes him back down. Attracted by the scene, a chorus of neighbors enters, commenting on Ford's skills as a commander ("Bravo, bravo, Generale"—*Bravo, general!*) as he directs a quasi-military assault on the screen. Behind that screen, Nannetta and Fenton sing ecstatically of their love and future together. Ford counts down for the assault, as Falstaff wails miserably for help; the screen is knocked down revealing not Alice and Falstaff, but Nannetta and Fenton. His mood already foul, Ford yells at his daughter, then to Fenton, that he's told him a thousand times Nannetta's not for him. Thinking he has spotted Falstaff on the stairs, Bardolfo yells, "È là! Ferma!"—*There he is—stop him!* The men dash off in the wrong direction to the fiddly theme, now roared out by the full orchestra with wild energy and force.

Alice, who has been offstage, returns, calling the servants to carry the basket to the river and empty it. Powerful tones for the full orchestra depict the unexpected weight of their lift. Alice sends her page to fetch Ford, whom she leads to the window. To a tense trill for the horns everyone watches what's taking place; to a mighty splash ("Patatrac!"), Falstaff goes into the Thames, offstage. The trumpets' glee in the quick orchestral postlude does not conceal its Beethoven-like bite and power.

Reminiscent of Beethoven, and Haydn, too, is the mighty prelude to act 3, where the demonic theme from the previous scene, which now characterizes Falstaff's turmoil, shows its full, furious potential. In forty-five seconds Verdi builds its relatively simple material into a fearful din. Begun by the low strings, it moves up the timbral ladder as instrumental groups join, moving to slashing chords and a few desolate repeats of its primary phrase. To a fanfare, a bedraggled Falstaff calls for the innkeeper ("Ehi, Taverniere!"). Thus begins the third of the three great monologues in *Falstaff*, where the knight reflects gloomily to growls from low woodwinds and brass on "Mondo ladro. Mondo rubaldo. Reo mondo!"—*Thieving world. Scoundrelly world. Wicked world!* Piteously, he orders mulled wine. Still holding some self-esteem, though, and calling himself "Audace e destro Cavaliere"—*A brave and skillful knight*—Falstaff reflects darkly on his treatment, which he compares to the drowning of "catellini ciechi"—*blind kittens.* Without the paunch that kept him afloat he surely would have drowned, an abhorrent death ("Brutta morte. L'acqua mi gonfia"—*Water swells me up*), he sings to a watery rising scale on a cut off high E, depicting the swelling. As the orchestra growls he thinks on the evil world again. Like an old man—as we have never seen him—he reflects, "Tutto declina"—*Everything's in decline.* To a minor-key version of the complacent march from act 2 scene 1, Falstaff takes another view of "Vecchio John," that he must go his way until he dies, when "Allor scomparirà la vera virilità dal mondo"—*Then true manhood will vanish from the world*—more typically Falstaffian vanity. He comments bleakly that he's getting too fat and has gray hairs.

To a repeat of the fanfare, the innkeeper brings Falstaff's wine, which he takes eagerly ("Versiamo un po' di vino nell' acqua del Tamigi"—*Let's pour a bit of wine into the Thames water*), as a broad, boldly harmonized phrase for the strings again suggests moving liquid, this time the wine. Verdi softens the harmony as the alcohol steals into Falstaff's veins, improving his outlook instantly. Then, as he reflects ever more cheerfully on the qualities of good wine, the strings followed by more instruments whisper and then shout their agreement. Falstaff sings that it chirps like a cricket ("grillo") in the brain, which when drunk ("brillo") makes the whole world resound like a trill ("trillo") as the full orchestra roars out one of the grandest trills in music. Entering to her musical curtsey ("Reverenza!"), Quickly starts to say something about the fair Alice, but Falstaff cuts her off fiercely: "Al diavolo te con Alice bella!"—*To hell with you and fair Alice!* She tries to speak, but Falstaff spits out an indictment of his treatment in a blazing *declamato*. Blaming the servants for his mishap, Quickly repeats that Alice is still in love with him ("Povera donna," the rhythm of which dominates the orchestra through the next passage) and hands him a letter from her. To a magical change in instrumentation and tone, Alice, Meg, Nannetta, Fenton, Ford, and Cajus peep out from around the corner of the inn, unseen by Falstaff. They watch him read the letter, commenting variously to a stealthy march that he's taking the hook again, or in Alice's case that "L'uomo non si corregge"—*Men never learn.* Falstaff reads her invitation to meet in the royal park at Herne's Oak at midnight. Now Verdi creates a mock-eerie atmosphere as Quickly, then Alice recite the legend of the Black Huntsman to weird harmonies and spooky, widely spaced orchestration, including the piccolo set against the horns as they growl in their deepest register. In a sprightly phrase Alice, joined by Meg and Nannetta, dismisses it all as "Fandonie"—*Fables*—told by grandmothers to put children to sleep. Ford chimes in that he'll be thrilled to see Falstaff wearing the horns of the Huntsman of the legend. Alice warns Ford that he, too, deserves punishment, which he humbly acknowledges, even though he continues to plot. To a magical passage that presages the fairy music of the final scene, Verdi deploys the woodwinds breathtakingly, to perform wonders as alone and in small groups as they underline ethereally the characters each will play in the night's masquerade: Nannetta will be the Fairy Queen; Meg, a wood nymph; and Quickly, a witch. Alice will bring children disguised as sprites, imps, and goblins. All this Verdi accomplishes with transparent textures and no fuss, each phrase spare and perfect. A new, exquisitely accented march that sets the mood for what will follow takes over until the end of the scene. The women bid one another good night; Ford and Cajus conspire to use the masquerade to marry Cajus and Nannetta, but they do not know that Quickly has overheard their plotting; "Stai fresco"—*We'll see about that*—she says. To some of the most fine-boned music Verdi ever wrote, the dainty little march winds down.

The final scene of *Falstaff*, set in Windsor Forest at midnight, shows the protagonist's second comeuppance of the day in a more broadly paced ceremony. The scene opens with atmospheric horn calls from offstage, representing the royal gamekeepers, alternating with exquisite phrases, mostly by the woodwinds except for a magical trill for the violins that are part of Fenton's great aria, "Dal labbro il canto estasiato vola"—*From my lips my song of ecstasy flies*—which follows. Set in three verses, this is the full version of the madrigal from which Nannetta and Fenton detached the last two lines ("Bocca baciata non perde ventura . . .") in their interrupted duet in act 1 scene 2. Set by Verdi with stylized melancholy, profound beauty, and a delicacy the composer has never before displayed, certainly in a tenor aria, although echoes of Radamès in *Aida*'s closing scene may be detected. The singer must possess taste and use restraint to put it over, as the composer marks the line to be sung "*dolcissimo*"—very sweetly—five times in the first ten bars. This is also perhaps Verdi's most gloriously orchestrated aria, indeed one of the most beautifully scored in any opera. The English horn is a continual companion lending a nocturnal atmosphere to what is much like a nocturne, in Chopin's sense, of an Italianate melody—there are few more so—set over a rich and delicate accompaniment. Within the second verse ("E innamorando l'aer antelucano"—*And filling the predawn air with love*) the trembling flutes suggest both a predawn chill and the sound world of *Aida*. The English horn murmurs ineffably alongside Fenton's surging Puccinian melodic line as the final verse ("Quivi ripiglia suon"—*Thence the sound begins anew*), to a more driving rhythm from the harp, catches the melody like a leaf in a stream, pulling it inevitably toward the clinching line ("Bocca baciata . . ."). Nannetta now joins, in, running eagerly toward him, with her reply ("Anzi rinnova come fa la luna") on several pretty A-flats. They embrace, but their love duet is interrupted again as Alice puts herself firmly between them ("Nossignore!

Tu indossa questa cappa"—*No, sir! Put on this cloak*), cooling them down as she hands Fenton his disguise.

The magical mood broken for the moment, scampering strings and winds accompany a few instructions by the women as they summarize their plot to scotch the betrothal to Cajus that Ford has treacherously planned for Nannetta, and to ensure that she and Fenton wind up together. Falstaff is seen coming: "Zitto! Viene il pezzo grosso!"—*Quiet! Here comes Fatso!*—Alice whispers. Falstaff's entrance with antlers and wrapped in a huge cloak draws a big laugh in performance. The strings play the simple musical element of a turn, making it impressive with eight carefully varied iterations. Falstaff counts off the twelve chimes sounding midnight to an eerie and harmonically bold chord sequence for the strings. The turns are brought back as he prays for protection, recalling the myth of Europa in which Jove "ti trasformasti in bove"—*transformed himself into a bull*—for his love; Verdi marking Falstaff's vocal line with a bellowing jump. Falstaff is joking about his horns, while his own bull-like size is the joke on him. Alice enters, calling him sweetly, as Falstaff excitedly replies, "L'amor m'infiamma"—*Love inflames me*. Once again Alice raises Meg as her nemesis, exciting Falstaff even more, as to barbaric yawps from the brass, timpani, and strings he cries that they'll have to share him, "Squartatemi come un camoscio a mensa"—*Tear me apart like venison*. Meg cries that the evil spirits are coming, and she and Alice flee the stage.

Magic returns, though, as led by Nannetta ("Ninfe! Elfi! Silfi!"—*Nymphs! Elves! Sylphs!*), the "fairies" enter to a slow call for woodwinds over trembling strings. Terrified, Falstaff throws himself to the ground ("Sono le Fate. Chi le guarda è morto."—*It's the fairies. Whoever looks at them will die*). The ensemble enters, to a springing figure for the harp and strings, answered by a slightly giddy giggle by the flutes and piccolo. Nannetta and some of her disguised entourage enter as Alice spots Falstaff on the ground, instructing everyone, "Non ridiam"—*Don't laugh*. Nannetta's aria "Sul fil d'un soffio etesio"—*On the breath of a fragrant breeze*—matches Fenton's aria for delicacy. It's declaimed but ethereal, set to a carefully gauged chamber-size ensemble in which shimmering muted violins dominate. She instructs the elves to dance, which they do, slowly, to the quiet chant of the chorus ("La selva dorme"—*The wood is asleep*). The aria's second verse, "Erriam sotto la luna"—*Let us wander beneath the moon*—is longer as the composer repeats the melodic material, expanding it in the middle with flowing harp figuration; again the chorus sings its closing verse in a drowsy harmony and tempo.

Verdi turns a delicate three-note figure for the strings into an energetic transition to the next passage, where Falstaff is "discovered" and punished. After trying to lift him to his feet ("Portatemi una grue! Non posso!"—*Bring a crane, I can't!*—Falstaff cries), they declare him a corrupt and impure human, and Bardolfo, acting for the moment the part of a sorcerer, conjures sprits to torment Falstaff in a mock-stormy invocation. Falstaff notices that the hooded sorcerer "puzzi come una puzzola"—*stinks like a polecat*. The children and choristers playing the elves and spirits now attack Falstaff, pinching and poking him in a memorable chorus ("Pizzica, stuzzica"—*Pinch him, sting him*) as he yelps in discomfort. The principals, led by Bardolfo and Pistola, accuse Falstaff in various insults ("Ghiotton! Pancion!"—*Glutton! Potbelly!*) as they pull him up to his knees. They finally get Falstaff to repent ("Ahi, ahi! Mi pento!"), then pray in a satiric mock-ecclesiastic call and response for his reform ("Domine, fallo casto"—*Lord, make him chaste*), to which he replies in kind that his belly be spared ("Ma salvagli l'addomine"—*But spare my belly*). The men mount a last, raucous assault on Falstaff's dignity ("Globo d'impurità! Rispondi!"—*Globe of filth! Answer!*) marked by blasts from the trumpets and trombones. "Ben mi sta"—*It serves me right*—he answers, meekly. But Falstaff, who is not stupid after all, again notices the tormentor with a familiar stink, and, as Bardolfo's hood falls back, the knight spits a litany of fire back at him to the same melody to which he was just roasted: "Naso vermiglio!"—*Scarlet nose!* The others relent as Quickly spirits Bardolfo off to dress him in preparation for the final turnaround. Ford approaches Falstaff, asking ironically how it feels to wear the horns. Recognizing "Master Brook," Falstaff sings his cordial greeting ("Caro Signor Fontana") from act 2 scene 1. Alice introduces him as her husband. Quickly reintroduces herself, "Cavaliere"—*Sir knight*—to her musical curtsey, which Falstaff now sings back to her. In light tones, Quickly asks whether he really believed two sensible women would damn themselves for him, as Alice and Meg chime in. Falstaff admits that he does seem to have acted like an ass, his vocal line set to a donkeylike braying. Everyone agrees that he was indeed "un mostro raro"—*a rare monster*—in a vehement Rossinian climax for the full ensemble and orchestra. Bravely, Falstaff points out that for all the present arrogance toward him, "L'arguzia mia crea l'arguzia degli altri"—*I'm not only witty in myself, but cause wit in other men*—his defense restoring our esteem for him. In bad spirit, Ford agrees then says it's time to move on to the marriage of the Fairy Queen. To a sublime minuet set for the flutes and stings, Dr. Cajus and someone veiled in white enter as the happy couple. Another couple, actually Nannetta and Fenton in disguise, are presented by Alice as asking to be married, too. Grandly, Ford agrees ("E sia"—*So be it*). The minuet expresses growing anticipation, as the four are unmasked and unveiled to a huge orchestra guffaw. Ford is not happy ("Tradimento!"—*Betrayed!*); and Cajus (a terrific character role) screeches, "Ho sposato Bardolfo!"—*I've married Bardolfo!* Alice points out without sympathy that Ford set the trap himself, and Falstaff now ironically asks Ford who is wearing the ass's ears. Cajus and Ford point at each other, as Quickly adds Falstaff, too, to their ranks; Nannetta asks publicly for his forgiveness, and Ford is in no position to say no.

Stepping out of the drama Falstaff sings, "Un coro e terminiam la scena"—*A chorus to end our play!*—as Ford agrees, "Poi con Sir Falstaff, tutti, andiamo a cena"—*Then we'll all feast with Sir John*. Falstaff himself opens the great choral fugue "Tutto nel mondo è burla"—*All the world's a joke*—that ends the opera, a stunning demonstration of Verdi's compositional technique—as if one were needed. Boito's text, which states that the world is a joke and man a jester, is harshly brilliant rather than funny, and Verdi's setting opens with panache but gives voice to its darker side. The idea of ending the opera with a fugue was Verdi's, and the irony of the master of Italian opera ending his last opera, a comedy among tragedies, with this learned and supposedly Germanic technique was entirely conscious, a decision of pure and intentional art.

Characters and chorus add lines to the whirling uproar in flawless counterpoint. Listen for the lyrical episode based on triplets early on, and for the mocking countersubject ("Tutti gabbati"—*All are gulled*), which takes on a laughing note, then a sharper force. "Tutti gabbati" receives a mock-serious treatment that builds to a ferocious cutoff climax on "Ma ride ben chi ride la risata final"—*But he who laughs last laughs best*—as Falstaff restarts the fugue again on "Tutti gabbati." This leads to the final, ascending episode, after which the brass and low strings roar out the subject imperially but with no flagging of the tempo; and once again the final cadences show Verdi's imagination at its most explosive.

# Listening to Verdi

s you must suspect, reading about Verdi's music is one thing; hearing it, in all its power, passion, beauty, and eloquence is another. Fortunately for Verdians, new and old, the composer's popularity ensures countless fine and great performances to hear. Many are recent, but some go back to the dawn of the age of recordings; such is the mix on the CD at the back of the book, with older recordings dominating.

One such is CD Track 2, "Vieni meco" from *Ernani*, by Mattia Battistini (born in 1856!), recorded in 1906, just five years after the composer's death. Battistini's silken delivery is clear, and some of his rich voice does make it through the primitive sound. Since a steady diet of these prehistoric vocal recordings becomes tiring, I've tried to use those made in the 1910s, '20s, and '30s, by which time technology had improved sufficiently to eliminate the shrill, boxy quality of the first generation of recordings. For example, you'll notice a big difference in quality between the Battistini excerpt and the 1911 one, "Ah, fors'è lui . . . Sempre libera" from *La traviata* (CD Track 7) by Luisa Tetrazzini. Be aware that Tetrazzini cuts the aria and interpolates coloratura and high notes not in the score. Tetrazzini also dispatches Oscar's "Saper vorreste" from act 3 of *Ballo* (CD Track 10) with admirable spirit and rhythmic verve, interpolating trills and coloratura here, as well. The oldest recordings demonstrate nineteenth-century singing styles.

The twentieth century was a golden age for Verdi singing, too, and we are fortunate to have some of the its most revered singers represented on the CD, including two of the greatest Verdi sopranos, the American Rosa Ponselle and the Italian Claudia Muzio. Ponselle's voice and vocal technique were so prodigious that according to one (possibly apocryphal) story, Maria Callas banned the playing of this very performance of

"Ernani, Ernani, involami" (CD Track 1) in her presence. Muzio's skill as a singing actress is clear from the primal intensity of this famous and justly revered excerpt "Teneste la promessa . . . Addio del passato" from act 3 of *Traviata* (CD Track 8); and, while her delivery is matchless, her big, dark-hued voice is a thing of beauty, as well. Although the recorded sound is a bit rough, Muzio again shines as a singing actress in the excerpt from *Ballo*, "Ma dall'arido stelo divulsa" (CD Track 9) and a ravishing, though abridged "O patria mia" from *Aida* (CD Track 14), where the clarity and weight of the declaimed phrases demonstrates how she never wasted a note in her characterizations, and yet again sets her apart as a great dramatic presence. The other Ponselle recordings include a mind-blowing "Pace, pace, mio Dio" from *La forza del destino* (CD Track 11), where the grandeur of the material and the singer's voice are well matched. A crippling stage fright helped to push Ponselle into an early retirement, but we must be grateful that the studio didn't faze her, as her beautiful and moving performance of the "Willow Song" from *Otello* (CD Track 17) shows her voice in its full glory and her delivery persuasive, if not at Muzio's mimetic pitch.

Those who want a lesson in the passionate Italian style of singing and delivery will appreciate Mario del Monaco in the 1955 excerpt from *Luisa Miller*, "Quando le sere al placido" (CD Track 3), as well as those performances—"Bella figlia dell'amore" from *Rigoletto* and "Se m'ami ancor . . . ai nostri monti" from *Il trovatore* (CD Tracks 5 and 6)—featuring Enrico Caruso, whose tenor in 1912 and 1913 had darkened to a remarkable baritonal sheen, while still holding its brilliance and displaying his aristocratic phrasing. Mariano Stabile, who sang the role of Falstaff many times, remains one of its greatest exponents, as his magnificent rendition of the "L'onore!" monologue (CD Track 18) demonstrates. But the less familiar Giacomo Rimini is impressive in "Quand'ero paggio" (CD Track 19) and the ensuing dialogue with Alice. Giovanni Martinelli's voice shows the *squillo*—metallic brilliance—that the role of Otello demands in "Esultate!" (CD Track 15); note that this recording includes the chorus ("Evviva! Vittoria!") conducted at breakneck tempo by Ettore Panizza, as well as Iago's opening exchange with Roderigo, wonderfully sung by Lawrence Tibbett.

The American Tibbett, one of the finest Verdi baritones, is also represented with Iago's "Credo" (CD Track 16), a magnificently sung and acted 1938 performance from the Metropolitan Opera in New York, in which the character's malignant intelligence is fully displayed without descending into moustache-twirling excess. To demonstrate further that great Verdi singers are hardly the province of Italy alone, the excerpt from *Simon Boccanegra* sung by the Bulgarian bass Boris Christoff, "A te, l'estremo addio...Il lacerato spirito" (CD Track 12), shows all the grandeur of the role of Jacopo Fiesco as well as the glory of his "black" voice. Christoff was also one of the best singers of King Philip in *Don Carlo*, a role he performed and recorded numerous times. The Austrian-born Ernestine Schumann-Heink, who sings Azucena (to Caruso's Manrico) in the hair-raising excerpt from the fourth act of *Trovatore*, makes a profound effect, even though her voice is no longer fresh, with convincing phrasing and acting that demonstrate high artistry. The German Meta Seinemeyer takes an admirably spacious approach with "Tu, che le vanità" from *Don Carlo* (CD Track 13); and finally, "La donna è mobile," recorded in French as "Comme la plume au vent" by Edmond Clément (CD Track 4), demonstrates that Verdi's music stands up to being sung in another language, definitively proving its universality.

Assuming that you're just beginning your journey through Verdi—and, perhaps, the rest of the operatic repertory—this CD should help you on your way. Be aware that it will be hard to get out once you're in, and that listening to Verdi, and to opera generally, is an open-ended process. Some performances (such as the Toscanini-led *Otello* or the 1977 *Simon Boccanegra* under Claudio Abbado) are so compelling that they do seem to set the standard, and to define for many how the opera should sound. But that doesn't mean new challengers never appear: the 1956 Karajan *Falstaff* with Tito Gobbi in the title role remains as good as it can be, but Abbado's 2001 recording with Bryn Terfel is no slouch. And the world of live performances may open another galaxy for you. You'll develop favorites of your own and pick up recordings with those singers, in which you'll find others whose singing you admire. Then, when you spot a performance with one or two good singers, you'll know that it's worth hearing, probably pretty good, and possibly great.

Ultimately, however, the best way to experience opera is to watch it performed onstage, in an opera house if you have one nearby, or on DVD if not. The Metropolitan Opera Live in HD broadcasts, via which audiences in remote locations (generally movie theaters) watch live performances, provide a new and valuable means of viewing live opera.

# Notes

## Chapter 1: Verdi and the Culmination of Italian Opera

1. Richard Crocker, *A History of Musical Style*, p. 473.

## Chapter 2: Verdi's Life and Character

1. Frank Walker, *The Man Verdi*, pp. 400–406.
2. Charles Osborne, *Verdi: A Life in the Theatre*, p. 231; Walker, pp. 280–281; Mary Jane Phillips-Matz, *Verdi: A Biography*, pp. 601–602.
3. Quoted by Phillips-Matz, p. 309.
4. Osborne, p. 54.
5. Mary Jane Phillips-Matz, "Verdi's Life: A Thematic Biography," in *The Cambridge Companion to Verdi*, ed. Scott L. Balthazar, p. 8.
6. Quoted in Osborne, p. 154.
7. Osborne, pp. 159–160.
8. Osborne, pp. 209–213.
9. Phillips-Matz, *Verdi*, p. 596.
10. See Osborne, pp. 231–233.

## Chapter 3: The Major Early Operas: *Nabucco, Ernani*, and *Macbeth*

1. Julian Budden, *The Operas of Verdi*, vol. 1, p. 112.
2. Mary Ann Smart, "Verdi, Italian Romanticism, and the Risorgimento," in *The Cambridge Companion to Verdi*, ed. Balthazar, p. 34.
3. Osborne, p. 29.
4. Budden, vol. 1, p. 163.
5. Quoted in Budden, vol. 1, p. 270.
6. See Budden, vol. 1, pp. 276–278.
7. Budden, vol. 1, p. 289.

## Chapter 4: The "Galley" Operas

1. Quoted in Osborne, p. 154.
2. Budden, vol. 1, pp. 69–87.
3. Budden, vol. 1, p. 72.
4. Julian Budden, program notes to Philips recording of *Jérusalem* (412 613-2), p. 15.
5. Osborne, p. 54.
6. Budden, vol. 1, pp. 316–318.

## Chapter 5: The Transition to the Middle Period: *Luisa Miller* and *Stiffelio; Aroldo*

1. Mary Ann Smart, "Verdi, Italian Romanticism, and the Risorgimento," in *The Cambridge Companion to Verdi*, ed. Balthazar, p. 32.
2. Luke Jensen, "An Introduction to Verdi's Working Methods," in *The Cambridge Companion to Verdi*, ed. Balthazar, p. 259.
3. Phillips-Matz, p. 262.
4. Peter Dyson, entry on *Stiffelio*, in *The St. James Opera Encyclopedia*, ed. John Guinn and Les Stone, p. 779.
5. Budden, vol. 1, pp. 269–270.

## Chapter 6: The Big Three of the Middle Period: *Rigoletto, Il trovatore,* and *La traviata*

1. Quoted in Budden, vol. 2, p. 64.
2. Cormac Newark, "'Ch'hai di nuovo, buffon?' or What's New with *Rigoletto*," *The Cambridge Companion to Verdi*, ed. Balthazar, pp. 197–208.
3. Budden, vol. 1, p. 485.
4. Budden, vol. 2, p. 82.

## Chapter 7: Broadening the Scope: *I vespri siciliani* and *Un ballo in maschera*

1. Budden, vol. 2, pp. 223–224.
2. Budden, vol. 2, p. 392.

## Chapter 9: Choral Works: The Manzoni Requiem and the *Quattro pezzi sacri*

1. See p. 14.
2. Phillips-Matz, pp. 745–747.

## Chapter 10: The Great Political Tragedy: *Don Carlo*

1. Budden, vol. 3, p. 68.
2. Budden, vol. 3, pp. 119–120.

## Chapter 11: A Farewell to Grand Opera: *Aida*

1. George Martin, "Verdi and the Risorgimento," in *The Verdi Companion*, ed. Weaver and Chusid, p. 41.

## Chapter 12: Shakespearean Tragedy: *Otello*

1. Joseph Kerman, *Opera as Drama*, p. 149.

## Chapter 13: Shakespearean Comedy: *Falstaff*

1. *Encounters with Verdi*, ed. Marcello Conati, pp. 292–293.
2. James Hepokoski, *Falstaff*, pp. 41–42.

# Selected Bibliography

Abbate, Carolyn, and Roger Parker. *A History of Opera*. New York: W. W. Norton, 2012.

Balthazar, Scott. L., ed. *The Cambridge Companion to Verdi*. Cambridge, UK: Cambridge University Press, 2004.

Budden, Julian. *The Operas of Verdi*. Vol. 1, From Oberto to Rigoletto. Revised edition. Oxford: Oxford University Press, 1992.

————. *The Operas of Verdi*. Vol. 2, *From Il Trovatore to La Forza del Destino*. Revised edition. Oxford: Oxford University Press, 1992.

————. *The Operas of Verdi*. Vol. 3, *From Don Carlos to Falstaff*. Revised edition. Oxford: Oxford University Press, 1992.

Conati, Marcello, ed. *Encounters with Verdi*. Translated by Richard Stokes. Ithaca, NY: Cornell University Press, 1984.

Crocker, Richard. *A History of Musical Style*. New York: Dover, 1986.

Cross, Milton. *The New Milton Cross' Complete Stories of the Great Operas*. Revised and enlarged edition. Garden City, NY: Doubleday, 1955.

Dean, Winton. *Essays on Opera*. Oxford: Oxford University Press, 1990.

Gossett, Philip. *Divas and Scholars: Performing Italian Opera*. Chicago: University of Chicago Press, 2006.

Guinn, John, and Les Stone, eds. *The St. James Opera Encyclopedia*. Detroit: Visible Ink Press, 1997.

Hepokoski, James A. *Falstaff*. Cambridge Opera Handbooks. Cambridge, UK: Cambridge University Press, 1983.

————. *Otello*. Cambridge Opera Handbooks. Cambridge, UK: Cambridge University Press, 1987.

Kennedy, Michael, ed. *The Oxford Dictionary of Music*. 2nd ed. Oxford: Oxford University Press, 1994.

Kerman, Joseph. *Opera as Drama*. New York: Vintage Books, 1956.

————. *Opera and the Morbidity of Music.* New York: New York Review Books, 2008.

Libbey, Ted. *The NPR Listener's Encyclopedia of Classical Music.* New York: Workman, 2006.

Osborne, Charles. *Verdi: A Life in the Theatre.* New York: Alfred A. Knopf, 1987.

Phillips-Matz, Mary Jane. *Verdi: A Biography.* Oxford: Oxford University Press, 1993.

Verdi, Giuseppe. Operas. *The Vocal Scores, 2-CD Set.* Milwaukee: Hal Leonard, 2006.

————. *Aïda.* Full score. New York: Dover, 1989.

————. *Falstaff.* Full score. New York: Dover, 1980.

————. *Don Carlo (5 atti).* Vocal score. Milan: Ricordi, 1993.

————. *Don Carlos.* Full score of the 5-act revision in Italian. New York: Dover, 2001.

————. *Il trovatore.* Full score. New York: Dover, 1994.

————. *I vespri siciliani.* Vocal score. Milan: Ricordi. Reprint, 2010.

————. *La forza del destino.* Full score. New York: Dover, 1991.

————. *La traviata.* Full score. New York: Dover, 1990.

————. *Luisa Miller.* Vocal score. Milan: Ricordi. Reprint, 2007.

————. *Macbeth.* Vocal score. Milan: Ricordi. Reprint, 2010.

————. *Otello.* Full score. New York: Dover, 1986.

————. *Rigoletto.* Full score. New York: Dover, 1992.

————. *Simon Boccanegra.* Vocal score. Milan: Ricordi. Reprint, 1997.

————. *Stiffelio.* Vocal score. Critical edition. Milan: Ricordi/University of Chicago Press, 2005.

————. *Un ballo in maschera.* Full score. New York: Dover, 1996.

Walker, Frank. *The Man Verdi.* Chicago: University of Chicago Press, 1982.

Weaver, William, and Martin Chusid, eds. *The Verdi Companion.* New York: W. W. Norton, 1979.

# CD Track Listing

1. *Ernani*: "Surta è la notte . . . Ernani, Ernani, involami" (4:29)
   Rosa Ponselle (Elvira); Rosario Bourdon, conductor; 1928
   From Naxos CD 8.110728

2. *Ernani*: "Vieni meco" (2:28)
   Mattia Battistini (Don Carlo), Emilia Corsi (Elvira); La Scala orchestra,
   Carlo Sabajno, conductor; 1906
   From Romophone CD 82008-2

3. *Luisa Miller*: "Oh! Fede negar potessi . . . Quando le sere al
   placido" (4:44)
   Mario Del Monaco (Rodolfo); Orchestra of Santa Cecilia, Rome, Alberto
   Erede, conductor; 1955
   From Naxos CD 9.80001

4. *Rigoletto*: "Comme la plume au vent" (2:25)
   Edmond Clément (Duke of Mantua); 1904
   From Romophone CD 82016-2

5. *Rigoletto*: "Bella figlia dell'amore" (3:42)
   Enrico Caruso (Duke of Mantua), Luisa Tetrazzini (Gilda), Josephine
   Jacoby (Maddalena), Pasquale Amato (Rigoletto); Victor Orchestra,
   Walter B. Rogers, conductor; 1912
   From Naxos CD 8.110724

6. *Il trovatore*: "Se m'ami ancor . . . Ai nostri monti" (4:26)
   Enrico Caruso (Manrico), Ernestine Schumann-Heink (Azucena); Victor
   Orchestra, Gaetano Scognamiglio, conductor; 1913
   From Naxos CD 8.110724

7. *La traviata*: "Ah, fors'è lui . . . Sempre libera" (4:40)

   Luisa Tetrazzini (Violetta); Victor Orchestra, Josef A. Pasternack, conductor; 1911
   From Romophone CD 81025-2

8. *La traviata*: "Teneste la promessa . . . Addio del passato" (4:35)

   Claudia Muzio (Violetta); Lorenzo Molajoli, conductor; 1935
   From Romophone CD 81015-2

9. *Un ballo in maschera*: "Ma dall'arido stelo" (3:22)

   Claudia Muzio (Leonora); 1918
   From Romophone CD 81010-2

10. *Un ballo in maschera*: "Saper vorreste" (2:54)

    Luisa Tetrazzini (Oscar); Victor Orchestra, Josef A. Pasternack, conductor; 1911
    From Romophone CD 81025-2

11. *La forza del destino*: "Pace, pace, mio Dio" (4:43)

    Rosa Ponselle (Leonora); Rosario Bourdon, conductor; 1928
    From Naxos CD 8.110728

12. *Simon Boccanegra*: "A te, l'estremo addio . . . Il lacerato spirito" (5:52)

    Boris Christoff (Fiesco); Rome Opera Chorus and Orchestra, Vittorio Gui, conductor; 1957
    From Nimbus CD NI7961-63

13. *Don Carlo*: "Tu, che le vanità" (8:13)

    Meta Seinemeyer (Elisabetta); Berlin State Opera Orchestra, Frieder Weissmann, conductor; 1927
    From Haenssler CD 94.511

14. *Aida*: "O patria mia" (2:57)

    Claudia Muzio (Aida); 1918
    From Romophone CD 81010-2

15. *Otello*: "Esultate! . . . Vittoria! . . . Ebben, Roderigo, che pensi?" (4:43)

   Giovanni Martinelli (Otello), Lawrence Tibbett (Iago), Giovanni Paltrinieri (Roderigo); Metropolitan Opera Chorus and Orchestra, Ettore Panizza, conductor; 1938
   From Naxos CD 8.111018-19

16. *Otello*: "Credo" (5:09)

   Lawrence Tibbett (Iago); Metropolitan Opera Chorus and Orchestra, Ettore Panizza, conductor; 1938
   From Naxos CD 8.111018-19

17. *Otello*: "Piangea cantando" (4:34)

   Rosa Ponselle (Desdemona); Rosario Bourdon, conductor; 1924
   From Naxos CD 8.110728

18. *Falstaff*: "L'onore!" (4:11)

   Mariano Stabile (Falstaff); La Scala Orchestra, Victor de Sabata, conductor; 1952
   From Music and Arts CD 1104

19. *Falstaff*: "Quand'ero paggio" (0:54)

   Giacomo Rimini (Falstaff), Pia Tassinari (Alice); La Scala Orchestra, Lorenzo Molajoli, conductor; 1932
   From Naxos CD 8.110198-99

Musical recordings under license from Naxos of America, www.Naxos.com.

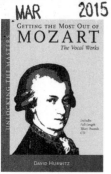